跟奥巴马学英语系列丛书

（英汉双语对照）

奥巴马的魅力演讲

——2012年每周六例行讲话全集

学习英文及演讲技巧的最好范例，
了解美国现状及奥巴马传奇的绝佳读本

附光盘

独家赠送
奥巴马原声光盘

[美国总统] 巴拉克·奥巴马 著
龙金顺 苏宗文 编译

北京航空航天大学出版社
BEIHANG UNIVERSITY PRESS

图书在版编目（CIP）数据

奥巴马的魅力演讲. 2012 年每周六例行讲话全集：英汉对照 / 龙金顺，苏宗文编译 . -- 北京：北京航空航天大学出版社，2013.10

ISBN 978-7-5124-1263-7

Ⅰ. ①奥…　Ⅱ. ①龙…　②苏…　Ⅲ. ①英语—汉语—对照读物 ②奥巴马，B. —演讲—汇编　Ⅳ. ① H319.4：D

中国版本图书馆 CIP 数据核字 (2013) 第 222066 号

奥巴马的魅力演讲——2012 年每周六例行讲话全集

[美国总统] 巴拉克·奥巴马　著

龙金顺　苏宗文　编译

责任编辑　江小珍

*

北京航空航天大学出版社出版发行

北京市海淀区学院路 37 号(邮编 100191)　http://www.buaapress.com.cn

发行部电话：(010)82317024　传真：(010)82328026

读者信箱：bhpress@263.net　邮购电话：(010)82316936

涿州市新华印刷有限公司印装　　各地书店经销

*

开本：710×960　1/16　印张：14.75　字数：339 千字

2013 年 10 月第 1 版　2013 年 10 月第 1 次印刷

ISBN 978-7-5124-1263-7　定价：38.80 元（含光盘 1 张）

若本书有倒页、脱页、缺页等印装质量问题，请与本社发行部联系调换。联系电话：(010)82317024

前言

美国第44任总统巴拉克•奥巴马身世复杂，于不同地方与不同文化背景的人共同生活过。早年，由于其多种族背景，很难取得社会认同。家境的困顿，前途的无望，使得十几岁的他过了一段荒唐的日子，干了很多愚蠢的事，比如逃学、吸毒、泡妞等。然而，在认识到生命的真正意义之后，就是这个不折不扣的“坏小子”，告别昨天，经过一番奋斗与抗争，终于有所作为，有所建树，成为一颗冉冉上升的政治明星，并于2009年1月问鼎美国总统宝座，且于2012年成功连任。

一脸帅气，一脸灿烂，奥巴马上任以后，与他的前任一样，每周星期六早晨都要发表一个例行演讲，就国内外某些热点问题等阐述其观点，表明其立场。一如他的其他一些讲话，这些演讲观点清晰鲜明，语言优美生动，语音纯正地道，内涵深刻丰富。这些演讲饱含激情，或令人痴迷，或催人奋进，或发人深省，极具魅力。诚如教育部高校外语教学指导委员会主任、南京大学外国语学院院长王守仁教授所言：透过奥巴马的演说词，你可以发现他那平实明了的英语极富表现力，叙事娓娓道来，说理周密细致，节奏收放自如，气势贯通，动人心弦。英语学习者认真学习奥巴马驾驭语言的技巧，会使自己的英语水平有很大程度的提升。

本书悉数收集奥巴马总统2012年每周六例行演讲53篇，并加以注释和翻译，还配有奥巴马原声MP3光盘。诚然，通过认真研读这些讲话，刻苦模仿讲话的语音语调，科学且充分地利用本书，对于了解美国社会与当今世界，拓宽视野，提高综合素质；对于今后比较顺利地收听收看英语国家的电视与广播以及与英语国家人士交流与互动；对于进一步提振学习英语的兴趣，熟悉英语演讲技巧，全面提升英语听说写读译能力；对于应对雅思、托福、英语专业四级和八级、研究生英语、大学英语四级和六级等各类各级英语考试，较大幅度地提高考试成绩，都有着不容置疑的积极作用。其姊妹篇《奥巴马的魅力演讲——2009年每周六例行讲话全集》、《奥巴马的魅力演讲——2010年每周六例行讲话全集》和《奥巴马的魅力演讲——2011年每周六例行讲话全集》面市之后，受到了读者的热捧与厚爱，一度在当当网英语读物热卖榜中位居第六、第四与第三。毋庸讳言，本书必将与此前出版的其他三册构成一个完整的系列，成为研究当今美国政治，研究奥巴马以及学习第一手英语、学习英语名人演讲不可多得的鲜活材料。

作者在编写本书的过程中，参考并借鉴了国内外大量中外文图书资料。由于所涉及的范围甚广，难以逐一列举与彰显，特此说明，并向原编著者表示诚挚的谢意；与此同时，编者还有幸得到了美国友人 William Walsh 先生，Barbara Toews 女士，Tennant Wright先生以及James Pongrass先生的鼎力支持与悉心指导；集美大学和其他一些高校的同仁也对本书的编译提出了不少宝贵的建议。值此本书付梓之际，同此表示由衷的感谢。

编者

2013 年 8 月

目录

第1周

Continuing to Grow the Economy in the New Year

January 07, 2012

在新年里力促经济持续增长

2012 年 1 月 7 日

【摘要导读】

在本周的广播电视讲话中，巴拉克•奥巴马总统与美国人民一起分享了他新年的决心：千方百计地促进经济增长，确保中产阶级家庭恢复其过去十年里失去的安全感。正是因为如此，本周奥巴马总统任命理查德•科德雷(*Richard Cordray*[①])为*消费者金融保护局*[②]局长，以为美国消费者提供保护。尽管美国经济的私营部门就业岗位持续增加——2011年全年新增190多万个——但奥巴马认为还需要采取更多的措施来促进经济增长。奥巴马同时也宣布他将在白宫主持一场“美国就业岗位内包”的论坛，倾听那些将就业岗位从海外带回国内的企业家们的声音，并商榷如何让其他企业家借鉴效仿。

演讲再现 Original Text

Words & Expressions

regardless of 不管，不顾

deserves [di'zə:v] *vt.* 值得，应得

1* Happy new year, everybody.

2 This week, I traveled to *Cleveland*[③], Ohio, to talk with folks about the biggest challenge we face as a country – rebuilding our economy so that, once again, hard work pays off, responsibility is rewarded, and anyone, regardless of who they are or where they come from, can make it if they try. That's the economy America deserves. That's the economy I'm fighting every day to build.

3 Now, to get there, the most important thing we need to do is get more Americans back to work. And over the past three years, we've made steady progress. We just learned that our economy added 212,000 private sector jobs in December.

* 书中演讲原文及译文中的段落编号为编译者考虑读者阅读时便于对照所加。

After losing more than 8 million jobs in the recession, we've added more than 3 million private sector jobs over the past 22 months. And we're starting 2012 with manufacturing on the rise and the American auto industry on the mend.

4 We're heading in the right direction. And we're not going to let up. On Wednesday the White House will host a forum called "Insourcing American Jobs." We'll hear from business leaders who are bringing jobs back home and see how we can help other businesses follow their lead.

5 Because this is a make or break moment for the middle-class and all those working to get there. We've got to keep at it. We've got to keep creating jobs. And we've got to keep rebuilding our economy so that everyone gets a fair shot, everyone does their fair share — and everyone plays by the same rules. We can't go back to the days when the financial system was stacking the deck against ordinary Americans. To me, that's not an option. Not after all we've been through.

6 That's why I appointed Richard Cordray as our nation's new consumer watchdog this week. Richard's job is simple: to look out for you. Every day, his sole mission is to protect consumers from potential abuses by the financial industry and to make sure that you've got all the transparent information you need to make the important financial decisions in your lives.

7 I nominated Richard for this job last summer. And yet, Republicans in the Senate kept blocking his confirmation — not because they objected to him, but because they wanted to weaken his agency. That made no sense. Every day we waited was a day you and consumers all across the country were at greater financial risk.

8 So this year, I'm going to keep doing whatever it takes to move this economy forward and to make sure that middle-class families regain the security they've lost over the past decade. That's my New Year's resolution to all of you. Thanks, and have a great weekend.

on the mend（病情或事态）正在好转中

let up 停止，放松，减少

forum [ˈfɔːrəm] *n.* 论坛，讨论会，法庭，公开讨论的广场

insourcing [ˈinsɔːsiŋ] *n.* 内销，内包

a make or break moment 一个决定胜负的时刻，一个成败的关头

get a fair shot 得到一个公平的机会

do one's fair share 完成本职工作，完成分内工作

stack the deck 暗中布局（使情况对某人有利或不利），预先做手脚，暗中策划

watchdog [ˈwɔtʃdɔg] *n.* 监督委员会，监督委员会委员，看门狗

look out for 当心，警戒，提防，照料，照看

nominate [ˈnɔmineit] *vt.* 提名，任命，提议，确定

confirmation [ˌkɔnfəˈmeiʃən] *n.*（进一步）确定，确认，批准，证据，证明

object to 对…反对

resolution [ˌrezəˈluːʃən] *n.* 决心，决定，决议，解决

背景知识注释 Background Notes

1. Richard Cordray　理查德•科德雷，曾担任过俄亥俄州立大学法学院的兼职教授和俄亥俄州司法部长。美国总统奥巴马于2012年1月4日任命前俄亥俄州司法部长理查德•科德雷为消费者金融保护局局长。奥巴马2011年7月曾宣布提名理查德•科德雷出任这一职，但参议院当年12月否决了这项提名。这次奥巴马绕过国会对科德雷进行任命，时值国会正处于休会期，因为根据美国宪法，总统在国会休会期间有权进行人事任命。

2. 消费者金融保护局　即the Consumer Financial Protection Bureau，设立该局是2010年7月生效的美国金融监管改革法案的重要内容。该机构拥有广泛的监管权力，旨在帮助消费者避开金融机构隐性收费和欺骗性借贷等金融欺诈行为。

3. Cleveland　克里夫兰，美国俄亥俄州东北部城市，位于伊利湖南岸，距离宾夕法尼亚边界100公里。这个城市始建于1796年，历史上是制造业中心。

中文译文 Chinese Version

1　嗨，各位好！

2　本周，我造访了俄亥俄州克利夫兰市(Cleveland)，与这里的人们探讨了我国当前面临的最大挑战——重建我们的经济，再次让勤奋工作有回报，认真履职有奖赏。任何人，无论他是谁、来自何方，只要他努力付出就能如愿以偿。这才是美国所应有的经济。这才是我每天都为之奋斗的经济。

3　现在，为达到这一目的，我们需做的最重要的事情就是让更多的美国人重返工作岗位。在过去三年中，我们取得了稳步的进展。我们刚获悉，12月份我们新增了21.2万个私营部门的就业岗位。在经济衰退中我们失去了800多万个就业岗位，但在过去的22个月里我们在私营部门新增了300多万个就业岗位。2012年伊始，我们的制造业持续回暖，汽车工业也逐渐好转。

4　我们正朝着正确的方向迈进。而且我们也不会有所懈怠。下周三白宫将举办以“美国就业岗位内包”为主题的论坛。届时我们能倾听到那些将就业岗位带回国内的企业家们的声音，并商议如何让其他企业借鉴效仿。

5　现在中产阶级和那些努力成为中产阶级的人们正处于成败的关键时刻，因此我们必须坚持不懈，继续创造就业岗位。我们必须继续重建我们的经济，让每个人都得到公平的机会，让每个人都能完成自己的本职工作——让每个人都在相同的规则下竞争。我们不能重回让金融系统暗算普通民众的时代。对我来说，这绝不是选择的问题。毕竟我们都曾经历过。

6　正是因为如此，本周我任命理查德•科德雷担任新的全国消费者监护机构的监管人。理查德的工作很简单：就是为大家提供保护。他每天的唯一使命就是保护消费者免受金融业滥用职权，确保你们在生活中得到所需的透明信息来做出重要的财务决定。

7 我去年夏天提名了理查德先生来担当此职。然而参议院的共和党人一直阻挠对他的任命——并不是因为他们对他持异议，而是他们想要削弱这个机构的职能。这毫无道理。我们每等待一天你们及全国各地的消费者们都将遭遇更大的金融风险。

8 因此，今年，我将继续采取一切措施推进经济增长，确保中产阶级家庭恢复其过去十年中失去的安全感。这就是我在新年里对你们所有人所表达的决心。谢谢大家，周末愉快！

第2周

Helping American Businesses Succeed

January 14, 2012

推动美国企业成功

2012 年 1 月 14 日

【摘要导读】

在本周的广播电视讲话中，巴拉克•奥巴马总统告诉美国民众，正在实施"内包"计划的企业主动将工作岗位带回美国并新增投资。为有力推动这一举措，奥巴马本周在白宫举办论坛邀请实施"内包"计划的企业领导参会，为其他企业借鉴效仿。他也承诺帮助一些企业将就业岗位带回国内。他表示不久他还将宣布一项税收提案，褒奖那些在美国投资的企业，同时削减将就业岗位输出海外的企业的税收优惠。另外，他还将推出一项提案来简化政府办事流程，让大小企业在国内外销售产品时更方便地获得政府支持。奥巴马还说他将继续采取措施促进经济增长，帮助美国人民就业。

演讲再现 Original Text

1 As you can see, I brought a few things with me for this week's video. A padlock. A pair of boots. A candle. And a pair of socks.

2 No, we're not having a *yard sale* [1]. And these products may not appear to have much in common. But they're united by three proud words: "Made in America." They're manufactured by American workers, in American factories, and shipped to customers here and around the world.

3 The companies that make these products are part of a hopeful trend: they're bringing jobs back from overseas. You've heard of outsourcing — well, this is insourcing. And

Words & Expressions

padlock [ˈpædlɔk] *n.* 挂锁

manufacture [ˌmænjuˈfæktʃə] *vt.* （大规模）制造，生产，加工，捏造

outsourcing [ˈautˌsɔːsiŋ] *n.* 外包，外购，外部采办

in this make or break moment for the middle-class and those working to get into the middle-class, that's exactly the kind of commitment to country that we need.

4 This week, I invited executives from businesses that are insourcing jobs to a forum here at the White House. These are CEOs who take pride in hiring people here in America, not just because it's increasingly the right thing to do for their bottom line, but also because it's the right thing to do for their workers and for our communities and our country.

5 I told those CEOs what I'll tell any business leader: ask yourself what you can do to bring more jobs back to the country that made your success possible. And I'll make sure you've got a government that does everything in its power to help you succeed.

6 That's why, in the next few weeks, I will put forward new tax proposals that reward companies that choose to do the right thing by bringing jobs home and investing in America — and eliminate tax breaks for companies that move jobs overseas.

7 It's also why on Friday, I called on Congress to help me make government work better for you. Right now, we have a 21st century economy, but we've still got a government organized for the 20th century. Over the years, the needs of Americans have changed, but our government has not. In fact, it's gotten even more complex. And that has to change.

8 That's why I asked Congress to reinstate the authority that past presidents have had to streamline and reform *the Executive Branch* ②. This is the same sort of authority that every business owner has to make sure that his or her company keeps pace with the times. It's the same authority that presidents had for over 50 years — up until *Ronald Reagan* ③. And let me be clear: I will only use this authority for reforms that result in more efficiency, better service, and a leaner government.

9 These changes will make it easier for small business owners to get the loans and support they need to sell their products around the world. For example, instead of forcing

CEO 首席执行官，总裁(全称为Chief Executive Officer)

take pride in 对…感到得意，以…自豪

bottom line 底线，最低限度，结果，概要，盈亏，决定因素

put forward 出示，提出，推举，促进

proposal [prəˈpəuzl] *n.* 推荐，申请，建议，提案，提议

tax break 减税优惠，税额优惠，减税特许，减税机会

call on 访问，拜访，号召，请求

reinstate [ˌriːinˈsteit] *vt.* 使复工，使复职，使复原，修复，使康复

streamline [ˈstriːmlain] *vt.* 使合理化，使成流线型 *n.* 流线，流线型 *adj.* 流线型的

leaner [ˈliːnə] *adj.* 精瘦的，贫乏的，简洁的（lean的比较级）

navigate [ˈnævigeit] *vt.* 航行于，飞越，驾驶，操纵

come up with 赶上，接近，提出，提议

patent [ˈpeitənt] *n.* 专利，专利品，专利证 *adj.* 专利的，特许的

warehouse [ˈweəhaus] *n.* 货栈，仓库，批发商店，大的零售商店

pay off 偿清(债务等)，有报偿，收到效果

paper profit 账面收益

speculation [ˌspekjuˈleiʃən] *n.* 思索，意见，推测，猜测，投机

small business owners to navigate the six departments and agencies in the federal government that focus on business and trade, we'll have one department. One place where entrepreneurs can go from the day they come up with an idea and need a patent, to the day they start building a warehouse, to the day they're ready to ship their products overseas.

10 And in the meantime, we're creating a new website — *BusinessUSA*④ — that will serve as a *one-stop shop*⑤ with information for businesses small and large that want to start selling their stuff around the world.

11 This means that more small business owners will see their hard work pay off. More companies will be able to hire new workers. And we'll be able to rebuild an economy that's not known for paper profits or financial speculation, but for making and selling products like these. Products "Made in America."

12 Thank you, and have a great weekend.

背景知识注释 Background Notes

1. yard sale　即 garage sale，宅前贱卖，庭院旧货出售。
2. the Executive Branch　行政部门，根据美国宪法，美国政府 (The Government) 由行政部门 (The Executive Branch)、立法部门 (The Legislative Branch) 和司法部门 (The Judicial Branch) 三部分组成。
3. Ronald Reagan　罗纳德•里根 (1911.2.6 ～ 2004.6.5) 美国政治家，第 33 任加利福尼亚州州长，第 40 任总统 (1981 ～ 1989)。他也是一名伟大的演讲家。在踏入政坛前，里根担任过运动广播员、救生员、报社专栏作家、电影演员、电视节目演员和励志讲师，并且是美国影视演员协会 (Screen Actors Guild) 的领导人。他的演说高明且极具说服力，他被媒体誉为"伟大的沟通者"(The Great Communicator)。历任总统之中，他就职年龄最大。他是历任总统中唯一一位演员出身的总统。里根影响了美国 1980 年代的文化，使得 1980 年代也常被称为"里根时代"。2005 年，美国在线探索频道组织评选了"最伟大的美国人"，结果里根名列第一。
4. BusinessUSA　商务美国，它是一个网站名称。美国商务部和小微企业署 2011 年 10 月 28 日宣布了两项帮助企业扩大和创造就业的总统备忘录，这是美国政府推出的又一项刺激经济增长的行政举措。根据这两项总统备忘录，奥巴马政府将加快把联邦实验室中的研究与

开发成果尽快市场化，还将创立一个新网站——商务美国 (BusinessUSA)。这是一个一站式综合网站，可帮助希望增加出口的各类规模企业获得联邦项目的信息，帮助企业省去在多个联邦机构搜索而耗费时间和精力。白宫表示，这些措施是奥巴马政府近期采取的一系列创造就业和推动经济增长的政策之一，因为政府已经等不及国会共和党采取行动。

5. one-stop-shop　一站式，一站式服务，单一服务点。简单地说，就是由某一组织提供相关的全套服务，比如汽车的 4S 店。

中文译文 Chinese Version

1　正如诸位所看到的，本周的讲话视频中我特地带来了几样东西。一把挂锁、一双靴子、一根蜡烛和一双袜子。

2　当然，我们不是在进行庭院旧货叫卖。这些产品似乎没有什么共通之处，但由于“美国制造”这四个字而使得它们紧密相连。它们都是由美国的工人，在美国的工厂制造的，并运往国内乃至世界各地的消费者。

3　制造这些产品的企业代表着充满希望的趋势：它们正在将工作岗位从海外带回来。你们肯定听说过外包——而这就是内包。中产阶级和那些努力成为中产阶级的人们现在处于成败的关键时刻，这一举措正是我们需要的对国家的承诺。

4　本周，我在白宫举办了一次论坛，邀请了内包就业岗位的企业管理层参加。他们都是一些以在国内雇用美国人为荣的总裁们，这不仅是因为他们这样做对他们自己有利，而且还因为他们做的是对他们的员工，对我们的社会和国家都有益的事情。

5　我告诫当时在场的总裁们，而且我还将告诫任何企业的领袖们：“扪心自问，你怎么做才能将更多的工作岗位带回国内，因为这是成就你们事业之地。我将确保你们拥有一个在其权力范围内竭尽所能帮助你们成功的政府。”

6　正是因为如此，在未来的几周我要推动一项税收提案，褒奖那些将就业和投资带回美国的企业，因为他们自愿做了好事；同时我也要削减将就业岗位输出海外的企业的税收优惠。

7　正是因为如此，上周五我呼吁国会协助我使政府更好地为民服务。目前，我们具有 21 世纪的经济，却依然保持着一个 20 世纪结构的政府。多年来，美国人的需求已经改变了，而政府却依然如故。实际上却变得更加复杂。这一局面必须改变。

8　正是因为如此，我要求国会恢复以前的总统所拥有的权力来理顺和改革行政部门。正是这份权力才使得每位企业主得以确保他们的企业与时俱进。这也是直到罗纳德•里根总统之前的 50 多年里各位总统所拥有的权力。让我说得直白一点：我将把这一权力只用于进行改革，以便获得更高的效率，提供更好的服务并建成更为精简的政府。

9　这些改变将让小微企业主更方便地获得所需贷款和支持以便将产品销往世界各地。

例如，过去小微企业主迫于在主管商业贸易的六个联邦政府部门机构间疲于奔波的事情，将在一个部门即可完成。仅在一个部门企业家们就可以在一天之内办完从提出想法，申请专利，开建仓库，准备将产品运输到海外的所有手续。

10 与此同时，我们也正在创建一个全新的网站：商务美国，这里将作为一站式服务点为那些希望把产品销往世界各地的大小企业提供他们所需的各种信息。

11 这意味着更多的小微企业主将看到自己的辛勤劳动能得到回报。更多的企业将能雇用新员工。我们将能重建我们的经济，它不是以账面效益和金融投机而出名，而是以制造并销售那些标有“美国制造”的产品而著称。

12 谢谢各位，周末愉快！

第3周

Creating Jobs by Boosting Tourism

January 21, 2012

提振旅游观光业，创造就业岗位

2012年1月21日

【摘要导读】

在本周的广播电视讲话中，巴拉克•奥巴马总统向民众阐述了当局在方便更多游客到访美国方面所采取的措施，因为持续增长的旅游业将帮助美国国内经济支撑更多企业扩张和雇用员工。这项提振旅游业的计划是奥巴马在没有国会协助下采取的一系列措施中的一部分，因为他认为需要帮助经济增长和创造就业，这不能再等了。奥巴马总统同样提到了下周的*国情咨文*①，他将就领导层和所有美国人民如何共同努力创造一个可持续发展的经济体发布蓝图计划。

演讲再现 Original Text

1 Hello, everybody. On Thursday, I went down to Florida to visit *Disneyworld*② . To Sasha and Malia's great disappointment, I was not there to hang out with Mickey or ride Space Mountain. Instead, I was there to talk about steps we're taking to boost tourism and create jobs.

2 Tourism is the number one service we export. Every year, tens of millions of tourists come from all over the world to visit America. They stay in our hotels, eat at our restaurants, and see all the sights America has to offer.

3 That's good for local businesses. That's good for local economies. And the more folks who visit America, the more Americans we get back to work. It's that simple.

Words & Expressions

boost [bu:st] *vt.* 升，提，抬，促进，支持，提升，激励，改善

hang out with sb. 与某人闲逛，与某人一起闲混

Space Mountain 太空山，太空飞车

4 We can't wait to seize this opportunity. As I've said before, I will continue to work with Congress, states, and leaders in the private sector to find ways to move this country forward. But where they can't act or won't act, I will. Because we want the world to know that America is open for business. And that's why I announced steps we're taking to promote America and make it easier for tourists to come and visit.

5 Frequent travelers who pass an extensive background check will be able to scan their passports and fingerprints and skip long lines at immigration at more airports. We're going to expand the number of countries where visitors can get pre-cleared by *Homeland Security* ③ so they don't need a tourist visa. And we're going to speed up visa processing for countries with growing middle-classes that can afford to visit America — countries like China and Brazil.

6 We want more visitors coming here. We want them spending money here. It's good for our economy, and it will help provide the boost more businesses need to grow and hire. And we can't wait to make it happen.

7 Too often over the last few months, we've seen Congress drag its feet and refuse to take steps we know will help strengthen our economy. That's why this is the latest in a series of actions I've taken on my own to help our economy keep growing, creating jobs, and restoring security for middle-class families.

8 In September, we decided to stop waiting for Congress to fix *No Child Left Behind* ④ and give states the flexibility they need to help our kids meet higher standards. We made sure that small businesses that have contracts with the Federal Government can get paid faster so they can start hiring more people. We made it easier for veterans to get jobs and put their skills to work. We took steps to help families whose home values have fallen to refinance their mortgages and save up to thousands of dollars a year. We sped up the loan process for companies that want to rebuild our roads and bridges — putting construction workers back on the job. And I appointed Richard Cordray to be America's consumer watchdog and protect working Americans from the worst

seize [si:z] *vt.* 突然抓住，抓住(机会等)，利用，理解，攻占

fingerprint ['fiŋgəprint] *n.* 指纹，指印

pre-clear 预净化，事先申报

drag one's feet 慢吞吞地走，故意拖拉，勉强行事，逃避责任，消极怠工

strengthen ['streŋθən] *vt.* 加强，使强壮，使坚强有力，巩固

flexibility [ˌfleksi'biliti] *n.* 灵活性，弹性，适应性

veteran ['vetərən] *n.* 老兵，老军人，老战士，退伍军人

refinance [ˌri:fai'næns] *vt.* 为…再提供资金，为…筹集额外的资金或贷款

mortgage ['mɔ:gidʒ] *n.* 抵押，抵押单，抵押贷款，抵押权

abuses of the financial industry.

9 These are good steps. Now we need to do more.

10 On Tuesday evening, I'll deliver my State of the Union Address, where I'll lay out my blueprint for actions we need to take together — not just me, or Congress, but every American — to rebuild an economy where hard work and responsibility are rewarded. An economy that's built to last.

11 I hope you'll tune in. In the meantime, I'm going to keep doing everything I can to make this country not only the best place to visit and do business — but the best place to live and work and build a better life.

12 Thanks for watching. Have a great weekend. And I'll see you on Tuesday.

deliver [di'livə] *vt.* 发表
lay out 安排，布置，设计，展示，花钱，提议
blueprint ['blu:print] *n.*（建筑或工程设计用的）蓝图，详尽的行动计划（规划、大纲）
tune in 使协调，收听，收看，使和谐

背景知识注释 Background Notes

1. 国情咨文　即 State of the Union Address 国情咨文演讲，国情咨文原名“年度咨文”，是宪法布置给总统向国会报告的任务，是咨文的一种，是美国统治阶级的施政纲领，主要阐明美国总统每年面临的国内外情况，以及政府将要采取的政策措施。按照美国惯例，每年年初，现任总统都要在国会做年度报告，阐述政府的施政方针，被称为“国情咨文”。国情咨文本是平常的政府工作报告，但现在已成为一项重大的游说宣传。美国在开国初期就有了“国情咨文”这种形式，其传统可追溯到1790年。那一年，美国首任总统乔治•华盛顿按宪法要求发表了当时被称做“年度咨文”的报告。

2. Disneyworld　迪斯尼世界，位于佛罗里达州中部，它是世界上最大的综合游乐场。迪斯尼世界的诞生，首先要归功于富于想象力和创造精神的美国动画片大师沃尔特•迪斯尼。1955年他在洛杉矶附近创办了第一座现代化的游乐园，取名迪斯尼乐园。1964年人们开始筹建一座更大规模的游乐公园，这就是迪斯尼世界。经过五年营造，迪斯尼世界终于1971年10月向公众开放了。它耗资7.66亿美元，占地面积达109平方公里，是一座老少咸宜的游乐中心。在迪斯尼世界中，设有中央大街、小世界、海底两万里、明天的世界、拓荒之地和自由广场等。迪斯尼世界不仅是个游乐场，同时又是一个旅游中心，游客来此还可以到附近的海滩游泳、滑冰、驾帆船，到深海捕鱼，乘气球升空，或是参观附近的名胜古迹。这些丰富多彩的节目，给迪斯尼世界更增添了几分魅力。

3. Homeland Security　(United States Department of Homeland Security, 缩写为 DHS)（美国）国土安全部，为美国政府的一个部门，负责国内安全及防止恐怖活动，是“9•11事件”之

后新成立的美国联邦部门，其总部位于内布拉斯加大道广场。2002 年 11 月 25 日，美国总统小布什在白宫签署《2002 年国土安全法》，宣布成立国土安全部。成立国土安全部是美国自 1947 年成立国防部以来最大规模的一次政府机构调整。

4. *No Child Left Behind* 《有教无类法案》/《不让一个孩子掉队法案》。2001 年 1 月 23 日，布什总统发布了题为《不让一个孩子掉队法案》的教育改善计划，提出将电子学习 (e-Learning) 作为美国基础教育信息化发展的新战略。

中文译文
Chinese Version

1 嗨，大家好。星期三，我造访了佛罗里达州的迪斯尼乐园。不过让萨莎和玛莉亚失望的是我并不是到那里与米奇 (Mickey) 玩耍或坐太空山 (Space Mountain) 去了。相反，我是去讨论我们如何振兴旅游业和创造就业的方案。

2 旅游业是我们最重要的出口服务。每年都有数千万来自世界各地的游客造访美国。他们在我们的宾馆逗留，在我们的餐馆就餐，并游览我们的风景名胜。

3 这对我们国内的企业和经济都是个福音。造访美国的游客越多，重返工作岗位的美国人也就越多。这个道理就这么简单。

4 机不可失，时不再来。正如我以前所说的，我将继续与国会、各州以及私营部门的领袖们密切合作，寻求使国家向前发展的途径。但是倘若他们不能或不想作为的话，我一定要有所作为。因为我们希望全世界都知道美国始终开门迎客。正是因为如此，我宣布了数项措施以提升美国形象，使游客更为便利地造访美国。

5 须经全面背景检查的常客们将能在更多机场的移民入境管理部门通过护照和指纹扫描，这样就免去了排长队的烦恼了。我们将增加游客通过国土安全部的事先审查而无需旅游签证的国家数量。有些国家，比如中国和巴西，中产阶级日益增加且有实力造访美国，我们将加快对这些国家游客的签证速度。

6 我们欢迎更多游客的到来。我们需要他们在此花钱。这对我们的经济是有益的，也将有助于为更多需要发展和雇用人员的企业提供更多支撑。对此我们都翘首以盼。

7 在过去的数月中，我们常常能看到国会故意拖拉，拒绝采取众所周知的可以巩固我们经济的措施。因此，最近我自主采取一系列措施以保持经济增长、创造就业岗位并恢复中产阶级家庭的安全感。

8 9 月份，我们决定不再等待国会对《不让一个孩子掉队法案》进行修订，就赋予各州所需的灵活性来帮助我们的孩子达到更高的标准。我们确保那些与联邦政府签有合同的小微企业能更快得到款项支付，以方便他们雇用更多的员工。我们使退伍老兵更便捷地找到工作，让他们的技能得以发挥。我们采取措施让房产价值缩水的家庭重新安排自己的抵押贷款从而每年节省数千美元。我们加快了对重建道路和桥梁的企业的贷款流程，让更多建筑工人重返工作岗位。我还任命理查德·科德雷为美国消费者监察机构领导，保护美国人民免受金融行业最严重的侵权行为。

9 这些措施很稳妥。但现在我们要做的还有很多。

10 下周二晚，我将发表国情咨文，我还将发布施政蓝图，实现这一愿景需要我们——不仅是我或是国会，而且包括全体美国人——团结一致，重建一种勤劳和责任心都能得到奖赏的经济，一种可持续发展的经济。

11 届时，我希望你们都能收看。与此同时，我也将继续竭尽所能来确保我们国家成为不仅是最适合旅游和经商的地方，也是最适合生活、工作和追求更美好人生的地方。

12 谢谢收看，周末愉快。下周二再见。

第4周

Blueprint Includes Renewal of *American Values*[①]

January 28, 2012

施政蓝图包含重拾美国价值观

2012 年 1 月 28 日

【摘要导读】

在本周的广播电视讲话中，巴拉克•奥巴马总统探讨了他在本周发表的国情咨文中提出的关于建设可持续发展经济的施政蓝图。在过去三天里连续关注美国制造业、能源产业以及美国人的劳动技能之后，在本周六的讲话中他又强调了对重拾美国价值观的承诺。奥巴马要求华盛顿的各位领导人，以美国的军人为榜样，结束政治僵局，摒弃个人野心，开始把重要的事情做好。

演讲再现
Original Text

1 On Tuesday, in my State of the Union Address, I laid out a blueprint for an economy built to last — an economy built on American manufacturing, American energy, skills for American workers, and a renewal of American values.

2 This week, I took that blueprint across the country, and what I saw was people who work hard and believe in each other. They believe in the America that's within our reach. But they're not sure that the right thing will get done in Washington this year, or next year, or the year after that. And frankly, when you look at some of the things that go on in this town, who could blame them for being a little cynical?

3 Just two days ago, a senator from Utah promised to obstruct every single American I appoint to a judgeship or public service position — unless I fire the consumer watchdog

Words & Expressions

cynical ['sinikəl] *adj.* 玩世不恭的，愤世嫉俗的，爱挖苦人的

obstruct [əb'strʌkt] *vt.* 阻塞，堵塞（道路等），阻碍，妨碍，阻止

judgeship ['dʒʌdʒʃip] *n.* 法官（或审判员）的职位

I put in place to protect the American people from financial schemes or malpractice.

4 For the most part, it's not that this senator thinks these nominees are unqualified. In fact, all of the judicial nominees being blocked have bipartisan support. And almost 90 percent have unanimous support from *the Judiciary Committee*②.

5 Instead, one of his aides told reporters that the senator plans to, and I'm quoting here, "Delay and slow the process in order to get the President's attention."

6 This isn't about me. We weren't sent here to wage perpetual political campaigns against each other. We were sent here to serve the American people. And they deserve better than gridlock and games. One senator gumming up the works for the whole country is certainly not what our founding fathers envisioned.

7 The truth is, neither party has been blameless in tactics like these. But it's time for both parties to put an end to them. I'm asking Congress, both Democrats and Republicans, to stop this kind of behavior by passing a rule that allows all judicial and public service nominations *a simple up-or-down vote*③ within 90 days.

8 We should also stem the corrosive influence of money in politics. The House and Senate should send me a bill that bans insider trading by Members of Congress, and I will sign it immediately. They should limit any elected official from owning stocks in industries they impact. And they should make sure people who bundle campaign contributions for Congress can't lobby Congress, and vice versa.

9 During my Address on Tuesday night, I spoke about the incredible example set by the men and women of our armed forces. At a time when too many of our institutions have let us down, they exceed all expectations. They're not consumed with personal ambition. They don't obsess over their differences. They focus on the mission at hand. They work together.

10 If you agree with me that leaders in Washington should follow their example, then make your voice heard. Tell

scheme [ski:m] *n.* 策划，方案，阴谋，诡计

malpractice [ˌmælˈpræktis] *n.* 失职行为，医疗事故

for the most part 多半，大部分

nominee [ˌnɔmiˈni:] *n.* 被提名者，被任命者

bipartisan [ˌbaipɑ:tiˈzæn] *adj.* 两党的，两派的

unanimous [ju:ˈnænimәs] *adj.* 意见相同的，一致同意的，全体一致的

aide [eid] *n.* 助手

perpetual [pәˈpetʃuәl] *adj.* 永远的，长期的，终身的

gridlock [ˈgridlɔk] *n.* 僵局

gum up [美国俚语]搞乱，弄糟，使…困惑

envision [inˈviʒәn] *vt.* 想象，设想，预想，展望

tactic [ˈtæktik] *n.* 战术，策略，手法，手段

stem [stem] *vt.* 阻止，遏止

corrosive [kәˈrәusiv] *adj.* 腐蚀性的，讽刺的

insider trading 暗箱操作

bundle [ˈbʌndl] *vt.* 收集，为…提供或供应

lobby [ˈlɔbi] *vt.* 对（议员）进行游说

institution [ˌinstiˈtju:ʃәn] *n.* 社会公共机构，制度，习俗

let... down 使失望，辜负…的期望

obsess over 为…拖累，被…困扰

your Member of Congress that it's time to end the gridlock, and start tackling the issues that really matter — an economy built on American manufacturing, American energy, American skills and education, and a return to American values. An economy built to last.

11 Thank you, God bless you, and have a great weekend.

背景知识注释 Background Notes

1. American Values 美国人的价值观，美国200多年建国和强国的历史，也是美国人价值观形成和发展的历史。美国人的价值观包括：

（1）今世我做主。美国人不相信天命。认为事在人为，没有不可能的事。

（2）求变。在美国人看来，变化是同成长、发展、改进、进步联系在一起的。

（3）惜时如金。时间，对美国人来说，是最最重要的。

（4）公平公正。人人生而平等，意味着生活中人人享有平等的成功的机会。

（5）张扬个性。无论是思想，还是行动，美国人处处表现出与众不同。

（6）自由竞争。美国人相信，竞争能产生挑战和压力，只有竞争，才有最好。

2. the Judiciary Committee （美国国会参议院常设）司法委员会。

3. a simple up-or-down vote 一个简单的投票表决。这种程序进行的是只投赞成票或反对票的直接表决。

中文译文 Chinese Version

1 本周二，在我的国情咨文演讲中，我提出了建立一种可持续发展的经济的施政蓝图。这种经济依托于美国的制造业、美国的能源产业、美国人的劳动技能以及美国价值观的复兴。

2 本周，我将施政蓝图带到了全国各地，我目睹了辛勤劳动和彼此信任的人们，他们都认为，在美国实现这一目标是切实可行的。只是不太确定今年或者明年抑或是后年才能办妥此事。坦率而言，当你看到事情正在向前发展时，谁还能去责备他们有一点愤世嫉俗呢？

3 就在两天前，一位来自犹他州的参议员信誓旦旦地声称：除非我取消所设置的用来保护美国人民免受金融系统的欺诈和渎职侵害的消费者监护机构，否则他将阻止我在司法部门或公共服务部门任命任何美国人。

4 在极大程度上，该参议员并不是认为这些提名人选不够格。实际上，所有受到阻挠的司法部门提名人选都有着两党的共同支持，而且有 90% 的人选都得到了司法委员会的一致支持。

5 然而，他的一位助手却还告诉媒体，我在这里援引他的话，称这位参议员还将“阻碍和延迟程序流程以引起总统的注意。”

6 这不能与我个人扯在一起。选民将我们送到这里，不是让我们来进行无休止的政治争斗。我们当选的宗旨就是为美国人民服务。政治僵局和争斗并不是他们应得的东西。一个把国家的事情搞得一团糟的参议员绝对不是我们的开国元勋们所期许的。

7 事实是，任何一个党派在这些争斗中都不是无可责备的。但现在两党应该共同结束这一局面。我现在要求国会、民主党人和共和党人，通过一项规定终止这些行为，对所有的司法部门和公共服务部门的提名人选在 90 天内要进行简单的投票表决。

8 我们同样还要遏制金钱对政治的腐蚀影响。众参两院应该向我提交一份法案来阻止国会议员之间的暗箱操作，我将尽快让它签署生效。国会还应限制任何民选官员拥有他们所能影响到的行业企业的股票，还应确保为竞选提供赞助的人不能对国会议员进行游说，反之亦然。

9 在周二晚上的讲话中，我谈到了我们的军队指战人员们所树立的杰出榜样。尽管曾有太多的部门机构让我们失望，而他们却超出了我们的期望。他们并没有被个人野心所吞噬，他们并不被彼此的分歧所困扰。他们关注自己身边的任务。他们团结奋进。

10 倘若你们同意我的看法，认为华盛顿的领袖们应该以他们为榜样，那么就尽量表达你们的心声。告诉你们的国会议员们，该是结束政治僵局，开始解决重大问题的时候了。我们要建立一种以美国制造业、美国能源产业、美国人的技能与教育以及美国价值观回归为基础的经济。建立一种可持续发展的经济。

11 谢谢各位，上帝保佑你们，周末愉快！

第5周

It's Time for Congress to Act to Help Responsible Homeowners

February 4, 2012

现在正是国会出手帮助信誉良好的房屋贷款人的好时机

2012年2月4日

【摘要导读】

在本周的广播电视讲话中，巴拉克•奥巴马总统继续呼吁重拾公平与平等等美国价值观，作为其建立可持续发展经济的施政蓝图的有机部分。因此，他向国会提出一项计划，向有信誉的房屋贷款人提供重新安排抵押贷款的机会，利用历史低位的利率节省数千美元的资金而且不需增加任何财政赤字。房贷危机是对当前经济复苏的最大拖累，尽管本届美国政府采取了各种措施来帮助有信用的房贷人将其抵押贷款寻求再融资，保留他们的住所，但现在国会必须尽更大的努力来帮助这些房屋贷款人，促进经济复苏。奥巴马总统请求全体美国人民敦促他们所选的官员们通过这项计划，以此来保证更多家庭有房可居，让更多社区生活兴旺美满。

演讲再现 Original Text

1 Over the last couple of weeks, I've been traveling around the country and talking with folks about my blueprint for an economy built to last. It's a blueprint that focuses on restoring the things we've always done best. Our strengths. American manufacturing. American energy. The skills and education of American workers.

2 And most importantly, American values like fairness and responsibility.

3 We know what happened when we strayed from those values over the past decade — especially when it comes to our housing market.

4 Lenders sold loans to families who couldn't afford them. Banks packaged those mortgages up and traded them for phony profits. It drove up prices and created an unsustainable bubble that burst — and left millions of families who did everything right in a world of hurt.

5 It was wrong. The housing crisis has been the single biggest drag on our recovery from the recession. It has kept millions of families in debt and unable to spend, and it has left hundreds of thousands of construction workers out of a job.

6 But there's something even more important at stake. I've been saying this is a make-or-break moment for the middle-class. And the housing crisis struck right at the heart of what it means to be middle-class in this country: owning a home. Raising our kids. Building our dreams.

7 Right now, there are more than 10 million homeowners in this country who, because of a decline in home prices that is no fault of their own, owe more on their mortgages than their homes are worth. Now, it is wrong for anyone to suggest that the only option for struggling, responsible homeowners is to sit and wait for the housing market to hit bottom. I don't accept that. None of us should.

8 That's why we launched a plan a couple years ago that's helped nearly one million responsible homeowners refinance their mortgages and save an average of $300 on their payments each month. Now, I'll be the first to admit it didn't help as many folks as we'd hoped. But that doesn't mean we shouldn't keep trying.

9 That's why I'm sending Congress a plan that will give every responsible homeowner the chance to save about $3,000 a year on their mortgages by refinancing at historically low rates. No more red tape. No more endless forms. And a small fee on the largest financial institutions will make sure it doesn't add a dime to the deficit.

10 I want to be clear: this plan will not help folks who

Words & Expressions

stray from 失散，偏离

package [ˈpækidʒ] *vt.* 包装，把…打包，把…装箱

phony [ˈfəuni] *adj.* 假的，欺骗的

drove up 开车赶到，抬高，迫使…上升

unsustainable [ˌʌnsəˈsteinəbl] *adj.* 不能证实的，不支持的

bubble [ˈbʌbl] *n.* 泡影，妄想，（欲表达的）一点感情

at stake 在危急关头，在危险中，成问题

struck right at the heart of 撞击在…要害之处

hit bottom= touch bottom 降到最低点，到达最低点，达到最坏程度，不幸到极点

red tape 繁文缛节，官样文章

deficit [ˈdefisit] *n.* 逆差，亏损，赤字，缺乏，不足

bought a house they couldn't afford and then walked away from it. It won't help folks who bought multiple houses just to turn around and sell them.

11 What this plan will do is help millions of responsible homeowners who make their payments every month, but who, until now, couldn't refinance because their home values kept dropping or they got wrapped up in too much red tape.

12 But here's the catch. In order to lower mortgage payments for millions of Americans, we need Congress to act. They're the ones who have to pass this plan. And as anyone who has followed the news in the last six months can tell you, getting Congress to do anything these days is not an easy job.

13 That's why I'm going to keep up the pressure on Congress to do the right thing. But I also need your help. I need your voice. I need everyone who agrees with this plan to get on the phone, send an email, tweet, pay a visit, and remind your representatives in Washington who they work for. Tell them to pass this plan. Tell them to help more families keep their homes, and more neighborhoods stay vibrant and whole.

14 The truth is, it will take time for our housing market to recover. It will take time for our economy to fully bounce back. But there are steps we can take, right now, to move this country forward. That's what I promise to do as your President, and I hope Members of Congress will join me.

15 Thanks, and have a great weekend.

multiple ['mʌltipl] *adj.* 多个的，多重的，多层次的，多倍的

get wrapped up in 沉溺于，陷入

tweet 推特，推文，微博信息

vibrant ['vaibrənt] *adj.* 震颤的，响亮的，充满生命力的，活泼的

bounce back 弹回，康复，复原，好转，回升

中文译文 Chinese Version

1 在过去的数周里，我走遍了全国各地，与人们共同商讨我提出的建立可持续发展经济的施政蓝图。该蓝图特别关注要恢复那些我们一直做得最好的事情。我们的实力、美国的制造业、美国的能源产业，以及美国劳动者所具有的技能和所受的教育。

2 而尤为重要的是，还有诸如公平和责任心等美国价值观。

3 众所周知，在过去的十年里我们偏离了这些价值观之后——尤其是在房地产领域——所发生的一切。

4 放贷人将贷款发放给那些无力偿还的家庭。银行将这些抵押贷款打包后进行交易以

寻求虚假的利润，这推动了价格的飞涨，导致了不稳定泡沫的形成并最终破裂——让数百万家庭蒙冤受害。

5 这是不正当的行为，房贷危机现在是我们经济复苏过程中最大的拖累。它让数百万家庭债台高筑无力消费，使数十万建筑工人遭遇失业。

6 但还有些事情更加利害攸关。我曾说过此时中产阶级正处于成败的关键时刻。但房贷危机却恰好撞在了美国意义上的中产阶级命门：拥有一套住房、养育儿女以及追求自己的梦想。

7 目前，我国有1,000多万房屋贷款人背负着比他们房屋价值高得多的贷款，这都源自房屋价格的下跌，而他们本身却毫无过错。现在，倘若有人说对于处境艰难而信用良好的房贷人来说唯一抗争的选择就是坐等房产市场的触底反弹，这种看法我持异议。任何人都不应该这么认为。

8 正是因为如此，两年前我们提出了一项计划，帮助将近100万有信用的房贷人将其抵押贷款寻求再融资，以此为其每月均省300多美元的还款额。现在，我首先要承认的是这一计划并没有帮助到我们希望中的那么多人。但这并不意味着我们不应该继续努力。

9 正是因为如此，我向国会提交了一项计划，让所有信誉好的房贷人有机会将其抵押贷款寻求再融资，以历史上最低的利率每年为他们节省3,000美元。不再有官僚的繁文缛节，不再有无休止的表格。只是会给最大的金融机构增添一些费用，但不会增加一分钱的财政赤字。

10 需要说明的是：该计划不能帮助那些无力承担贷款却又逃避的购房者，也不会帮助那些购买多套房产只是等着行情转好就出手卖个好价的人。

11 这项计划的宗旨就是帮助那些信誉好的房贷人能够每月正常还贷，但直到现在，这些人还不能将其抵押贷款寻求再融资，因为他们的房产价格一直在下降，或者他们陷入了繁文缛节的包围之中难于抽身。

12 这就是问题所在：为了降低数百万美国人民的房贷还款额，我们需要国会有所作为。我们需要他们通过这一计划。但过去的6个月的事实告诉我们，如今要让国会采取行动的确并非易事。

13 正是因为如此，我要持续向国会施压，使他们做些该做的事情。但我仍需要大家的帮助。我需要你们的声援。我需要同意这一计划的每个人拨通电话、发送电子邮件或者推特、登门拜访，用这些方式提醒你们那些为华盛顿效力的代表们，告诫他们要通过这项计划，告诫他们要帮助更多家庭保住房产，使更多社区的生活兴旺美满。

14 事实是，房产市场的复苏有待时日。我们的经济要完全复苏也有待时日。但我们现在可以采取行动来推动我们国家向前发展。这是我作为总统所做出的承诺，我也希望国会议员们都能与我携手并进。

15 谢谢各位，周末愉快。

第6周

Extending the Payroll Tax Cut for the Middle-Class

February 11, 2012

为中产阶级延长工资税减免政策

2012 年 2 月 11 日

【摘要导读】

在本周的广播电视讲话中，巴拉克•奥巴马总统敦促国会尽快通过对工资税减免政策的延期，以避免增税使1亿6千万辛勤的美国人受到冲击，他们依然处在自*大萧条*[①]以来最严重的经济衰退的恢复期中。他表示现在不是在复苏道路上自我伤害或给中产阶级家庭添加重负的时候，因此，民主党和共和党都必须尽快通过这一合乎常理的减税政策，不能有丝毫的阻挠或拖延。另外，奥巴马总统再次呼吁全美人民告诫自己选出的领导人要做好本职工作，把党派利益搁置一边，为中产阶级延长这一减税政策。

演讲再现 Original Text

1 Hello, everybody.

2 In recent weeks, we've seen signs that our economy is growing stronger and creating jobs at a faster clip. While numbers and figures will go up and down in the coming months, what cannot waver is our resolve to do everything in our power to keep stoking the fires of the recovery.

3 And the last thing we should do is let Washington stand in the way.

4 You see, at the end of the month, taxes are set to go up on 160 million working Americans. If you're one of them, then you know better than anyone that the last thing you need right now is a tax hike. But if Congress refuses to act, middle-

Words & Expressions

at a faster clip 以更快的速度

waver [ˈweivə] *vi.* 摇动，犹豫不决，动摇，颤抖

stoke the fires of... 点燃…之火，火上浇油，推波助澜

stand in the way 阻碍，妨碍，影响

tax hike 赋税增加，增税

class taxes will go up. It's that simple.

5 Now, if this sounds familiar, it's because we've been here before. Back in December, Congress faced this exact same predicament. Ultimately, thanks to your voices, they did the right thing — but only after a great deal of bickering and political posturing that put the strength of our economy and the security of middle-class families at risk. We can't go through that again.

6 Congress needs to stop this middle-class tax hike from happening. Period. No drama. No delay. And no ideological side issues that have nothing to do with this tax cut. Now is not the time for self-inflicted wounds to our recovery. Now is the time for common-sense action. And this tax cut is common-sense. If you're a family making about $50,000 a year, this tax cut amounts to about $1,000 a year. That's about $40 in every paycheck. I know there are some folks in this town who think $40 isn't a lot of money. But to a student or a senior who's trying to stretch the budget a little bit further? To a parent who's filling up the tank and looking at rising gas prices? To them, $40 can make all the difference in the world.

7 And so can your voice. I hope you'll pick up the phone, send a tweet, write an email, and tell your representative that they should get this done before it gets too late. Tell them not to play politics again by linking this debate to unrelated issues. Tell them not to manufacture another needless standoff or crisis. Tell them not to stand in the way of the recovery. Tell them to just do their job. That's what our middle-class needs. That's what our country needs.

8 In the wake of the worst economic crisis of our lifetimes, we're getting things going again. And we're going to keep at it until everyone shares in America's comeback.

9 Thanks, and have a great weekend.

predicament [priˈdikəmənt] *n.* 处境，(尤指)困境，危境，险境

bickering [ˈbikəriŋ] *n.* 口角，争吵，争论

posturing[ˈpɔstʃəriŋ] *n.* 故作姿态，摆姿势，并非由衷的言行

put... at risk 将…置于风险中

ideological [ˌaidiəuˈlɔdʒikəl] *adj.* 思想上的，思想意识的，意识形态的

self-inflicted [ˈselfinˈfliktid] *adj.* 自己造成的，自身受到的，加于自身的

stretch the budget 提高预算

make all the difference = make a world of difference 关系重大，大不相同

manufacture [ˌmænjuˈfæktʃə] *vt.* (大规模)制造，生产，捏造，虚构

standoff [ˈstændɔf] *n.* 平局，停工，冷漠

in the wake of 紧跟，随着…而来，作为…的结果，效仿

背景知识注释 Background Notes

1. 经济大萧条　即 the Great Depression 经济大衰退，指 1929 年至 1933 年之间全球性的经济大衰退。大萧条的影响比历史上任何一次经济衰退都要来得深远。这次经济萧条是以农产品价格下跌为起点的。它首先发生在木材的价格上 (1928 年)，这主要是由于苏联木材竞争的缘故；但更大的灾难是在 1929 年到来，加拿大小麦的过量生产，美国强迫压低所有农产品产地基本谷物的价格。不管是欧洲、美洲还是澳洲，农业衰退由于金融的大崩溃而进一步恶化，尤其在美国，一股投机热导致大量资金从欧洲抽回，随后在 1929 年 10 月发生了令人恐慌的华尔街股市暴跌。1931 年法国银行家收回了给奥地利银行的贷款，但这并不足以偿还债务。这场灾难使中欧和东欧许多国家的制度破产了：它导致了德国银行家为了自保，而延期偿还外债，进而也危及了在德国有很大投资的英国银行家。资本的短缺，在所有的工业化国家中，都带来了出口和国内消费的锐减：没有市场必然使工厂关闭，货物越少，货物运输也就越少，这必然会危害船运业和造船业。在所有国家中，经济衰退的后果是大规模失业：美国 1,370 万，德国 560 万，英国 280 万 (1932 年的最大数据)。大萧条对拉丁美洲也有重大影响，使得在一个几乎被欧美银行家和商人企业家完全支配的地区失去了外资和商品出口。

中文译文 Chinese Version

1　嗨，各位好！

2　最近数周，我们目睹了经济持续好转、就业加速上升的迹象。尽管统计数字在未来数月中会有起伏，但我们竭尽所能保持经济复苏势头的强大决心绝不动摇。

3　我们极不情愿看到的就是华盛顿阻碍我们前进的步伐。

4　众所周知，本月末，1 亿 6 千万美国工薪人员的税金将要上涨。倘若你是他们中的一员，你一定比任何人都更清楚，眼下你最不需要的就是税金上涨。但倘若国会拒绝采取行动，中产阶级的税金就将面临上涨。事实就是如此。

5　现在，倘若说这些似乎耳熟能详，那是因为我们曾遭遇过此类情况。回顾去年 12 月，国会也面临同样的困境。由于大家的声援，他们最终做出了正确的选择——但却经历了大量的争论和政治伎俩，将我们经济发展的活力和中产阶级的安全置于风险之中。这一切我们再也无法忍受了。

6　国会应阻止向中产阶级增税的事情发生。立即行动，不玩伎俩，绝不拖延。这项减税政策与意识形态方面的问题毫不相关。现在不是在我们复苏的道路上自我伤害的时候，而是要采取合理行动的时候。而这一减税政策就是合理行为。倘若你的家庭年收入约 5 万美元，这项减税政策每年将为你节约 1,000 美元。平均到每份工资单就是 40 美元。我想有人会认为

40 美元算不上什么大数目。但对于一位想把预算稍做一点精打细算的学生或老人而言呢？对于一位瞅着油价上涨却需要每天加油的父母而言呢？对他们而言 40 美元就大为可观了。

7 你们的声援也关系重大。我希望你们拿起电话，或发送推特，或发送电子邮件，告诫你们的议员代表们，要他们尽快把这件事办妥。告诫他们不要再玩弄政治手段，不要将这件事和不相干的问题放到一起辩论。告诫他们不要人为制造不必要的僵局或危机。告诫他们不要阻挠经济复苏的步伐。告诫他们做好自己的本职工作。这就是我们中产阶级所需要的，也是我们的国家所需要的。

8 经历我们人生之中最为严重的经济危机之后，我们正在使局面逐渐好转。我们也将坚持不懈，让每个人都能参与到美国复兴的事业中去。

9 谢谢各位，周末愉快！

第7周

Continuing to Strengthen American Manufacturing

February 18, 2012

进一步夯实美国制造业的基础

2012年2月18日

【摘要导读】

巴拉克·奥巴马总统在波音公司位于华盛顿州埃弗雷特市的工厂发表了本周的广播电视讲话，内容涉及如何努力夯实美国的制造业和创造就业的基础。他还描述了如何支持一些诸如波音这样在全国拥有数千名职工的公司，那就是采取措施将以前给向海外输出就业机会的公司提供的税收优惠政策取消，转而将这些政策提供给那些在国内创造就业机会的公司。他承诺将继续协助企业在全球推销其产品，美国也正在为实现奥巴马5年内达到出口翻一番的目标而继续前行。奥巴马认为，通过提振美国制造业，支持这些创造就业的公司，美国就一定能建立一种可持续发展的经济。

演讲再现 Original Text

1 Hello, everybody.

2 I'm speaking to you this week from the Boeing Plant in *Everett*①, Washington. Boeing has been in this community for half a century. But it's what they're doing here today that has folks really excited; because at this plant they're building the plane of the future — *the Dreamliner*②. It's an impressive sight. And, to be honest, part of why I came was to see it up close. But I also came because this is a great example of how we can bring jobs and manufacturing back to America.

3 You see, the last few decades haven't been easy for manufacturing in this country. New technology has made businesses more efficient and productive — and that's good

Words & Expressions

impressive [im'presiv] *adj.* 给人深刻印象的，令人难忘的，令人敬畏的，威严的

up close 很近距离内地，仔细地

— but it's also made a lot of jobs obsolete. The result has been painful for a lot of families and a lot of communities. Factories where people thought they'd retire have left town. Jobs that provided a decent living have been shipped overseas. And the hard truth is that a lot of those jobs aren't coming back.

4 But that doesn't mean we have to settle for a lesser future. I don't accept that idea. In America, there's always something we can do to create new jobs and new manufacturing and new security for the middle-class. In America, we don't give up, we get up.

5 Right now, that's exactly what we're doing. Over the past 23 months, businesses have created 3.7 million new jobs. And manufacturers are hiring for the first time since the 1990s. It's now getting more expensive to do business in places like China. Meanwhile, America is more productive than ever. And companies like Boeing are realizing that even when we can't make things cheaper than China, we can make things better. That's how we're going to compete globally.

6 For Boeing, business right now is booming. Last year, orders for commercial aircraft rose by more than 50 percent. To meet that rising demand, they've put thousands of folks to work all over the country. We want to see more of this. We need to make it as easy as we can for our companies to create more jobs in America, not overseas. And that starts with our tax code.

7 No company should get a tax break for outsourcing jobs. Instead, tax breaks should go to manufacturers who set up shop here at home. Bigger tax breaks should go to high-tech manufacturers who create the jobs of the future. And if you relocate your company to a struggling community, you should get help financing that new plant, that new equipment, or training for new workers. It's time to stop rewarding businesses that ship jobs overseas, and start rewarding businesses that create jobs here in America. And Congress should send me that kind of tax reform right away.

8 Another thing we're doing is to make it easier for companies like Boeing to sell their products all over the world, because more exports mean more jobs. Two years ago,

obsolete [ˈɔbsəliːt] *adj.* 废弃的，淘汰的，陈腐的，过时的

decent [ˈdiːsənt] *adj.* 合乎礼仪的，得体的，体面的，合宜的

settle for 满足于，勉强接受，将就

boom [buːm] *vi.* 发隆隆声，急速发展，兴旺

tax break 减税优惠，税额优惠，减税特许

set up shop 开业

relocate [ˌriːləuˈkeit] *vt.* 重新定位，迁移，重新安置

I set a goal of doubling U.S. exports over five years. And we're on track to meet that goal — ahead of schedule.

9 We have a big opportunity right now to build not only an economy that will help us succeed today, but an economy that will help our kids and their kids succeed tomorrow. We know what we need to do. We need to strengthen American manufacturing. We need to invest in American-made energy and new skills for American workers. And above all, we need to renew the values that have always made this country great: Hard work. Fair play. Shared responsibility.

10 We can do this. Ask the folks in Everett. Right here, a few years ago, the first Dreamliner took off on its maiden trip. Thousands of employees came to watch. One was an executive office administrator named Sharon O'Hara. As Sharon saw that first plane take flight — a result of so much hard work — she got goose bumps. In her words, she said, "We said we would do it and we did." That's the story of America. We said we would do it, and we did. That's the can-do spirit that makes us who we are. We've seen challenging times before. But we always emerge from them stronger. And that's what we're going to do again today. Thanks, and have a great weekend.

be on track to 正在…，在…的途中，往…方向发展，走上…的正轨

ahead of schedule（比原计划或规定时间）提前，提早

above all 首先，首要，尤其是，最重要的是

maiden ['meidən] *adj.* 少女的，处女的，首次的

take flight 飞行，逃走

get goose bumps 全身起鸡皮疙瘩，非常感动

背景知识注释 Background Notes

1. Everett　埃弗雷特市，美国华盛顿州西北部城市，波音公司的飞机装配厂位于该市，波音公司的 787 梦想客机 (Dreamliner) 就是在这个工厂制造的。

2. the Dreamliner　波音 787，亦称梦幻客机，是波音公司最新型号的具有远程直飞能力的广体中型客机，由波音民用飞机集团负责开发，于 2011 年投入服务。787 可载 210 至 330 人，视座位编排而定。燃料消耗方面，787 比以往的产品省油，效益更高。此外在用料方面，787 是首款主要使用复合材料建造的主流客机。787 是波音公司 1990 年启动波音 777 计划后十多年来推出的首款全新机型，航空公司可利用它为不适合使用大型飞机的远程航线提供不经停服务。波音 787 在客舱环境方面的改善，尤其是客舱湿度的提高，全面提高了乘客的乘机舒适性。

中文译文
Chinese Version

1 嗨，各位好！

2 此刻我正在波音公司位于华盛顿州埃弗雷特市 (Everett) 的工厂向大家发表本周的广播电视讲话。波音公司在这个区域扎根了半个世纪。但公司里的工人所做的事情着实让人激动不已，因为他们在生产未来的飞机——梦幻客机（波音 787）。该机真是蔚为壮观。坦率而言，我来此地的部分原因就是要近距离地观察她。但另外的原因就是这为我们如何将就业和制造业带回国内树立了一个绝佳的范例。

3 众所周知，我国的制造业在过去的几十年中并非一帆风顺。新技术使企业效率和产量都得到提高，虽然这是好事，但同时也使得大量工作岗位遭废弃。结果对许多家庭和全社会而言是痛苦的。人们曾指望得以退休的工厂离开了城市。为人们提供体面生活的工作岗位转移至海外。残酷的事实就是大量这类工作再也没有回到国内。

4 但这并不意味着我们要面临更为暗淡的前景。我不认可这样的观点。在美国，我们总能做些事情为中产阶级创造新的就业岗位，创立新的制造业和创建新的安全生活。在美国，我们从不放弃，我们绝不趴下。

5 这正是眼下我们在做的事情。在过去的 23 个月里，企业创造了 370 万个新的就业岗位。制造业自 20 世纪 90 年代以来首次开始在雇用员工。如今在像中国这类新兴市场做生意的成本正在上升。而同时美国却比以往更有生产效率。像波音这样的公司就意识到，即使我们生产的产品不比中国的便宜，但我们可以让产品的质量更优。这将是我们在国际竞争中制胜的法宝。

6 就波音公司而言，目前的业务蓬勃发展。去年，商用飞机的订单增长超过 50%。为满足不断增长的需求，公司在全国各地招聘了数千员工投入生产。我们希望看到更多这样的情形。我们要尽可能地使我们的企业更方便地在国内而不是海外创造就业。这就要从我们的税收政策上开始做文章。

7 将就业外包出去的公司不应该得到税收优惠。相反，应将税收优惠政策提供给那些在国内设厂的制造商们。而且应给那些为未来创造就业的高科技制造商们提供更大的税收优惠。倘若你在艰难度日的地区重新部署你的公司，你在新厂建设、新设备购买以及新员工培训等多方面都应得到资金支持。现在应该停止奖励那些把就业岗位输出到海外的企业，并开始奖励那些在国内创造就业的企业。国会应尽快将这样的税改方案呈交给我。

8 我们正在做的另一件事情就是要让像波音这样的公司更方便地在全球销售其产品，因为更多的出口就意味着更多的就业机会。两年前，我设定了在 5 年内美国的出口要翻一番的目标。现在我们正超越预期地朝着实现这一目标继续前行。

9 我们目前拥有绝佳的机遇，创建一种不仅能有助于我们赢得今天的经济，而且能创建一种有助于我们的后代赢得未来的经济。我们需要做什么大家都心知肚明。我们需要夯实美国的制造业基础。我们需要投资于美国制造的能源产业和美国工人新技能的提升。但最重要的，我们需要重拾那些曾让我们国家变得伟大的价值观：努力工作、公平竞争以及共担责任。

10 这点我们能够做到。只要问问埃弗雷特的百姓就知道。几年前，第一架梦幻客机就从这里首航。成千上万的员工前来观看。其中就有一位叫莎朗•奥哈拉 (Sharon O'Hara) 的管理层人员。当看到这一凝结了这么多人辛勤汗水的飞机首航起飞时，莎朗心中感到无比激动。用她的话来说："我们说过我们可以做到，我们真的做到了。"这就是美国传奇。我们说过我们可以做到，我们做到了。这种我能做到的精神成就了我们的为人。我们曾经面临过多次挑战。但我们总能战胜挑战变得更强。这正是我们目前又要做的事情。谢谢。祝大家周末愉快！

第8周

An All-Of-The-Above Approach to American Energy

February 25, 2012

美国全面的能源计划

2012 年 2 月 25 日

【摘要导读】

在本周的广播电视讲话中，巴拉克•奥巴马总统向美国民众阐释了解决美国面临能源挑战采取全面战略的重要性。奥巴马说：由于只有全世界2%的石油储量，美国不能像华盛顿某些人建议的那样，仅靠开采石油来降低油价这一条路；美国必须制定一项利用一切可能的能源的长远战略，包括石油、天然气、风能、太阳能、核能以及生物燃料等。同时美国人民也必须认识到提高汽车的能源利用效率在降低美国对石油的依赖性和节约消费者的油费方面所发挥的重要作用。此外，奥巴马提到当石油公司赚取着空前的巨额利润而普通家庭却支付着空前的高额油价时，美国必须永远终结这些公司所享有的每年40亿美元的税收优惠。

演讲再现 Original Text

1 Hello, everybody.

2 In the State of the Union, I laid out three areas we need to focus on if we're going to build an economy that lasts: new American manufacturing, new skills and education for American workers, and new sources of American-made energy.

3 These days, we're getting another painful reminder why developing new energy is so important to our future. Just like they did last year, gas prices are starting to climb. Only this time, it's happening earlier. And that hurts everyone — everyone who owns a car; everyone who owns a business. It

Words & Expressions

lay out 提出

means you have to stretch your paycheck even further. Some folks have no choice but to drive a long way to work, and high gas prices are like a tax straight out of their paychecks.

4 Now, some politicians always see this as a political opportunity. And since it's an election year, they're already dusting off their three-point plans for $2 gas. I'll save you the suspense: Step one is drill, step two is drill, and step three is keep drilling. We hear the same thing every year.

5 Well the American people aren't stupid. You know that's not a plan — especially since we're already drilling. It's a bumper sticker. It's not a strategy to solve our energy challenge. It's a strategy to get politicians through an election.

6 You know there are no quick fixes to this problem, and you know we can't just drill our way to lower gas prices. If we're going to take control of our energy future and avoid these gas price spikes down the line, then we need a sustained, all-of-the-above strategy that develops every available source of American energy — oil, gas, wind, solar, nuclear, biofuels, and more. We need to keep developing the technology that allows us to use less oil in our cars and trucks; in our buildings and plants. That's the strategy we're pursuing, and that's the only real solution to this challenge.

7 Now, we absolutely need safe, responsible oil production here in America. That's why under my Administration, America is producing more oil today than at any time in the last eight years. In 2010, our dependence on foreign oil was under 50% for the first time in more than a decade. And while there are no short-term silver bullets when it comes to gas prices, I've directed my administration to look for every single area where we can make an impact and help consumers in the months ahead, from permitting to delivery bottlenecks to what's going on in the oil markets.

8 But over the long term, an all-of-the-above energy strategy means we have to do more. It means we have to make some choices.

9 Here's one example. Right now, four billion of your tax dollars subsidize the oil industry every year. Four billion

stretch [stretʃ] *vt.* 展开，延伸，拉紧，绷紧

paycheck ['peitʃek] *n.* 薪水

dust off 抹去灰尘，掸净，擦净，重新使用

save sb. the suspense 打消某人的疑虑，不想吊某人的胃口

bumper sticker =bumper strip（汽车）保险杠上的标贴，张贴在汽车保险杠上的小标语（或政党候选人的名字）

spike [spaik] *vi.* 钉子般突出，迅速上升（或上涨）*n.* 墙头钉，尖刺

sustained [sə'steind] *adj.* 持续的，持久的

biofuel ['baiəu'fju:əl] *n.* 生物燃料

pursue [pə'sju:] *vt.* 追赶，追捕，追击，追求，继续

silver bullet 银弹，良方，高招

bottleneck ['bɔtlnek] *n.* 瓶颈，阻碍，障碍

over the long term 从长远来看

subsidize ['sʌbsidaiz] *vt.* 发给…补助金，资助

dollars.

10 Imagine that. Maybe some of you are listening to this in your car right now, pulling into a gas station to fill up. As you watch those numbers rise, know that oil company profits have never been higher. Yet somehow, Congress is still giving those same companies another four billion dollars of your money. That's outrageous. It's inexcusable. And it has to stop.

11 A century of subsidies to the oil companies is long enough. It's time to end taxpayer giveaways to an industry that's never been more profitable, and use that money to reduce our deficit and double-down on a clean energy industry that's never been more promising. Because of the investments we've already made, the use of wind and solar energy in this country has nearly doubled — and thousands of Americans have jobs because of it. And because we put in place the toughest fuel economy standards in history, our cars will average nearly 55 miles per gallon by the middle of the next decade — something that, over time, will save the typical family more than $8,000 at the pump. Now Congress needs to keep that momentum going by renewing the clean energy tax credits that will lead to more jobs and less dependence on foreign oil.

12 Look, we know there's no silver bullet that will bring down gas prices or reduce our dependence on foreign oil overnight. But what we can do is get our priorities straight, and make a sustained, serious effort to tackle this problem. That's the commitment we need right now. And with your help, it's a commitment we can make. Thanks.

outrageous [aut'reidʒəs] *adj.* 蛮横的，残暴的

inexcusable [ˌinik'skju:zəbl] *adj.* 无法辩解的，难以原谅的，不可宽恕的

giveaway ['givəˌwei] *n.* 泄漏，免费样品，不正当的交易，有奖问答节目

double-down on 变本加厉，双管齐下，加倍专注于

put in place 放置，落实到位，正在实施

fuel economy standards 燃料节约标准

average ['ævəridʒ] *vt.* 平均为，平均是 *adj.* 平均的

over time 有朝一日，归根结底，最后

momentum [məu'mentəm] *n.* 动力，力量，势头

tax credit = tax offset 税额减免

priority [prai'ɔrəti] *n.* 优先，重点，[复数]优先权，优先考虑的事

tackle ['tækl] *vt.* 着手处理，解决，应付

中文译文 Chinese Version

1 嗨，各位好！

2 为建立一种可持续发展的经济，我在国情咨文中提出了需要重点关注的三个领域：美国的新制造业、美国劳动者的新技能与教育、美国造的新能源。

3 开发新能源为什么对我们的未来如此重要——近来我们又受到了沉痛的警示。正如去年的情形那样，油价又开始上涨。只不过这次出现得更早了。这让每个人都受到伤害——每个人都是车主或企业主。这意味着你要在薪水方面精打细算才行。但有些人要开车走很远的路去上班，他们别无选择，高油价就像从他们的薪水中直接抽税一样。

4 现在，有些政客总是将这一问题看成是政治机遇。由于大选年到来，他们总是重新提出 2 美元油价的 3 点计划。还是我来给你们介绍吧：第一步是钻探；第二步是钻探；第三步依然是持续钻探。这样的方案我们每年都能听到。

5 美国人民又不是傻瓜。大家都知道这根本就不是什么计划，尤其是在我们已经钻探的情况下。这只不过是条宣传的小标语，并不是可以解决我们的能源挑战的战略方案，而是让政客为了赢得胜选的计谋而已。

6 众所周知，解决这一问题没有锦囊妙计，而且我们也不能仅靠开采石油来降低油价。倘若我们想要掌控我们的能源未来并避免油价一路飙升对我们的影响，我们就需要一项可持续的、最高的能源战略，开发一切可以利用的美国能源，包括石油、天然气、风能、太阳能、核能以及生物燃料等等。我们需要持续开发各种技术让我们的汽车、建筑以及植物上使用的石油更少。这才是我们追求的战略，也是解决我们面临的挑战的唯一现实方案。

7 现在，我们国内十分需要安全的、有保障的石油生产。正是因为如此，在本届政府的努力下，美国石油产量比过去 8 年的任何时候都要高。2010 年，我们对海外石油的依赖度 10 多年来首次降低到 50% 以下。但由于对油价问题没有短期的良方妙药，我已指示本届政府寻找每一个我们可以施加影响的领域，并在未来数月中给消费者提供帮助，包括从消除运输瓶颈到关注石油市场变化等方面。

8 但长期来看，一项最高的能源战略意味着我们必须做的事情更多，也意味着我们必须做出某些选择。

9 举例而言，目前，你们每年纳税中的 40 亿美元作为补助提供给了石油公司。40 亿美元啊。

10 试想一下。也许你们当中有人正开着车收听我的讲话。当你驶入加油站加油的时候，看着数字不断上升，你可知道石油公司的利润是有史以来最高的。然而，国会却一直每年为这些公司提供 40 亿美元的补贴，而钱都来自于你们纳税人。这是无法容忍的。这是不可饶恕的。必须加以制止。

11 给石油公司一个世纪的补贴已经够长了。现在该是终止用纳税人的钱为一个利润空前高的行业提供补贴了，用这些钱来降低我们的赤字，加倍专注于希望无限的清洁能源产业。由于我们已经做出的投资，风能和太阳能在我国的使用已将近翻番——成千上万的美国人因此得到了工作。同时由于我们制定了史上最为严厉的燃料节约标准，我们的汽车在未来十年的中期每加仑汽油平均行驶的里程将达到约 55 英里。最终，一个普通家庭将在油费上节省 8,000 美元。现在，国会要保持强劲势头继续向清洁能源产业实施税收优惠政策，这将为我们提供更多就业岗位并降低对海外石油的依赖度。

12　众所周知，对于降低油价或降低我们对海外石油的依赖度等问题并没有在一夜间能加以解决的良方妙药。这一问题的解决需要持续认真的努力，但我们可以将一些优先的事情办妥。这是我们此刻需要做出的承诺。只要大家鼎力相助，我们一定能够兑现这一承诺。谢谢大家。

第9周

Taking Control of Our Energy Future

March 3, 2012

掌控我们的能源未来

2012年3月3日

【摘要导读】

在本周的广播电视讲话中，巴拉克·奥巴马总统告诉美国人民，经过三年的扶持，美国的汽车产业挽救了100多万个工作岗位，汽车产业得以复兴，汽车制造也达到历史最高水平。在过去的两年半时间里，整个行业共新增20多万个就业岗位，由于政府的新燃油效率标准出台，各公司生产的汽车将能为每个家庭在油费方面节约资金，同时也能降低美国对海外石油的依赖。奥巴马呼吁必须终结对利润巨大的石油公司每年40亿美元的税收优惠。另外，他还呼吁所有人告诫所选官员们要终结这一企业福利，并为可实现的清洁能源未来努力。

演讲再现 Original Text

Words & Expressions

shed [ʃed] *v.* 流出；摆脱；散发；倾吐

on the brink of 将要，濒于，将陷于（灾难、死亡或其他）

go bankrupt 破产

1 Hello, everybody. Earlier this week, I spent some time with the hardworking men and women of the American auto industry, who are busy writing a new chapter in America's story.

2 Just a few years ago, their industry was shedding hundreds of thousands of jobs. Two of the Big Three — GM and Chrysler — were on the brink of failure. If we had let this great American industry collapse — if we had let Detroit go bankrupt — more than one million Americans would have lost their jobs in the middle of the worst recession since the Great Depression.

3 I refused to let that happen. These jobs are worth

more than just a paycheck — they're a source of pride and a ticket to the middle-class. These companies are worth more than just the cars they build — they're a symbol of American innovation and a source of our manufacturing might.

4 So in exchange for help, we demanded responsibility. We got the companies to retool and restructure. Everyone sacrificed. And three years later, the American auto industry is back. Today, GM is the number one automaker in the world. Chrysler is growing faster in America than any other car company. Ford is investing billions in American plants and factories, and plans to bring thousands of jobs back home. All told, the entire industry has added more than 200,000 new jobs over the past two and a half years.

5 And they're not just building cars again — they're building better cars. Thanks to new fuel efficiency standards we put in place, they're building cars that will average nearly 55 miles per gallon by the middle of the next decade. That's almost double what they get today. That means folks will be able to fill up every two weeks instead of every week, saving the typical family more than $8,000 at the pump over time. That's a big deal, especially as families are yet again feeling the pinch from rising gas prices.

6 So what's happening in Detroit will make a difference. But it won't solve everything. There's no silver bullet for avoiding spikes in gas prices every year. There's no shortcut to taking control of our energy future. We have to pursue an all-of-the-above strategy that helps develop every source of American energy. And we have to do it now.

7 The good news is, we've been making progress. Take a look at this chart. Six years ago, 60% of the oil we used was imported. Since I took office, America's dependence on foreign oil has decreased every single year. In fact, in 2010, for the first time in thirteen years, less than half the petroleum we consumed was imported. Part of that is because we're producing more oil here at home than at any time in the last eight years.

8 But we can't just drill our way out of this problem. While we consume 20 percent of the world's oil, we only have

might [mait] *n.* 体力，精力，能力，威力，力量，强权，势力，权势

in exchange for 作为（对…的）交换（或替换）

retool [riːˈtuːl] *vi.* 重新装备，改组，调整

restructure [riːˈstrʌktʃə] *vt.* 重新构成，重建，调整，改组

sacrifice [ˈsækrifais] *n.* 祭献，供奉，牺牲，为…献身

feel the pinch 感到经济困难（或手头拮据）

make a difference 有（重要）作用，有影响，有关系

sliver bullet 速效良方

spike [spaik] *n.* 剧增

2 percent of the world's oil reserves. We've got to develop new technology that will help us use new forms of energy. That's been a priority of mine as President. And because of the investments we've made, our use of clean, renewable energy has nearly doubled — and thousands of Americans have jobs because of it.

9 Now we need to keep at it. And to do that, we need to make the right choices.

10 Here's one choice we can make right now. Every year, $4 billion of your tax dollars go to subsidizing the oil industry. These are the same companies making record profits — tens of billions of dollars a year. I don't think oil companies need more corporate welfare. Congress should end this taxpayer giveaway. If you agree with me, I'm asking you to e-mail, call, or Tweet your representative. Tell them to stop fighting for oil companies. Tell them to start fighting for working families. Tell them to fight for the clean energy future that's within our reach. Because the sooner we all get started, the sooner we'll get there together. Thanks and have a great weekend.

oil reserve 石油储量，石油储备

record profits 创纪录的利润

corporate [ˈkɔːpərit] *adj.* 社团的，法人的，公司的

中文译文 Chinese Version

1 嗨，各位好。本周早些时候，我与美国汽车业界昧旦晨兴的人们进行了接触，他们正忙于书写美国传奇的新篇章。

2 就在几年前，这一产业流失了数十万的工作岗位。三大巨头中的两家：通用和克莱斯勒公司濒临破产。倘若我们当时任由这一美国的支柱产业倒闭，倘若我们任由底特律破产，那么就会有 100 多万美国人会在大萧条后的这场最为严重的经济衰退中失去工作。

3 我决不让这种情形发生。这些工作的价值远超过其工资本身，它们代表着一份尊严，代表着通往中产阶级的途径。这些公司的价值也远超它们制造的汽车本身，它们是美国创新的标志，是美国制造业力量的源泉。

4 因此，作为援助条件，我们要求它们担当起责任，并责令这些公司开始重组改革。每个人都付出了牺牲。三年后的今天，美国汽车产业复兴了。今天，通用是全球最大的汽车制造商。克莱斯勒在国内的增长速度比其他任何一家汽车公司都快。福特投资数十亿美元在美国建厂，这些计划将为国内带来数千个工作岗位。总之，整个汽车产业在过去两年半里新

增20多万个就业岗位。

5 它们不仅又在生产汽车——而且是在生产更好的汽车。由于新燃油效率标准的实施，它们生产的汽车将在未来5年内实现每加仑燃油平均行驶近55英里（约合23公里/升，百公里油耗4.28升）的目标。这几乎是当前行驶里程的一倍。这也意味着人们可以每两周加一次油而不用每周都去，随着时间推移为一般家庭在油费上节约8,000美元。这是一笔不小的金额，尤其是在因为油价上涨各家各户再次感到经济拮据的时候。

6 因此，底特律所发生的事情影响深远。但并不能解决所有问题。避免油价每年的上涨并没有速效良方。在掌控我们的能源未来上也无捷径可走。我们必须寻求全面的能源战略帮助我们开发美国的各种能源，而且现在就要行动。

7 令人振奋的是，我们一直不断地取得进展。请看这张图表。六年前，我们使用的石油60%是进口的。自我就职以来，美国对海外石油的依赖度每年都在下降。事实上，在2010年，我们13年来首次实现进口石油占我们消耗石油总量的一半以下。部分原因就是我们国内石油的产量比过去八年的任何时候都多。

8 但我们不能仅依靠开采国内石油的方式来摆脱困境。我们的石油消费占全球的20%，而我们的石油储量却只有全球储量的2%。我们必须发展新技术来帮助我们利用新形式的能源。这是我作为总统优先考虑的事情。由于我们已经做出的投资，我们对清洁可再生能源的使用将近翻倍——同时也有数千美国人因此而获得了工作。

9 现在我们需要保持这一发展势头。为达到这一目的，我们需要做出正确选择。

10 我们现在就能做出一个正确选择。每年，40亿美元的税金作为补贴提供给了石油业。而正是这些公司每年却在获取数百亿美元的创纪录利润。我认为石油公司的企业福利已经够多的了。国会应该终结用纳税人的钱对它们进行补助。倘若你们同意我的看法，那么我请求你们通过电子邮件、电话或者推特告诫你们的议员们。告诉他们要为工薪家庭谋利。告诉他们要为我们可实现的清洁能源的未来奋斗。因为我们行动越迅速，我们的目标也实现得越快。谢谢各位，周末愉快。

第10周

Investing in a Clean Energy Future

March 10, 2012

对清洁能源的未来进行投资

2012年3月10日

【摘要导读】

在本周的广播电视讲话中，巴拉克•奥巴马总统在弗吉尼亚州匹兹堡市的一家工厂向美国民众发表讲话，内容涉及企业为国内创造更多就业岗位，同时也生产出更好的产品这一增长趋势。他表示企业开发的新技术在降低美国对海外石油的依赖性并节省普通家庭的油费支出上起到非常重要的作用。奥巴马还呼吁国会终止对石油公司每年40亿美元的补贴，以便将这些钱投资到清洁能源技术上。他说解决高油价问题没有锦囊妙计，但只要美国人民齐心协力就能够战胜现有的能源挑战，并创造出新的就业岗位。

演讲再现 Original Text

1 Hi, everybody. I'm speaking to you this week from a factory in Petersburg, Virginia, where they're bringing on more than 100 new workers to build parts for the next generation of jet engines.

2 It's a story that's happening more frequently across the country. Our businesses just added 233,000 jobs last month — for a total of nearly four million new jobs over the last two years. More companies are choosing to bring jobs back and invest in America. Manufacturing is adding jobs for the first time since the 1990s, and we're building more things to sell to the rest of the world stamped with three proud words: Made in America.

3 And it's not just that we're building stuff. We're building better stuff. The engine parts manufactured here in Petersburg will go into next-generation planes that are lighter, faster, and more fuel-efficient.

4 That last part is important. Because whether you're paying for a plane ticket, or filling up your gas tank, technology that helps us get more miles to the gallon is one of the easiest ways to save money and reduce our dependence on foreign oil.

5 The recent spike in gas prices has been another painful reminder of why we have to invest in this technology. As usual, politicians have been rolling out their three-point plans for two-dollar gas: drill, drill, and drill some more. Well, my response is, we have been drilling. Under my Administration, oil production in America is at an eight-year high. We've quadrupled the number of operating oil rigs, and opened up millions of acres for drilling.

6 But you and I both know that with only 2% of the world's oil reserves, we can't just drill our way to lower gas prices — not when consume 20 percent of the world's oil. We need an all-of-the-above strategy that relies less on foreign oil and more on American-made energy — solar, wind, natural gas, biofuels, and more.

7 That's the strategy we're pursuing. It's why I went to a plant in North Carolina earlier this week, where they're making trucks that run on natural gas, and hybrid trucks that go further on a single tank.

8 And it's why I've been focused on fuel efficient cars since the day I took office. Over the last few years, the annual number of miles driven by Americans has stayed roughly the same, but the total amount of gas we use has been going down. In other words, we're getting more bang for our buck.

9 If we accelerate that trend, we can help drivers save a significant amount of money. That's why, after 30 years of inaction, we finally put in place new standards that will make sure our cars average nearly 55 miles per gallon by the middle of the next decade — nearly double what they get today. This

Words & Expressions

roll out 导入，推出，实施，滚出

drill [dril] *vt.* 开采

quadruple [ˈkwɔdrupl] *adj.* 四部分(组成)的，四方的，四倍的，四重的

oil rig 石油钻塔，油井设备

pursue [pəˈsjuː] *vt.* 追赶，追捕，实行，寻求，追求

hybrid truck 混合动力卡车

bang [bæŋ] *adj.* 惊人的成功，引人注目的结果，突然的效果

buck [bʌk] *n.* 美元

accelerate [əkˈseləreit] *vt.* 使增速，使加快，促进

significant [sigˈnifikənt] *adj.* 重要的，意义重大的，大量的

inaction [inˈækʃən] *n.* 不活动，不行动，不活跃，懒散

wasn't easy: we had to bring together auto companies, and unions, and folks who don't ordinarily see eye to eye. But it was worth it.

10 Because these cars aren't some pie in the sky solution that's years away. They're being built right now — by American workers, in factories right here in the U.S.A.. Every year, our cars and trucks will be able to go further and use less fuel, and pretty soon, you'll be able to fill up every two weeks instead of every week — something that, over time, will save the typical family more than $8,000 at the pump. We'll reduce our oil consumption by more than 12 billion barrels. That's a future worth investing in.

11 So we have a choice. Right now, some folks in Washington would rather spend another $4 billion on subsidies to oil companies each year. Well you know what? We've been handing out these kinds of taxpayer giveaways for nearly a century. And outside of Congress, does anyone really think that's still a good idea? I want this Congress to stop the giveaways to an oil industry that's never been more profitable, and invest in a clean energy industry that's never been more promising. We should be investing in the technology that's building the cars and trucks and jets that will prevent us from dealing with these high gas prices year after year after year.

12 Ending this cycle of rising gas prices won't be easy, and it won't happen overnight. But that's why you sent us to Washington — to solve tough problems like this one. So I'm going to keep doing everything I can to help you save money on gas, both right now and in the future. I hope politicians from both sides of the aisle join me. Let's put aside the bumper-sticker slogans, remember why we're here, and get things done for the American people.

13 Thank you, God bless you, and have a great weekend.

see eye to eye 意见完全一致

pie in the sky 不切实际的想法，梦想，空头支票，渺茫的幸福

tough [tʌf] *adj.* 坚韧的，坚强的，艰难的

aisle [ail] *n.* (教堂的)侧廊，走廊，过道

bumper-sticker slogans 汽车贴纸文化口号

中文译文

Chinese Version

1 各位好。本周我在弗吉尼亚州匹兹堡市的一家工厂向大家发表讲话，这家工厂带来了 100 多个新的工作岗位，他们正在生产下一代喷气发动机的零部件。

2 这样的事迹在全国各地层出不穷。上个月我们的企业就新增了 23.3 万个就业岗位，过去两年总共新增约 400 万个就业岗位。越来越多的企业选择回国投资并将工作岗位带回来。制造业也从 20 世纪 90 年代以来首次增加就业岗位，我们正在制造更多的产品并将其销往世界各地，产品上印着让我们引以为自豪的四个字：美国制造。

3 我们不仅仅是在制造产品，我们是在制造更好的产品。在匹兹堡这边生产的引擎零部件将用于更轻、更快、更节省燃料的下一代飞机上。

4 最后一个特点很重要。因为无论你是付款买机票还是给自己的汽车加油，增加单位燃料的行驶里程是帮助我们节省支出和降低对海外石油依赖的最简便的方法之一。

5 我们为什么必须要在这一技术上进行投资，最近油价的上涨是对我们又一次沉痛的警醒。一些政客一直在兜售他们实现 2 美元油价的三项计划：开采、开采以及更多的开采。好吧，我的回应是，我们一直都在开采。在本届政府的治理下，美国国内的石油产量处在 8 年来的最高点。我们开放了数百万英亩的开采区域，运转的石油钻井平台也增加了 4 倍。

6 但你我都明白我们仅仅拥有 2% 的世界石油储量，我们不能只在国内开采来降低油价，何况我们还消耗了全球 20% 的石油。我们需要一个全面的能源战略，以减少我们对海外石油的依赖，更多地使用国产能源：太阳能、风能、天然气以及生物燃料等等。

7 这正是我们追求的战略。这也是我本周早些时候造访北卡罗来纳州一家工厂的原因，那里的工人们正在生产使用天然气的卡车——混合动力卡车，它用一箱油能行驶得更远。

8 这也是我自就职以来一直关注高效能汽车的原因。在过去的几年中，美国人每年的汽车行驶里程基本保持不变，但总的汽油消耗量在不断下降。换句话说，花同样的钱，我们能获得更多的利益。

9 倘若我们加速推进这一趋势，我们就可以帮助驾驶员们节约一笔可观的费用。正因为如此，经过 30 年的无作为之后，我们终于实施了新的能效标准，这样就能确保在未来 5 年内实现汽车用 1 加仑汽油平均行驶近 55 英里的目标，几乎是目前的两倍。实现这一目标并非易事：我们必须将汽车生产厂家、工会以及意见通常有分歧的人们团结在一起。但这么做是值得的。

10 因为这样的汽车并不像前几年那样还是空中楼阁。美国工人现在就在国内的工厂生产这样的汽车。每年，我们的汽车都能用更少的油跑得更远。不久，你们将能每两周加一次油而不必每周都去加油站。这样经过一段时日，将为普通家庭节省油费达 8,000 多美元。我们将减少石油消费量达 120 多亿桶。这是值得我们投资的未来。

11 因此，我们要做出选择。但现在华盛顿有些人却宁愿每年再花 40 亿美元给石油公司提供补贴。你们可知道。我们已经用纳税人的钱给它们提供了将近一个世纪的补贴了。在国会之外，还有人真的会认为这是个好主意吗？我希望国会终止对利润已经创历史新高的石油产业的补贴，我们应该把这些钱投资到最有希望的清洁能源产业上。我们应该投资于生产高能效汽车和飞机的技术上，以避免我们年复一年受高油价的困扰。

12 结束不断上涨的油价这一恶性循环并非易事，也不能一蹴而就。但这正是你们选择我们来到华盛顿的原因，我们就是来解决这样的难题的。因此我将继续竭尽所能帮助你们节约油费支出，现在如此将来亦如此。我希望国会中两党的政客们都能与我携起手来。让我们把空洞的口号搁置一旁，牢记使命，为美国人民办些实事。

13 谢谢大家，上帝保佑你们，周末愉快！

第11周

Ending Subsidies for Big Oil Companies

March 17, 2012

终止对大型石油公司的补贴

2012 年 3 月 17 日

【摘要导读】

在本周的广播电视讲话中，巴拉克•奥巴马总统号召全体美国人对国家的未来要充满信心。因为美国通过增加国内油气产量，提高汽车的燃油效率并投资于高科技和可替代能源从而降低了对海外石油的依赖性；因为对于高油价问题并没有锦囊妙计，奥巴马总统已经采取了数项措施为普通家庭节约油费支出，这其中包括签署华尔街改革方案终结了交易商通过不公平方式操纵能源市场；制定历史性的成倍提高汽车燃油效率的燃油节约标准，这样将为所有家庭节省1.7万亿的油费支出并减少120亿桶的石油消费量。奥巴马还指出：美国国内的石油产量也比过去8年中的任何时候都要高，但由于美国只有全球已探明石油储量的2%，仅仅加大开采量并不是解决办法。美国必须制定一个全面的能源战略，投资于新技术，并终止对获取巨额利润的石油公司每年40亿美元的补贴。奥巴马说倘若美国民众认为国会应该永远结束对石油公司的这项补贴，那么就应告诉他们选举出来的官员们，现在应该优先考虑的是中产家庭而不是大型石油公司的利益。

演讲再现 Original Text

1 Hi, everybody. As I know you've noticed over the past few weeks, the price at your local pump has been going up and up. And because it's an election year, so has the temperature of our political rhetoric.

2 What matters most to me right now is the impact that rising prices have on you. When you've got to spend more on gas, you've got less to spend on everything else. It makes things harder. So I wanted to take a minute this weekend to explain what steps my Administration is taking when it comes

Words & Expressions

political rhetoric 政治修辞，政治言论

to energy — most importantly, producing more of it while using less of it.

3 The truth is: the price of gas depends on a lot of factors that are often beyond our control. Unrest in the Middle East can tighten global oil supply. Growing nations like China or India adding cars to the road increases demand. But one thing we should control is fraud and manipulation that can cause prices to spike even further.

4 For years, traders at financial firms were able to game the energy markets, distort the price of oil, and make big profits for themselves at your expense. And they were able to do all that because of major gaps and loopholes in our regulations. When I took office, we did something about it.

5 The Wall Street reforms I signed into law are helping bring energy markets out of the shadows and under real oversight. They're strengthening our ability to go after fraud and to prevent traders from manipulating the market. So it's not just wrong, but dangerous that some in Congress want to roll back those protections and return to the days when companies like *Enron*[1] could avoid regulation and reap enormous profits, no matter who it hurt.

6 What's more, at a time when big oil companies are making more money than ever before, we're still giving them $4 billion of your tax dollars in subsidies every year. Your member of Congress should be fighting for you. Not for big financial firms. Not for big oil companies.

7 In the next few weeks, I expect Congress to vote on ending these subsidies. And when they do, we're going to put every single Member of Congress on record: They can either stand up for oil companies, or they can stand up for the American people. They can either place their bets on a fossil fuel from the last century, or they can place their bets on America's future. So make your voice heard. Send your representative an email. Give them a call. Tell them to stand with you.

8 And tell them to be honest with you. It's easy to promise a quick fix when it comes to gas prices. There just

unrest [ʌn'rest] *n.* 动荡，不安定

tighten ['taitn] *v.* 收紧，使绷紧

fraud [frɔ:d] *n.* 欺诈，骗子，诡计

manipulation [məˌnipju'leiʃn] *n.* 伪造，控制

game [geim] *n.* 游戏，比赛 *adj.* 勇敢的 *vi.* 赌博

distort [di'stɔ:t] *vt.* 歪曲，扭曲，变形

at your expense 由你支付，由你承担

loophole ['lu:phəul] *n.* 窥孔，透气孔，逃避的手段，（法律等条文中的）漏洞，空子

regulation [ˌregju'leiʃən] *n.* 规则，规章，条例，法规，管理，控制，调节，校准

oversight ['əuvəsait] *n.* 疏忽，忽略，照管，监督

roll back （使）滚回，（使）卷起，（使）退却，击退，（使）回忆起

reap [ri:p] *vt.* 收割，收获，获得，得到

put... on record 明确地说，立案，备案，记录

stand up for 坚决要求，争取，维护，支持，保卫

fossil fuel 矿物燃料，天然生成的燃料

a quick fix 速成法

isn't one. Anyone who tells you otherwise — any career politician who promises some three-point plan for two-dollar gas — they're not looking for a solution. They're just looking for your vote.

9 If we're truly going to make sure we're not at the mercy of spikes in gas prices every year, the answer isn't just to drill more — because we're already drilling more. Under my Administration, we're producing more oil here at home than at any time in the last eight years, that's a fact. We've quadrupled the number of operating oil rigs to a record high, that's a fact. And we've opened millions of acres on land and offshore to develop more of our domestic resources.

10 Those are the facts. But we can't just rely on drilling. Not when we use more than 20 percent of the world's oil, but still only have 2 percent of the world's known oil reserves. If we don't develop other sources of energy, and the technology to use less energy, we'll continue to be dependent on foreign countries for our energy needs. That's why we're pursuing an all-of-the-above strategy. As we develop more oil and gas, we're also developing wind and solar power; biofuels, and next-generation vehicles — and thousands of Americans have jobs right now because of it. We need to keep making those investments — because I don't want to see those jobs go to other countries. I want to create even more of them right here in the United States of America.

11 And after three decades of inaction, we raised fuel economy standards so that by the middle of the next decade, our cars will average nearly 55 miles per gallon. That's nearly double what they get today. That means you'll only have to fill up every two weeks instead of every week. And that will save the typical family more than $8,000 over the life of the car — just by using less gas.

12 Combined, these steps have helped put us on a path to greater energy independence. Since I took office, America's dependence on foreign oil has gone down every single year. In 2010, for the first time in 13 years, less than half the oil we used came from foreign countries.

at the mercy of 任凭…的摆布，完全受…的支配，在…掌握中

offshore [ˈɔfˈʃɔː] *adv.* 向海，离岸，在离岸一定距离的海面上

destiny ['destini] *n.* 命中注定，命运，定数，天数，天意

13 We can do even better. And we will. But what we can't do is keep being dependent on other countries for our energy needs. In America we control our own destiny. So that's the choice we face — the past, or the future. And America is what it is today because we have always placed our bets on the future. Thanks, and have a great weekend.

背景知识注释 Background Notes

1. Enron　即 Enron Corporation 安然有限公司，成立于 1930 年，曾是一家位于美国得克萨斯州休斯敦市的能源类公司。在 2001 年宣告破产之前，安然有限公司拥有约 21,000 名雇员，是世界上最大的电力、天然气以及电讯公司之一，2000 年披露的营业额达 1,010 亿美元之巨。公司连续六年被《财富》杂志评选为"美国最具创新精神公司"，然而真正使安然有限公司在全世界声名大噪的，却是这个拥有上千亿资产的公司 2002 年在几周内破产，持续多年精心策划、乃至制度化系统化的财务造假丑闻。安然欧洲分公司于 2001 年 11 月 30 日申请破产，美国本部于 2 日后同样申请破产保护。目前公司的留守人员主要进行资产清理、执行破产程序以及应对法律诉讼，从那时起，"安然"已经成为公司欺诈以及堕落的象征。

中文译文 Chinese Version

1　嗨，各位好。可以肯定，在过去的数周中，大家都注意到了我们各地的油价是一涨再涨。由于时逢大选年，当前政治言论的激辩程度也愈演愈烈。

2　就我而言，当下最紧要的是上涨的油价对大家的影响。倘若大家在油费上增加支出，那么肯定要减少其他方面的消费。这会使局势变得更加艰难。因此，本周末我想花点时间向大家讲解一下本届政府为应对目前能源问题所采取的一些措施——最为重要的就是减少能源的消耗，增加能源的效益。

3　然而事实是影响油价的许多因素往往非我们所能控制。中东地区的动荡使全球石油供应趋紧。而像中国和印度这样的新兴国家不断增长的汽车数量也增加了对石油的需求。但我们至少应该对引起油价进一步飙升的欺诈行为和恶意操纵加以控制。

4　数年来，金融公司的交易人员能够玩弄能源市场，扭曲石油价格，牺牲公众的利益而自己却攫取了巨额的利润。他们之所以能这么恣意妄为主要是由于我们监管上的缺失和漏洞。在我就职之后，我们对此采取了一些措施。

5　我签署生效的华尔街改革法案使能源市场摆脱一些金融危机的阴影，并使其得到有效的监管。这些改革法案增强了我们在追查欺诈和防止交易人员操纵市场方面的能力。因

此，一些国会议员希望撤销这些保护措施，重回让安然有限公司这样的企业可以规避监管，不顾他人死活而掠取巨额利润的日子，这不仅是错误的，而且是危险的。

6 更有甚者，当这些大型石油公司赚取着空前的利润的时候，我们依然每年用纳税人的钱给他们提供40亿美元的补贴。大家选出来的国会议员们应该为你们争取利益，而不是为大型金融企业，也不是为大型石油公司谋利。

7 在未来的数周里，我希望国会就终止这些补贴进行投票。与此同时，我们将让每个国会议员表明自己的立场：他们要么代表石油公司的利益，要么代表美国人民的利益。他们要么把赌注押到自上个世纪开始使用的化石燃料上，要么就押到美国的未来上。让议员们听到你们的心声。通过发邮件、打电话给议员们要他们站在你们这边。

8 告诫他们要对你们以诚相待。在油价问题上提出一个速效良方的承诺轻而易举。但这都是画饼充饥。任何人、任何职业政治家向大众承诺实现两美元油价的三步计划，都不是要寻求真正的解决方案。这种人只是想设法得到你们的投票。

9 倘若我们确切想要避免每年任由油价上涨的摆布，答案就不会仅仅是去开采——因为我们已经开采得够多。在本届政府的治理下，我们国内生产的石油比过去八年中的任何时候都要多，这是不争的事实。我们正在运转中的石油钻井平台的数量创纪录地翻了四倍，这也是不争的事实。我们开放了数百万英亩的陆地和近海区域来开发更多的国内资源。

10 事实就是如此。但我们不能仅仅依靠开采这一手段。尤其是当我们只有全球已探明石油储量的2%，却消耗了全世界20%的石油的时候，我们绝不能这么做。倘若我们不开发其他形式的能源，不利用技术减少能源使用，我们将因为我们的能源需求而继续依赖于其他国家。这正是我们要制定一个全面能源战略的原因所在。在我们生产更多石油和天然气的同时，我们也在发展风能、太阳能、生物燃料以及下一代的交通工具，这些也让成千上万的美国人现在有了就业机会。我们需要继续保持对这些领域的投资，因为我不希望看到这些工作机会流失到其他国家。我希望在国内创造更多这样的就业机会。

11 在经过了30多年的无所作为之后，我们提高了燃油节约标准，以便到下一个十年的中期，我们的汽车用1加仑油可以平均行驶55英里。这是现有水平的两倍。这也意味着你们只需每两周加一次油而不需每周都去。这也将为普通家庭在一辆车的使用寿命内节省8,000多美元，而这靠的就是减少用油。

12 综上所述，这些措施有助于让我们迈向一条能源更具独立性的大道。自我就职以来，美国对海外石油的依赖性每年都在下降。2010年是13年以来我们使用的石油首次还不到一半是来自别的国家的。

13 我们能够做得更好。一定能。但让我们的能源需求继续依赖于其他国家，这是我们无法容忍的事情。在美国，我们掌控着我们自己的命运。因此这就是我们面临的抉择：是回到过去还是面向未来。美国之所以有今天就是因为我们对自己的未来充满信心。谢谢大家，祝周末愉快！

第12周

President Obama Says House Must Pass Bipartisan Transportation Bill

March 24, 2012

奥巴马总统称众议院必须通过两党联合交通法案

2012 年 3 月 24 日

【摘要导读】

在本周的广播电视讲话中，巴拉克•奥巴马总统号召美国众议院[①]议员们通过两党联合提出的交通法案，用以修复破损的道路和桥梁，并扶持全国各社区的建筑工人就业。根据最新的调查报告，美国建筑业员工中有90%都属于中产阶级。美国参议院[②]在民主党和共和党的共同支持下已经通过了这项法案，因为倘若这项法案在参议院受阻，那么建筑工地就会停工，工人们就得回家，美国的经济也将遭受冲击。因此，奥巴马总统号召所有人都力促自己所选的官员要通过这一长期的交通法案，扶持美国的建筑工人就业，并助推美国的经济增长。

演讲再现 Original Text

Words & Expressions

run for office 竞选公职

1 Hello, everybody. This week, I traveled across the country to talk about my all-of-the-above energy strategy for America — a strategy where we produce more oil and gas here at home, but also more biofuels and fuel-efficient cars; more solar power and wind power and other sources of clean, renewable energy.

2 Now, you wouldn't know it by listening to some of the folks running for office today, but producing more oil at home has been, and will continue to be, a key part of my energy strategy. Under my Administration, we're producing more oil than at any other time in the last eight years. We've

quadrupled the number of operating oil rigs to a record high. And we've added enough oil and gas pipeline to circle the entire Earth and then some. Those are the facts.

3 But as I've been saying all week, even though America uses around 20 percent of the world's oil, we only have around 2 percent of the world's known oil reserves. So even if we drilled everywhere, we'd still be relying on other countries for oil.

4 That's why we're pursuing an all-of-the-above strategy. We're producing more biofuels. More fuel-efficient cars. More solar power. More wind power. This week, I was in *Boulder City*③, Nevada, where they've got the largest solar plant of its kind anywhere in the country. That's the future. I was at *Ohio State University*④, where they've developed the fastest electric car in the world. That's the future. I don't want to cede these clean energy industries to China or Germany or any other country. I want to see solar panels and wind turbines and fuel-efficient cars manufactured right here in America, by American workers.

5 Now, getting these clean energy industries to locate here requires us to maintain a national commitment to new research and development. But it also requires us to build world-class transportation and communications networks, so that any company can move goods and sell products all around the world as quickly and efficiently as possible.

6 So much of America needs to be rebuilt right now. We've got crumbling roads and bridges. A power grid that wastes too much energy. An incomplete high-speed broadband network. And we've got thousands of unemployed construction workers who've been looking for a job ever since the housing market collapsed.

7 But once again, we're waiting on Congress. You see, in a matter of days, funding will stop for all sorts of transportation projects. Construction sites will go idle. Workers will have to go home. And our economy will take a hit.

8 This Congress cannot let that happen. Not at a

solar panel 太阳能电池板（或组）

wind turbine（由风力驱动的）风力涡轮机，风轮机，风力机

locate [ləu'keit] *vt.* 安置，把…设置在，确定…的位置，确定…地点

crumbling ['krʌmbliŋ] *adj.* 破碎的，崩溃的

power grid 高压电力网，电力输送网

broadband ['brɔːdbænd] *n.* 宽波段，宽频带

wait on 服侍，焦急地等待

funding ['fʌndiŋ] *n.* 财政支持，资金，基金

go idle 闲置

take a hit 遭受打击，受到影响

time when we should be doing everything in our power — Democrats and Republicans — to keep this recovery moving forward. The Senate did their part. They passed a bipartisan transportation bill. It had the support of 52 Democrats and 22 Republicans. Now it's up to the House to follow suit; to put aside partisan posturing, end the gridlock, and do what's right for the American people.

9 This is common sense. Right now, all across this country, we've got contractors and construction workers who have never been more eager to get back on the job. A long term transportation bill would put them to work. And those are good jobs. We just released a report that shows nearly 90 percent of the construction, manufacturing and trade jobs created through investments in transportation projects are middle-class jobs. Those are exactly the jobs we need right now, and they'll make the economy stronger for everybody.

follow suit 学样，照别人的方式去做

partisan posturing 党派立场

contractor [ˈkɔntræktə] *n.* 立约人，订约人，承包人，承包商，承揽人

10 We've done this before. During the Great Depression, America built the *Hoover Dam*[⑤] and the *Golden Gate Bridge*[⑥] After World War II, we connected our states with a system of highways. Democratic and Republican administrations invested in great projects that benefited everybody, from the workers who built them to the businesses that still use them today.

11 So tell Congress that if we invest in new technology and new energy; in new roads and bridges and construction projects, we can keep growing our economy, put our people back to work, and remind the world why the United States is the greatest nation on Earth.

12 Thanks and have a great weekend.

背景知识注释 Background Notes

1. 美国众议院　即 the House of Representatives，为美国国会两院之一，另一院为参议院。美国各州在众议院中拥有的席位比例以人口为基准，但至少会有一名议员。院内议员总数经法律明定为 435 名。众议员任期两年，无连任限制。众议院议长由议员选举产生，亦称多数党领袖。据美国总统继位条例，众议院议长继位总统之顺序仅次于兼任参议院议长的副

总统，为政坛上第三重要的领袖人物。两院制国会的起源是因为建国者希望拥有一个贴近且跟随民意公论的“人民议院”，并受代表各州政府、不太受大众情绪干扰的参议院制衡。美国宪法规定法案须经两院批准方能通过。

2. 美国参议院　即 United States Senate，是美国的立法机构——美国国会的两院之一，另一院为众议院。美国每一州于参议院中均有两位议员作为代表，与各州人口无关。所以全院员额为 100 名议员。参议员任期六年，相互交错，故每隔两年改选约三分之一的席位。美国副总统任参议院议长，无参议员资格；参议院公认较众议院更为审慎；参议员名额较少而任期较长，容许学院派看法与党派之见，较众议院更易置外于公共舆论。参议院拥有若干表列于宪法而未授予众议院的权力。其中最重要的是，美国总统批准条约或任命重要人事时，须“采酌参议院之建议并得其认可”(美国宪法第一修正案)。

3. Boulder City　博尔德城，又译“石砾城”、“巨石城”，位于美国的内华达州，被誉为沙漠中的清洁绿洲。该城位于拉斯维加斯城开外约 20 英里处，离胡佛水坝也只有几英里的路程，城市人口为 15,000 多。

4. Ohio State University　俄亥俄州立大学 (简称 OSU)，是一所四年制州立大学，成立于 1870 年，目前是美国最大的大学，由五所成员大学组成。它的宠物是一颗橡树。俄亥俄州立大学是美国一所顶尖的公立大学，在美国所有注重研究的大学里，综合排名第 15，其中位于哥伦布的学院，获评“全美 229 所国家级大学”之一。据《纽约时报大学指南》指出，该大学最好的学科有会计、化学、经济、教育、地理、工业设计、外文、物理、政治科学和工程。学生选修最多的学科，依次是商科管理 (19%)、工程 (10%)、社会科学 (9%)、教育 (9%)、大众传播 (9%)。

5. Hoover Dam　胡佛水坝，在内华达州及亚利桑那州的西北部交界处，从拉斯维加斯出发向东南方向行驶约 40 公里处。胡佛水坝于 1931 年 3 月 11 日动工，建造耗费了大量资金，动用了大批人力，于 1936 年竣工并交付使用。它是一座拱门式重力人造混凝土水坝。坝高 220 米，底宽 200 米，顶宽 14 米，堤长 377 米。这样巨大的水坝在世界上是不多见的，它宛如一条巨龙盘卧在大地上，显得十分威武。水坝建成后对工农业发展起着巨大的作用。因此它在世界水利工程行列中占有重要的地位。

6. Golden Gate Bridge　金门大桥，是世界著名大桥之一，于 1933 年动工，1937 年 5 月竣工，用了 4 年时间和 10 万多吨钢材，耗资达 3,550 万美元，被誉为近代桥梁工程的一项奇迹，也被认为是旧金山的象征。这个伟大的建筑奇迹同时又被认为是全球首选的自杀圣地。设计者为工程师约瑟夫•斯特劳斯，人们把他的铜像安放在桥畔，用以纪念他对美国做出的贡献。大桥雄峙于美国加利福尼亚州宽 1,900 多米的金门海峡之上。金门海峡为旧金山海湾入口处，两岸陡峻，航道水深，为 1579 年英国探险家弗朗西斯•德雷克发现，并由他命名。金门大桥的北端连接北加利福尼亚，南端连接旧金山半岛。巨大桥塔高 227 米，每根钢索重 6,412 吨，由 27,000 根钢丝绞成。整个大桥造型宏伟壮观、朴素无华。桥身呈朱红色，横卧于碧海白浪之上，华灯初放，如巨龙凌空，使旧金山市的夜空景色更加壮丽。

中文译文
Chinese Version

1 各位好。本周我巡游了全国各地，向人们阐述了美国的全面能源战略：这一战略包括在国内不仅生产更多的石油和天然气，而且还生产更多生物燃料和节能汽车，更多地利用太阳能、风能以及其他可再生清洁能源。

2 也许你们从参与竞选公职的人们中无法得知，但提高国内石油产量一直是，也将继续是我的能源战略的重要组成部分。在本届政府的治理下，我们的石油产量比过去8年中的任何时候都高。我们的石油钻井平台数量创纪录地增加了4倍。同时我们增铺了油气管道，其长度比绕整个地球一周都还要多。这些都是不争的事实。

3 但正如我本周一直所言，尽管美国的石油消费量占全球约20%，但我们的石油储量却只有全球已探明储量的约2%。所以即使我们在各地加大开采，我们仍不得不依赖其他国家的石油供应。

4 这正是我们力求奉行一项全面的能源战略的原因。我们正在生产更多的生物燃料和更多的节能汽车，更多地使用太阳能和风能。本周，我去了内华达州的博尔德市，那里有最大的全国各地可见的太阳能发电厂。这才是我们的未来。我在俄亥俄州立大学看到他们已经研发出世界上最快的电动汽车。这才是我们的未来。我不想让清洁能源产业让位于中国或者德国或者任何其他国家。我希望看到太阳能电池板、风力发电机和节能汽车就在美国本土由美国工人制造。

5 现在，让这些清洁能源产业在国内扎根不仅要求我们国家信守对新技术研发的承诺，同时还要求我们建立世界一流的交通设施和通信网络。这样，任何公司都能以最快的速度和最高的效率将产品运往世界各地销售。

6 现在美国需要重建的项目不胜枚举。我们的公路和桥梁已经破损不堪。陈旧电网浪费了太多能源。我们的高速宽带网络也不完备。而且自房地产市场崩溃以来，成千上万的建筑工人下岗待业，直到现在他们依然还在寻找工作。

7 但我们又一次要急盼着国会有所作为。众所周知，在数天之后，各类交通项目的资助就要停止运作。建筑工地就将停工。工人们就得回家待业。我们的经济也将遭受冲击。

8 国会绝应杜绝此类事情的发生。尤其是在民主共和两党都在竭尽所能保持经济复苏势头继续向前之时，我们更不应该这么做。参议院已经尽到了责任。他们已经通过了这一两党联合提出的交通法案。这项法案得到了52名民主党参议员和22名共和党参议员的支持。现在该轮到众议院也效法跟进；搁置党派立场分歧，结束僵局，做对美国人民有益的事情。

9 这是情理之中的事。眼下，全国各地的承包商和建筑工人们都热望着重返工作岗位。

一项长期的交通法案将使他们重新投入工作，而且这些岗位还都不错。我们刚刚发布的一项调查报告表明通过投资于交通基建项目带来的建筑业、制造业和贸易业的岗位中有将近 90% 的属于中产阶级。这些工作岗位正是我们眼下所需要的，它们将帮助我们每一个人，使我们的经济更加强劲。

10 以前我们也曾这么做过。在大萧条时期，美国修建了胡佛大坝和金门大桥。第二次世界大战后，我们建设了联系各州的公路网。民主党和共和党的各届政府都投资于惠及民生的重大项目，无论是昔日的建设者还是如今依旧在享用这些工程的企业都从中获益匪浅。

11 因此，请大家告诫国会，倘若我们投资于新技术和新能源，投资于新道路、新桥梁和基建工程，我们就能使经济持续增长，使人民重返工作岗位，并警示世人美国依然是这个星球上最伟大的国家。

12 谢谢，祝周末愉快！

Passing the *Buffett Rule* so that Everyone Pays Their Fair Share

March 31, 2012

通过《巴菲特条例》以确保人人公平纳税

2012年3月31日

【摘要导读】

在本周的广播电视讲话中，巴拉克•奥巴马总统号召国会通过《巴菲特条例》，利用这一公平原则确保亿万富豪们缴纳的税收相对于他们的收入而言不再低于中产家庭。奥巴马总统认为美国的体制必须让富豪们承担他们应该承担的义务，同时保护另外98%的美国人的税率免于上升。正是因为如此，他提出了《巴菲特条例》，这一条例将有助于让所有人都享有公平的机会，遵守相同的规则行事，公平承担纳税义务。

演讲再现 Original Text

Words & Expressions

settle for 满足于，勉强接受

one's fair share 公平的税赋，合理的份额

1 Over the last few months, I've been talking about a choice we face as a country. We can either settle for an economy where a few people do really well and everyone else struggles to get by, or we can build an economy where hard work pays off again — where everyone gets a fair shot, everyone does their fair share, and everyone plays by the same rules. That's up to us.

2 Today, I want to talk to you about the idea that everyone in this country should do their fair share.

3 Now, if this were a perfect world, we'd have unlimited resources. No one would ever have to pay any taxes, and we could spend as much as we wanted. But we live in the real world. We don't have unlimited resources. We have

a deficit that needs to be paid down. And we also have to pay for investments that will help our economy grow and keep our country safe: education, research and technology, a strong military, and retirement programs like Medicare and Social Security.

4 That means we have to make choices. When it comes to paying down the deficit and investing in our future, should we ask middle-class Americans to pay even more at a time when their budgets are already stretched to the breaking point? Or should we ask some of the wealthiest Americans to pay their fair share?

5 That's the choice. Over the last decade, we've spent hundreds of billions of dollars on what was supposed to be a temporary tax cut for the wealthiest two percent of Americans. Now we're scheduled to spend almost a trillion more. Today, the wealthiest Americans are paying taxes at one of the lowest rates in 50 years. *Warren Buffett*[②] is paying a lower rate than his secretary. Meanwhile, over the last 30 years, the tax rates for middle-class families have barely budged.

6 That's not fair. It doesn't make any sense. Do we want to keep giving tax breaks to the wealthiest Americans both like myself, or Warren Buffett, or Bill Gates — people who don't need them and never asked for them? Or do we want to keep investing in things that will grow our economy and keep us secure? Because we can't afford to do both.

7 Now, some people call this class warfare. But I think asking a billionaire to pay at least the same tax rate as his secretary is just common sense. We don't envy success in this country. We aspire to it. But we also believe that anyone who does well for themselves should do their fair share in return, so that more people have the opportunity to get ahead — not just a few.

8 That's the America I believe in. And in the next few weeks, Members of Congress will get a chance to show you where they stand. Congress is going to vote on what's called the *Buffett Rule*: If you make more than $1 million a year, you should pay at least the same percentage of your income in taxes as middle-class families do. On the other hand, if you

pay down 用现金支付，当场支付，付现款，偿还

budget [ˈbʌdʒit] *n.*（收支）预算，预算案 *vt.* 安排，预定，把…编入预算

be stretched to the breaking point 处于崩溃的重压之下，被绷紧到断裂点

temporary [ˈtempərəri] *adj.* 暂时的，临时的，一时的，无常的，短暂的

barely [ˈbeəli] *adv.* 只有，几乎不，简直没有，勉强

budge [bʌdʒ] *vi.* [用于否定句] 挪动，微微移动，推动，让步，屈从

warfare [ˈwɔːfeə] *n.* 战争，冲突，斗争，竞争

aspire to 渴求，追求

get ahead （使）领先，（使）走在前面，（使）超前，前进，成功

grocery ['grəusəri] *n.* 食品杂货店，食品杂货
scrape by 勉强维持，勉强度日

make under $250,000 a year — like 98 percent of American families do — your taxes shouldn't go up. You're the ones struggling with the rising cost of everything from college tuition to groceries. You're the ones who deserve a break.

9 So every Member of Congress is going to go on record. And if they vote to keep giving tax breaks to people like me — tax breaks our country can't afford — then they're going to have to explain to you where that money comes from. Either it's going to add to our deficit, or it's going to come out of your pocket. Seniors will have to pay more for their Medicare benefits. Students will see their interest rates go up at a time when they can't afford it. Families who are scraping by will have to do more because the richest Americans are doing less.

10 That's not right. That's not who we are. In America, our story has never been about what we can do by ourselves — it's about what we can do together. It's about believing in our future and the future of this country. So tell your Members of Congress to do the right thing. Call them up, write them a letter, pay them a visit, and tell them to stop giving tax breaks to people who don't need them and start investing in the things that will help grow our economy and put people back to work.

11 That's how we'll make this country a little fairer, a little more just, and a whole lot stronger. Thanks.

背景知识注释 Background Notes

1. the *Buffett Rule* 《巴菲特条例》。奥巴马总统再提向富人增税的建议，意在确保年收入超过100万美元的富人承担与中产阶级相同的税率。奥巴马将这一条建议称做《巴菲特条例》。先前，美国"股神"沃伦•巴菲特(Warren Buffett)抱怨美国国会"溺爱"超级富翁，要求政府向包括自己在内的富人多收税。
2. Warren Buffett 沃伦•巴菲特(1930.8.30 —)，美国投资家、企业家、慈善家。他毕业于宾夕法尼亚大学、哥伦比亚大学。现任伯克希尔•哈撒韦公司董事长及华盛顿邮报公司董事，一般人称他为"股神"。他借由睿智进行投资，汇聚了非常庞大的财富。在2008年的《福

布斯》排行榜上财富超过比尔•盖茨，成为世界首富。2006 年 6 月，巴菲特承诺将其资产捐献给慈善机构，其中 85% 将交由盖茨夫妇基金会来运用。巴菲特此一大手笔的慈善捐赠，创下了美国有史以来的纪录。

中文译文
Chinese Version

1 在过去的数月中，我一直在谈论我们国家所面临的抉择。我们要么建立一种仅满足于极少数人获得成功而其他人却要苦苦挣扎才能勉强度日的经济，要么我们就建立一种辛勤工作能再次得到回报，人人都享有公平的机会，人人都公平承担纳税的义务，人人都遵守相同规则行事的经济。这完全取决于我们自己。

2 今天，我想要与大家谈论的话题涉及关于我们国家的每个人如何承担自己的义务的观点。

3 倘若我们生活在一个理想的世界里，有取之不尽的资源。那么任何人都不必要纳税，我们可以按需求随意花费。但是我们是生活在现实的世界中。我们没有用之不竭的资源。我们还有赤字需要平衡。而且我们还必须在助推我们的经济增长和保证我们的国家安全等领域进行投资，这涉及教育、科学研究与技术研发、强大的军力以及诸如医保和社保这些退休保障计划。

4 这就意味着我们必须做出选择。当我们面临平衡赤字并同时投资于未来的时候，我们是让处在收支都很难平衡的临界点上的中产阶级缴纳更多赋税呢，还是让美国的富豪们承担他们合理的纳税义务呢？

5 这就要求我们做出选择。过去的十年中，我们已经为原本是一项针对占 2% 的美国富豪们的临时减税计划花费了数千亿美元。而现在我们预计还要为他们减税近 1 万亿。今天，美国的富豪们承担的税率处在 50 年来的最低水平。沃伦•巴菲特的税率比他的秘书的还要低。与此同时，过去 30 年以来，中产阶级的税率几乎从来没有调整过。

6 这既不公平也没道理。我们是希望给像我，或者沃伦•巴菲特，或是比尔•盖茨这些本身就不需要而且从来没有要求享有这种政策的人士继续提供税收减免呢？还是想在保持我们的经济增长和国家安全等领域继续进行投资呢？原因就在于我们不能同时承担起这两项任务。

7 现在，有些人称这是阶级斗争。但我认为让亿万富豪至少跟他们的秘书一样承担相同的税率是合乎情理的。在美国，我们并不嫉妒成功。我们追求成功。但同时我们也认为任何取得成就的人也应该承担责任回馈社会，以便有更多的人可以获取成功的机会——而不仅限于极少数人。

8 这就是我所信赖的美国。在未来的数周中，国会议员们将有机会展示自己的立场。国会将就《巴菲特条例》进行投票：倘若你每年收入超过 100 万美元，那么你就应该至少承担与中产家庭一样的收入所得税税率。另一方面，倘若你与98%的美国家庭一样年收入低于25万，那么你的税率将不会增加。因为你们一直在为从大学学费到日常用品等所有东西的价格上涨而苦苦挣扎。你们才是理应获得税务减免的人。

9 因此，每个国会议员都要公开表明自己的立场。倘若他们投票赞成继续给像我这样的人提供税收优惠，那么由于我们国家不堪承受这样的减税政策，他们就必须向公众解释这些钱要从哪里来。要么就是继续增加我们的赤字，要么就是从大家的腰包中掏取。其结果是老人将为医疗保险缴纳更多保险费；学生也将眼看贷款利率升高而无法承受。由于美国富豪们承担较低的税率，勉强度日的普通家庭就不得不背负较高的税率。

10 这既不合理也不合我们的本质。在美国，我们的历史从来就不是我们依靠自己单打独斗的历史，而是我们团结奋进的历史，是我们信赖我们的未来和国家的未来的历史。所以请告诫你们的国会议员们要采取理智的行动。打电话呼吁他们，写信给他们，登门拜访他们，告诫他们要停止为那些不需要税收优惠的人减税，告诫他们要开始为在助推我们的经济增长和让人们重返工作岗位等领域进行投资。

11 这正是我们让国家更加公平、更加公正、更加强大的途径所在。谢谢大家。

第14周

Easter[①] and Passover[②] Greetings from President Obama

April 7, 2012

奥巴马总统在复活节和逾越节的祝福

2012年4月7日

【摘要导读】

在本周的广播电视讲话中，巴拉克•奥巴马总统向周末欢度复活节和逾越节的人们致以最温馨的问候，并一起反思将大家紧密相连的这一人类共同脉络。奥巴马总统希望全体美国人都度过一个欢快的周末，关注美国独特的传统所创造的奇迹以及将美国人民团结起来的价值观。

演讲再现 Original Text

1 For millions of Americans, this weekend is a time to celebrate redemption at God's hand. Tonight, Jews will gather for a second *Seder*[③], where they will retell the story of the *Exodus*[④]. And tomorrow, my family will join Christians around the world as we thank God for the all-important gift of grace through the resurrection of His son, and experience the wonder of Easter morning.

2 These holidays have their roots in miracles that took place thousands of years ago. They connect us to our past and give us strength as we face the future. And they remind us of the common thread of humanity that connects us all.

3 For me, and for countless other Christians, Easter weekend is a time to reflect and rejoice. Yesterday, many of us took a few quiet moments to try and fathom the tremendous sacrifice Jesus made for all of us.

Words & Expressions

redemption [riˈdempʃən] *n.* 赎回，偿还，挽救，赎救

resurrection [ˌrezəˈrekʃən] *n.* 复活，复苏

miracle [ˈmirəkl] *n.* （神创造的）奇迹，不可思议的事

rejoice [riˈdʒɔis] *vi.* 欣喜，感到高兴

fathom [ˈfæðəm] *vt.* 测…的深度，弄清…真相，彻底了解，洞察

sacred ['seikrid] *adj.* 祭神的，宗教上的，神圣的

recommit ourselves to 再次承诺，重新做出承诺

rededicate [ri'dedikeit] *vt.* 再次奉献

humble ['hʌmbl] *adj.* 谦卑的，谦虚的，恭顺的

almighty [ɔːl'maiti] *adj.* 有无限权力的，有强大力量的，全能的，万能的

triumph over 征服，击败，战胜，克服

identify with 使等同于，把…看做一致，（使）与…有关，（使）支持

put sth. in perspective 正确地看待事物，对某事充满期待

4 Tomorrow, we will celebrate the resurrection of a savior who died so that we might live.

5 And throughout these sacred days, we recommit ourselves to following His example. We rededicate our time on Earth to selflessness, and to loving our neighbors. We remind ourselves that no matter who we are, or how much we achieve. We each stand humbled before an almighty God.

6 Christ's triumph over death holds special meaning for Christians. But all of us, no matter how or whether we believe, can identify with elements of His story. The triumph of hope over despair. Of faith over doubt.

7 The notion that there is something out there that is bigger than ourselves.

8 These beliefs help unite Americans of all faiths and backgrounds. They shape our values and guide our work. They put our lives in perspective.

9 So to all Christians celebrating the Resurrection with us, Michelle and I want to wish you a blessed and Happy Easter. And to all Americans, I hope you have a weekend filled with joy and reflection, focused on the things that matter most. God bless you, and may God bless the United States of America.

背景知识注释 Background Notes

1. Easter 复活节。它是西方相当重要的节日之一，是为了纪念耶稣基督在十字架受刑死后复活的节日，所以西方信基督教的国家都会过这个节。在西方教会传统里，春分过后第一次满月之后的第一个星期日即为复活节。东方教会则规定，倘若满月恰逢星期日，则复活节再推迟一周。因此，节期大致在3月22日至4月25日之间。复活节是最古老最有意义的基督教节日之一，庆祝的是基督的复活，世界各地的基督徒每年都要举行庆祝。复活节还象征着重生和希望。

2. Passover 逾越节，又称"无酵节"、"巴斯卦节"，是犹太教的主要节期之一，以纪念摩西成功地率领犹太人摆脱法老控制、离开埃及、举族返回迦南的经历，又叫做"自由节"。

逾越节是犹太历正月十四日白昼及其前夜，是犹太人的新年，犹太民族的四大节日之一（第二个是犹太历七月吹 角节—赎罪日—住棚节，一个节日系列；第三个为献殿节；第四个是普尔节）。

3. Seder　逾越节家宴（犹太历尼撒月 15 日和 16 日）。犹太人庆祝逾越节（Passover）的晚餐称为 Seder，是庆祝逾越节时吃的第一顿晚餐，也是庆祝逾越节的最主要活动。逾越节家宴 (Seder) 的程序很复杂，桌上的摆设也很讲究，有许多象征性的食物，比如象征泪水的苏打水，象征苦难的一种蔬菜，象征牺牲的羊骨，象征重生的鸡蛋等。

4. *Exodus*　《出埃及记》，《圣经•旧约》中的 (古代以色列人在摩西率领下的) 出埃及记，出埃及记的故事，或大迁徙。

中文译文
Chinese Version

1　对千百万美国人而言，这个周末是感谢上帝救赎的日子。今晚，犹太人将聚集一堂再次举行家宴，重新讲述出埃及记的故事。明天，我全家将和世界上所有基督徒一起感恩上帝通过其子复活所给予的盛大恩典，并见证复活节早上的奇迹。

2　这些节日起源于几千年前所发生的奇迹。正是它们将我们与过去联系在一起，并给予我们面对未来的力量。这些也让我们牢记将我们紧密联系在一起的这一人类共同脉络。

3　就我和无数基督徒而言，复活节周末是反省和愉悦的时刻。昨天，我们许多人都静静地花了些时间去领悟耶稣为我们所付出的巨大的牺牲。

4　明天，我们将一起庆祝救世主的复活，正因为他的离世我们才得以存活。

5　在这神圣的日子里，我们再次承诺要以他为楷模。再次将时间奉献在无私的事业和关爱邻里上。我们要不断地警醒自己：无论我们是谁，无论我们取得多大的成就，在全能的上帝面前，我们都要保持谦卑。

6　基督对死亡的征服对于基督徒而言有着特殊的意义。但我们所有人，无论我们信仰耶稣的方式如何，或者是否信仰，都能认同他故事中的所有内容。希望终将战胜绝望，信任定能消除怀疑。

7　存在某种精神的观念超越了我们自身。

8　这些信念有助于将不同信仰和背景的全体美国人团结在一起，塑造我们的价值观并指导我们的工作，使我们能正确地看待人生。

9　至此，米歇尔和我希望祝福所有与我们一起庆祝复活节的基督徒们，祝你们复活节幸福而又快乐。对于所有的美国人，我希望大家的周末充满愉快和反思，并关注那些最紧要的事情。愿上帝保佑大家，愿上帝保佑美利坚合众国。

第15周

It's Time for Congress to Pass the *Buffett Rule*

April 14, 2012

该是国会通过《巴菲特条例》的时候了

2012年4月14日

【摘要导读】

在本周的广播电视讲话中，巴拉克·奥巴马总统敦促国会通过《巴菲特条例》。根据这一条例，倘若年收入超过100万美元，那么至少应该按与中产家庭一样的税率缴纳所得税。同时，倘若像美国98%的家庭一样，年收入低于25万美元，那么税率将不会上浮。奥巴马总统一直在推动国会通过《巴菲特条例》，他认为这样有助于确保美国体制的公平，让人人都遵从同样的规则行事，让美国可以继续做出必要的投资推动经济的发展，帮助中产阶级以及那些试图加入中产阶级的人们。

演讲再现
Original Text

1 One of the fundamental challenges of our time is building an economy where everyone gets a fair shot, everyone does their fair share, and everyone plays by the same rules.

2 And as many Americans rush to file their taxes this weekend, it's worth pointing out that we've got a tax system that doesn't always uphold the principle of everyone doing their part.

3 This is not just about fairness. This is also about growth. It's about being able to make the investments we need to strengthen our economy and create jobs. And it's about whether we as a country are willing to pay for those investments.

4 In a perfect world, of course, none of us would have

Words & Expressions

fundamental [ˌfʌndəˈmentəl] *adj.* 基本的，基础的，根本的，实质的

file their taxes 报税，缴税

uphold [ʌpˈhəuld] *vt.* 举起，支撑，支持，维护，赞成

to pay any taxes. We'd have no deficits to pay down. And we'd have all the resources we needed to invest in things like schools and roads and a strong military and new sources of energy — investments that have always bolstered our economy and strengthened the middle-class.

5 But we live in the real world, with real choices and real consequences. Right now, we've got significant deficits to close. We've got serious investments to make to keep our economy growing. And we can't afford to keep spending more money on tax cuts for the wealthiest Americans who don't need them and didn't even ask for them.

6 Warren Buffett is one of the wealthiest men in the world. But he pays a lower tax rate than his secretary. That's just the way the system is set up. In fact, one in four millionaires pays a lower tax rate than millions of hardworking middle-class households.

7 As Warren points out, that's not fair and it doesn't make sense. It's wrong that middle-class Americans pay a higher share of their income in taxes than some millionaires and billionaires.

8 This week, Members of Congress are going to have a chance to set things right. They get to vote on what we call the *Buffett Rule*.

9 It's simple: If you make more than $1 million every year, you should pay at least the same percentage of your income in taxes as middle-class families do. On the other hand, if you make less than $250,000 a year — like 98 percent of American families do — your taxes shouldn't go up.

10 That's all there is to it. It's pretty sensible. Most Americans support this idea. One survey found that two-thirds of millionaires do, too. So do nearly half of all Republicans.

11 We just need some Republican politicians to get on board with where the country is.

12 I know they'll say that this is all about wanting to raise people's taxes. They probably won't tell you that if you belong to a middle-class family, then I've cut your taxes each year that I've been in office, and I've cut taxes for small

bolster [ˈbəulstə] *vt.* 支撑，加固，维持，鼓励，支持，加强，充实
consequence [ˈkɔnsiˌkwəns] *n.* 结果，后果，影响
household [ˈhaushəuld] *n.* 家庭，户，全家人，一家人
set things right 把事情纠正过来，拨乱反正，改正
sensible [ˈsensəbl] *adj.* 明智的，合理的，意识到的
survey [ˈsəːvei] *n.* 概况，调查，调查(或检验)报告，测量，审视
get on board with 和…一起踏上甲板，与…联合起来，参与

business owners 17 times.

13 But the thing is, for most Americans like me, tax rates are near their lowest point in 50 years. In 2001 and 2003, the wealthiest Americans received two huge new tax cuts. We were told these tax cuts would lead to faster job growth. Instead, we got the slowest job growth in half a century, and the typical American family actually saw its income fall.

14 On the flip side, when the most well-off Americans were asked to pay a little more in the 1990s, we were warned that it would kill jobs. Instead, tens of millions of jobs followed.

15 So we've tried this trickle-down experiment before. It doesn't work. And middle-class families have seen too much of their security erode over the past few decades for us to tell them they're going to have to do more because the wealthiest Americans are going to do less. We can't stop investing in the things that will help grow our economy and create jobs — things like education, research, new sources of energy — just so folks like me can get another tax cut.

16 So I hope you'll ask your Member of Congress to step up and echo that call this week by voting for the Buffett Rule. Remind them that in America, prosperity has never just trickled down from a wealthy few. Prosperity has always been built by a strong, thriving middle-class. That's a principle worth reaffirming right now.

17 Thanks. God bless you, and have a great weekend.

on the flip side 另一方面

well-off ['wel'ɔf] *adj.* 处境好的，富有的，宽裕的，繁荣昌盛的

trickle-down ['trikldaun] *adj.* 滴入论的，点滴受益论的，利益扩散论的

erode [i'rəud] *vt.* 腐蚀，侵蚀，磨损，损害，削弱

echo ['ekəu] *vt.* 发出…的回声，附和，重复 *n.* 反响，回音，共鸣 *vi.* 起反响，起共鸣

prosperity [prɔs'periti] *n.* 繁荣，昌盛，幸福，成功

thriving ['θraiviŋ] *adj.* 兴旺的，发达的，繁荣的，成功的

reaffirm [ˌriːə'fəːm] *vt.* 重申，再次肯定，再次确认

中文译文
Chinese Version

1 当前我们所面临的一个根本挑战就是建立一种人人都享有公平的机会，人人都承担公平的义务，人人都按同样规则行事的经济。

2 值得指出的是，本周末当许多美国民众纷纷赶去报税的时候，我们的税制体制却表现得并不足以维持每个人都公平纳税这一原则。

3 这不仅仅牵涉到公平的问题，还牵涉到经济的增长，牵涉到我们是否能够进行我们所必需的投资以夯实我们的经济基础并创造就业岗位，牵涉到我们国家是否有意愿做出这些投资。

4 当然，倘若是在完美的世界，我们任何人都不必要缴税。我们也不必要抵消赤字。我们拥有所需要的各种资源来投资于建设学校、公路、强大的军队和开发新能源，正是这些投资一直支撑着我们的经济并巩固了中产阶级的地位。

5 但是，我们是生活在现实的世界里，面对着切切实实的选择和影响。现在，我们有严重的赤字需要消除。我们还要做出重大的投资保持经济的增长。而且我们无法承受花费更多金钱继续为不需要甚至也没有相应要求的富豪们减免赋税。

6 沃伦•巴菲特现在是世界上最为富有的人士之一。但他所缴的税率却比他秘书的还要低。这就是我们的税制的现状。实际上，有四分之一的百万富翁的所缴税率比数百万辛勤工作的中产阶级家庭的要低。

7 正如沃伦所指出的，这既不公平也不合理。美国的中产阶级缴纳的税款占他们收入的比例要比一些百万富翁和亿万富翁还要高，这是不合理的。

8 本周，国会议员们将有机会纠正这一错误。他们就要对《巴菲特条例》进行投票。

9 道理很简单：倘若你年收入超过100万，那么你至少应该承担与中产阶级家庭一样的所得税税率。另一方面，倘若你与其他98%的中产阶级家庭一样，年收入低于25万美元，那么你的税率将不会上浮。

10 仅此而已，相当合理。大部分美国人都支持这一想法。一项调查报告显示：2/3的百万富翁们也希望如此，而且将近一半的共和党人也是支持的。

11 我们只是需要一些共和党的政治家们与这个国家协调一致，顺从民意。

12 当然，我知道反对者们会说这项条例最终就是要提高人民的税率。但他们很可能不会告诉你的是，倘若你属于中产阶级家庭，自我上任以来，我每年都为你们减税，而且还17次为小微企业减税。

13 但事实是，对像我一样的高收入美国人而言，我们的税率几乎处在50年来的最低值。在2001年和2003年，美国的富豪们得到了两项全新的巨额减税。我们被告知这些减税将加快就业增长。然而，我们的就业增长速度在这半个多世纪里却是最慢的，普通的美国家庭实际上都见证了自己的收入在下降。

14 另一方面，20世纪90年代，当美国的富豪们被要求多缴点税时，我们就受到警告称这样会伤害就业。然而，事实正相反，就业岗位却增加了数千万。

15 我们之前尝试过了这种涓滴模式的试验，根本就不奏效。过去几十年里，中产阶级家庭眼睁睁看着自己太多的安全保障受到侵害，而我们却告诉他们你们要承受更重的税率，因为富豪们承担的少了。我们不能终止在教育、科研以及新能源等有助于我们发展经济和创造就业方面的投资，尽管如此像我这类人还是能获得额外的减税。

16 因此，我希望你们要求你们的议员们挺身而出投票通过《巴菲特条例》，借此对本周的呼吁做出回应。要警醒他们：在美国，繁荣从来就不是依靠少数富裕人士滴入式获得的，繁荣总是根基于一个强大而兴旺的中产阶级。这是眼下值得重新确认的原则。

17 谢谢大家，上帝保佑你们，祝大家周末愉快。

第16周

Calling on Congress to Prevent Student Interest Rates from Doubling

April 21, 2012

呼吁国会要阻止助学贷款利率翻倍增长

2012 年 4 月 21 日

【摘要导读】

在本周的广播电视讲话中，巴拉克•奥巴马总统呼吁国会要在助学贷款利率翻倍生效前采取行动，否则740万学子将因此平均增加1,000美元的债务。他表示：接受高等教育从来没有显得这么重要，但也从来没有这么昂贵；当奥巴马政府采取一系列历史性措施为美国人提供公平的机会接受可承受的高等教育的同时，国会中的共和党人却将为百万富豪和亿万富豪们提供大规模新的减税政策列为优先事项；现在，国会有机会来决定两党应在哪一领域达成共识以阻止这种不必要的并具有破坏性的助学贷款利率的上涨，给美国的年轻人提供一个在当今和未来的职业生涯中获得成功的机会。

演讲再现 Original Text

1 Hi. This week, I got the chance to sit down with some impressive students at *Lorain County Community College* ① in Ohio. One of them was a woman named Andrea Ashley. Two years ago, Andrea lost her job as an HR analyst. Today, she's getting certified in the fast-growing field of electronic medical records. Before enrolling at Lorain, Andrea told me she was looking everywhere trying to find a new job. But without a degree, she said that nobody would hire her.

2 Andrea's story isn't unique. I've met so many Americans who are out there pounding the pavement looking for work only to discover that they need new skills. And I've

Words & Expressions

HR analyst 人力资源专员，人力资源分析师

certify ['sə:tifai] *vt.* 证明，证实，发证书批准

medical record 病历

enrol [in'rəul] *vi.* 登记

pound the pavement 四处奔走，找工作，努力苦干

met a lot of employers who are looking for workers, but can't find ones with the skills they're looking for.

3 So we should be doing everything we can to put higher education within reach for every American — because at a time when the unemployment rate for Americans with at least a college degree is about half the national average, it's never been more important. But here's the thing: it's also never been more expensive. Students who take out loans to pay for college graduate owing an average of $25,000. For the first time, Americans owe more debt on their student loans than they do on their credit cards. And for many working families, the idea of owing that much money means that higher education is simply out of reach for their children.

4 In America, higher education cannot be a luxury. It's an economic imperative that every family must be able to afford. That's why next week I'll be visiting colleges across the country, talking to students about how we can make higher education more affordable — and what's at stake right now if Congress doesn't do something about it. You see, if Congress doesn't act, on July 1st interest rates on some student loans will double. Nearly seven and half million students will end up owing more on their loan payments. That would be a tremendous blow. And it's completely preventable.

5 This issue didn't come out of nowhere. For some time now, I've been calling on Congress to take steps to make higher education more affordable — to prevent these interest rates from doubling, to extend the tuition tax credit that has saved middle-class families millions of dollars, and to double the number of work-study jobs over the next five years.

6 Instead, over the past few years, Republicans in Congress have voted against new ways to make college more affordable for middle-class families, and voted for huge new tax cuts for millionaires and billionaires — tax cuts that would have to be paid for by cutting things like education and job-training programs that give students new opportunities to work and succeed.

7 We cannot just cut our way to prosperity. Making it harder for our young people to afford higher education and

out of reach 遥不可及，无法控制的

imperative [im'perətiv] *n.* 必要的事，紧急的事，必要性 *adj.* 必要的，迫切的，强制的

at stake 在危急关头，在危险中，成问题

end up doing 以…而告终

come out of nowhere 不知从何而来，突然出现，凭空产生

tuition [tjuː'iʃən] *n.* 学费，辅导费

nothing more than 仅仅，不过是，无非是

shrink [ˈʃriŋkiŋ] *adj.* 收缩的，畏缩的，减少的

earn their degrees is nothing more than cutting our own future off at the knees. Congress needs to keep interest rates on student loans from doubling, and they need to do it now.

8 This is a question of values. We cannot let America become a country where a shrinking number of people do really well, while a growing number of people struggle to get by. We've got to build an economy where everyone gets a fair shot, everyone does their fair share, and everyone plays by the same set of rules. That's how the middle-class gets stronger. That's an economy that's built to last. And I'm not only going to take that case to college campuses next week — I'm going to take it to every part of the country this year. Thanks, and have a great weekend.

背景知识注释 Background Notes

1. Lorain County Community College　劳伦县社区学院，位于俄亥俄州伊利亚市 (Elyria)，是该州最大最好的社区大学，注册学生人数高达 12,000 人，包括来自 45 个国家的留学生。伊利亚市距离该州最大的城市克利夫兰市区仅半小时车程，距纽约、华盛顿乘飞机仅 1 个多小时，毗邻五大湖之一的伊利湖及美加边境。

中文译文 Chinese Version

1 各位好！本周，我有机会来到俄亥俄州劳伦县社区学院 (Lorain County Community College)，与一些品学兼优的学生们座谈。他们当中有一位叫安德拉·阿什利 (Andrea Ashley) 的女生。安德拉曾是一位人力资源分析师，两年前她失业了。今天，她在电子病历这一发展迅速的领域获得了认证证书。安德拉告诉我说，在入学之前，她也曾到处找过工作，但由于缺少文凭，没人想雇用她。

2 安德拉的故事并不是特例。我遇到过许多四处奔波寻找工作的美国人，结果他们都发现自己缺乏新的技能。我也遇到过许多雇主在寻找员工，但总是找不到他们所需要的具备相应技能的人员。

3 因此，我们应该竭尽全力地让所有美国人都有机会接受高等教育，因为当下至少拥有大学学历人群的失业率只是全国平均水平的一半，所以高等教育具有前所未有的重要性。但问题的症结是：学费也是空前昂贵。贷款上学的学生毕业后平均负债 2.5 万美元。这也是

第一次出现美国人在助学贷款上的债务要比信用卡的债务高的情况。对许多工薪家庭而言，高等教育需要负担如此沉重的债务这对他们的孩子而言简直是可想而不可及的了。

4 在美国，高等教育绝不是奢侈品。就经济上而言，它理应是每个家庭都能担负得起的必需品。这也是下周我将巡访全国一些大学的原因所在，我将与学生们一起讨论如何使高等教育能更让人负担得起，以及眼下倘若国会不对此采取措施将会发生什么危机等问题。众所周知，倘若国会不有所作为，从 7 月 1 日起，部分助学贷款利率将翻一番。将近 750 万学生将因此增加还款额度。这对他们将是一个巨大的打击，然而这完全是可以避免的。

5 这个问题并不是凭空而来的。一段时间以来，我一直在呼吁国会要采取措施使高等教育更让人负担得起，阻止贷款利率翻倍，并扩大学费税抵免范围，为中产阶级家庭节省数百万美元，同时将半工半读的助学岗位在未来 5 年里增加一倍。

6 然而，在过去数年中，国会的共和党人投票反对各种使中产阶级家庭更能承受得起大学教育的新措施，却支持对百万富豪和亿万富豪们减免巨额税款，而减免的这些税款的来源正是削减本来应该用于教育、职业培训计划上的资金，而这些本可以给学生们提供就业并取得成功的机会。

7 我们绝不能切断通向繁荣的道路。让年轻人更加艰难地承受高等教育的学费和获取学位无异于断送我们脚下的前程。国会不能让助学贷款利率翻倍，他们应该立即采取行动。

8 这是一个涉及价值观的问题。我们不能让美国成为一个只有越来越少的人获得成功而越来越多的人却只能挣扎度日的国度。我们必须建立一种人人都享有公平的机遇，人人都承担平等的义务，人人都按相同规则行事的经济。这才是让中产阶级壮大的途径。这才是建立一种可持续发展的经济的途径。我不仅要将这个观念带到我下周将造访的各个大学校园，我还将在今年把它带到全国各地。谢谢大家，祝周末愉快！

Helping Veterans and Servicemembers Make Informed Decisions about Higher Education

April 28, 2012

协助退伍老兵及现役军人在申请高等教育时做出明智选择

2012 年 4 月 28 日

【摘要导读】

在本周的广播电视讲话中，巴拉克·奥巴马总统告诉美国民众他于周五签署了一项新的行政命令，对那些损害退伍老兵和现役军人接受高等教育的恶劣行径进行严厉打击。因为这些英勇的军人们常常被校方所提供的欺骗性或误导性的信息轮番轰炸，例如贷款利率、信用转让和就业安置计划等。美国政府的这项新的行政命令将使退伍老兵和现役军人更容易就资金援助和大学学费等方面做出明智决定，并采取措施与某些机构的欺骗行径做斗争。奥巴马说他将一如既往地确保这些为国服务的人们得到他们应有的机遇。

演讲再现 Original Text

Words & Expressions

make it back 回来，返回

1 On Friday, I traveled to *Ft. Stewart* ① in Georgia to meet with soldiers from *the Third Infantry Division* ②.

2 These men and women have fought with bravery and honor in some of the most dangerous places on the planet. Some of them didn't make it back. But those who did are now fighting a different kind of battle here at home. They're looking for new jobs, new opportunities, and new ways to serve.

3 For many, that means going back to school — and America has a long tradition of making sure our veterans

and our men and women in uniform can afford to do that. After World War II, we helped a generation of Americans — including my grandfather — to go to school on *The GI Bill* ③. Now, thanks to *The 9/11 GI Bill* ④ and *the Tuition Assistance program* ⑤, last year we supported more than half a million veterans and over 300,000 service members who are pursuing a higher education degree.

4 That's progress. But it's not enough to just help our veterans and service members afford school — we need to make sure they have all the tools they need to make an informed decision when it comes to picking the right program.

5 The sad truth is that there are people out there who are less interested in helping our men and women in uniform get ahead and more interested in making a buck. They bombard potential students with emails and pressure them into making a quick decision. Some of them steer recruits towards high-interest loans and mislead them about credit transfers and job placement programs. One of the worst examples was a college recruiter who visited a Marine barracks and enrolled Marines with brain injuries so severe that some of them couldn't recall what courses the recruiter had signed them up for.

6 That's appalling. It's disgraceful. And even though the vast majority of schools do the right thing, we need to guard against the bad actors who don't.

7 That's why, on Friday, I signed an Executive Order making life a whole lot more secure for our service members, veterans and their families — and a whole lot tougher for anyone who tries to prey on them.

8 We're making sure veterans and service members get a simple fact sheet called "Know Before You Owe" that lays out all the information they need about financial aid and paying for college. We're requiring schools to offer counselling to help students finish their degree even if they have to move or deploy. And we're

make a buck 挣钱，赚钱

potential [pəu'tenʃəl] *adj.* 潜在的，有潜势，可能的，有可能性的

pressure sb. into doing sth. 迫使某人做某事

steer [stiə] *vt.* 掌舵，驾驶，操纵，引导

recruit [ri'kru:t] *n.* 新兵，新手，大学新生

placement ['pleismənt] *n.* 放置，安置，部署，安排，布置

college recruiter 大学的招生人员

marine [mə'ri:n] *n.* （美国）海军陆战队士兵（或军官）

barrack ['bærək] *n.* 兵营，营房，（工地等的）棚屋

sign up for 签约，报名参加

appalling [ə'pɔ:liŋ] *adj.* 可怕的，骇人的，骇人听闻的，极其低劣的

disgraceful [dis'greisful] *adj.* 丢脸的，可耻的，不光彩的

guard against 预防，提防，警惕

tough [tʌf] *adj.* 坚韧的，强健的，坚定的，倔强的，艰难的，劳累的

Know Before You Owe 贷款须知

counselling ['kaunsəliŋ] *n.* 忠告，建议，劝告，协商

deploy [di'plɔi] *vt.* 使展开，调度，配备，部署，利用

stepping up our efforts to fight dishonest recruiters by strengthening rules about who can come on base and making it easier to file complaints.

step up one's efforts 加大力度，加强工作，
file a complaint 投诉，提出控告，申诉

9 When our men and women in uniform succeed, our country succeeds. They have our back — now it's our turn to have theirs. And as long as I'm President, I'm going to make sure that anyone who serves this country gets every opportunity they deserve.

10 Thanks, and have a great weekend.

背景知识注释 Background Notes

1. Ft. Stewart 即 Fort Stewart 斯图尔特堡，是美国密西西比河东岸最大的军事基地。这块专用地从东到西约 39 英里（63 公里），从北到南 19 英里（31 公里）。二战期间，整个营地驻扎了 2,705 名警察和 37,267 名士兵。该基地紧靠东海岸，与佐治亚州的萨凡纳港（深 42 米）和南卡罗来纳州的查尔斯顿港（深 142 米）有两个深水港口毗邻。坦克、大炮、直升机和小型武器应有尽有，几乎全天候都能操练。
2. the Third Infantry Division 第三步兵师，始建于 1917 年，隶属于美国第十八空降军和美国陆军部队司令部。
3. The *GI Bill* 《退伍军人法》/《士兵福利法案》。美国联邦政府为了有效地解决战后退伍士兵面临的就业、培训、医疗保障等方面的问题，1944 年，罗斯福总统提出了《退伍军人法》(*The GI Bill*)，设立了一项特殊的奖学金，向退伍军人提供经济与教育方面的资助，资助那些战后退役军人接受高等教育，将服务和教育结合，有机会服务国家。该法案奠定了美国战后退伍士兵安置的法律基础，促使联邦政府大量的资金源源不断地流入到对退伍士兵的教育训练中去，有力地推动了战后美国各州教育尤其是成人教育的改革与发展进程。
4. *The 9/11 GI Bill* 《后 911 士兵福利法案》。9•11 事件后，美国国会通过了该法案，通过拨款已经帮助约 30 万退伍军人和他们的家庭成员追求他们的大学梦。同时，为了帮助退伍军人在经济困难时期找到工作，美国政府在岗位培训和安置上投入了新的资源。
5. the Tuition Assistance program 学费援助计划。

中文译文 Chinese Version

1 星期五，我造访了佐治亚州的斯图尔特堡 (Ft. Stewart)，会晤了第三步兵师的士兵们。

2 这些男女士兵们曾经在这个星球上最为危险的地方英勇而又光荣地战斗过，其中有些人从此一去不复还。但那些凯旋的现在却在国内进行一场不同类型的战斗。他们在寻找新的工作、新的机遇和新的为国效力的途径。

3 对他们许多人而言，这意味着要重返校园。美国有着确保退伍老兵和现役军人能完成学业的悠久传统。第二次世界大战之后，我们利用《退伍军人法》(*The GI Bill*) 帮助了一代美国人——包括我的祖父——回到校园。现在，有了《后 911 士兵福利法案》(*The 9/11 GI Bill*) 和学费资助计划，去年我们帮助 50 多万退伍老兵和 30 多万现役军人接受高等教育。

4 这就是进步。但仅仅帮助退伍老兵和现役军人能负担大学学费是不够的，我们还需要确保他们能获得所有的工具在选择正确的学习计划上做出明智的决定。

5 但可悲的事实是，总有些人对于帮助这些普通军人取得进步不那么感兴趣而更热衷于赚钱。他们用大量的 e-mail 信件围攻潜在的学员，施加压力迫使他们尽快做出决定。有些人甚至诱导新生们申请高利率贷款，并在信用转让和就业安置计划方面误导他们。举个最恶劣的例子，一位大学招生人员到访一个海军陆战队兵营专门招收那些脑部严重受损的陆战队员，而这些队员事后甚至无法回忆起招生人员跟他们签约了哪些课程。

6 这真是骇人听闻，太可耻了。尽管绝大多数学校做事正派，但我们还是需要提防这些害群之马。

7 因此，周五我签署了行政命令要确保我们的现役军人、退伍老兵及其家属能过上更加有保障的生活，并采取更加强硬的手段打击那些试图损害其利益的人。

8 我们要确保退伍老兵和现役军人得到一张简明真实的《贷款须知》表，详细列出他们在获取资金援助和支付学费等方面的所有信息。我们还要求学校提供咨询服务，帮助学生们即便在部队需要调动或部署的情况下完成学业。而且我们要加大力度打击不诚实的招生人员，加强进入军营的规章制度，让投诉渠道通畅无阻。

9 当我们的军人获得了成功，我们国家才能成功。他们作为我们的后盾——现在该轮到我们为他们提供保障了。只要我任总统一职，我就要确保每一个为国服役的人都能得到他们应有的机遇。

10 谢谢大家，祝周末愉快！

第18周

A New Chapter in Afghanistan

May 5, 2012

阿富汗的新篇章

2012 年 5 月 5 日

【摘要导读】

在本周的广播电视讲话中，巴拉克•奥巴马总统谈到了最近的阿富汗之行。他说他在那里会晤了美国官兵们，并与阿富汗签订了一项有助于结束这场战争的历史性协议，这项协议重新定义了两国关系，阿富汗人民将很快担当起自己国家安全的责任。他还表示当美国的部队凯旋，当美国人民在共同展望未来之际，国家的现状又是美国人民必须着重关注的焦点。因此他呼吁国会把因战争结束而剩余的资金的一半用于偿还债务，另一半用于重建国家。

演讲再现 Original Text

1 This week, I traveled to Afghanistan—to thank our troops serving far from home, and to sign an historic agreement that will help us complete our mission and end the war.

2 As Commander-in-Chief, nothing is more humbling or inspiring than the chance to spend some time with our troops. At *Bagram Air Base* ①, I visited with some of our outstanding men and women in uniform. I thanked them for their extraordinary service. And I let them know that America honors their sacrifice.

3 Because of their bravery and dedication, the tide of war has turned in Afghanistan. We have broken the Taliban's momentum. We've built strong Afghan Security Forces.

Words & Expressions

mission [ˈmiʃən] *n.* 外交使团，代表团，使命，天职

humbling [ˈhʌmbliŋ] *adj.* 谦卑的，谦虚的，谦恭的，恭顺的

dedication [ˌdediˈkeiʃən] *n.* 献身，热衷，奉献

momentum [məuˈmentəm] *n.* 动力，冲力，力量，势头

We have devastated *al Qaeda*[②]'s leadership. And one year ago, our troops launched the operation that killed *Osama bin Laden*[③]. The goal that I set — to defeat al Qaeda, and deny it a chance to rebuild — is within reach.

4 Because of the progress we have made, I was able to sign an historic agreement between the United States and Afghanistan that defines a new kind of relationship between our countries — a future in which Afghans are responsible for the security of their nation, and we build an equal partnership between two sovereign states; a future in which the war ends, and a new chapter begins.

5 The enormous sacrifices of our men and women in uniform are not over. But many of our troops are already coming home. Last year, we removed 10,000 U.S. troops from Afghanistan. Another 23,000 will leave by the end of the summer. As our coalition agreed, by the end of 2014, the Afghans will be fully responsible for the security of their country

6 And this is as it should be. Because after more than a decade of war, it is time to focus on nation building here at home.

7 As a new greatest generation returns from overseas, we must ask ourselves, what kind of country will they come back to? Will it be a country where a shrinking number of Americans do really well while a growing number barely get by? Or will it be a country where everyone gets a fair shot, everyone does their fair share, and everyone plays by the same set of rules — a country with opportunity worthy of the troops who protect us?

8 America has answered this question before. My grandfather, a veteran of *Patton's*[④] Army, got the chance to go to college on *The GI Bill*. My grandmother, who worked on a bomber assembly line, was part of a workforce that turned out the best products on Earth. They contributed to a story of success that every American had the chance to share in, the basic American promise that if you work hard, you could do well enough to raise a family, own a home, send your kids to college, and put a little away for retirement.

devastate [ˈdevəsteit] *vt.* 摧毁，破坏，蹂躏，劫掠，使荒芜，制服

sovereign state 主权国家

coalition [ˌkəuəˈliʃən] *n.* 联合，结合，结合体，联盟

bomber [ˈbɔmə] *n.* 轰炸机，投弹手

workforce [ˈwəːkfɔːs] *n.* 劳动力，工人总数，职工总数

turn out 出动，赶走，熄灭，生产，结果，原来是

put away 把…收起来，放回原处，储蓄，放弃

define [di'fain] *vt.* 给（词、短语等）下定义，明确说明，限定

generate ['dʒenəreit] *vt.*（使）产生，造成，引起，导致

entrepreneur [ˌɔntrəprə'nəː] *n.* 企业家，实业家，承包人，包办人

secure [si'kjuə] *vt.* 使安全，保卫，防护，保证 *adj.* 安心的，安全的，可靠的

be struck by 被…所侵袭（或袭击），为…所感动，被…打动，被…所迷惑

preserve [pri'zəːv] *vt.* 保护，维护，保存，保持

cherish ['tʃeriʃ] *vt.* 珍视，珍爱，热爱，钟爱

9 Keeping that promise alive is the defining issue of our time. But it means making responsible choices.

10 I don't think we should prioritize things like more tax cuts for millionaires while cutting the kinds of investments that built a strong middle-class.

11 That's why I've called on Congress to take the money we're no longer spending at war, use half of it to pay down our debt, and use the other half to rebuild America.

12 Because we've got more jobs to create. More students to educate. More clean energy to generate. More entrepreneurs with the next great idea, just looking for their shot at success. We've got to invest in things like education and medical research. We've got to build newer, faster transportation and communication networks. And we've got to secure the care and benefits our veterans have earned, so that we serve them as well as they have served us.

13 Every time I have the privilege of meeting with our troops, I'm struck by their courage, their commitment, their selflessness, and their teamwork. They have something to teach us. Recovering from the worst economic crisis since the Great Depression is a work in progress — but if we follow their example, then I have no doubt we will preserve the promise of this country, protect the freedoms we cherish, and leave for our children an America that's built to last.

14 God bless you, and have a great weekend.

背景知识注释 Background Notes

1. Bagram Air Base 巴格拉姆空军基地，位于阿富汗东部的帕尔旺省，距离该省首府恰里卡尔南部约 11 公里，距离首都喀布尔北部大约 47 公里，离中国西部边境只有 700 公里左右的路程。经美军 6 年苦心经营，基地的规模已比之前大了 1/3，总面积达到 5,000 亩左右。而且该基地容纳了美军在阿富汗驻兵的一半，目前大约 2.5 万人中有 1.3 万人在这里。巴格拉姆空军基地已成为美军在整个中亚地区屯兵最大的基地，也是美军在中国西大门外驻军最多的大型基地。巴格拉姆空军基地平时的一大任务就是确保阿富汗首都喀布尔的空中

安全，阻止任何反政府武装对首都发动大规模袭击。不仅如此，巴格拉姆基地还负责对其他地区反政府武装进行监视和打击，支持阿富汗政府军对全国的控制。近年来，美军已打死多名塔利班中高层指挥官，极大扰乱了塔利班的作战指挥能力。其中，许多空袭战机是从巴格拉姆空军基地起飞的。美国借反恐为名发动了阿富汗战争，随着战争的进行，美国在中亚的军事存在已成为现实。现在，美军把巴格拉姆基地扩建成中亚最大军事基地并试图长期驻军，用意无疑极为深远。

2. al Qaeda　基地组织，阿拉伯语 القاعدة，拉丁字母标记 Al Qaeda、Al-Qaida、Al-Qa' ida，极端的伊斯兰恐怖组织，其领袖为拉登，成立于 1988 年年底或 1989 年年初。拉登成立该组织的最初目的是以此组织为基地，来训练和指挥与入侵阿富汗的苏联军队战斗的阿富汗义勇军。苏军撤退后，目标转为美国和伊斯兰世界的“腐败政权”。该组织主要在中亚、中东地区活动。基地组织的最高领导是以拉登为首的中央委员会，下设有 4 个专门职能委员会。训练内容包括学习原教旨主义教义，学习使用轻型武器、使用电脑等。美国政府一直认为该组织策划了 9•11 恐怖袭击，并借此发动了阿富汗战争。2011 年 5 月 1 日本•拉登死亡。

3. Osama bin Laden　奥萨马•本•拉登（1957 年 3 月 10 日—2011 年 5 月 2 日），沙特阿拉伯王国利雅得行省人，是基地组织的首领，该组织被认为是全球性的恐怖组织。本•拉登笃信伊斯兰教逊尼派瓦哈比支派。本•拉登被美国政府指为 1998 年美国大使馆爆炸案和 2001 年酿成 2,998 人死亡的 9•11 袭击事件的幕后领导人，名列联邦调查局十大通缉要犯。他的亡命生涯于是开始，本•拉登本人立刻否认了这项指控，但 2002 年在阿富汗找到的一卷录像带显示他在讲话中谈到攻击这个词，该录像带强烈暗示他至少是 9•11 袭击的主要策划者之一。2011 年 5 月 2 日，美国总统奥巴马声称本•拉登在巴基斯坦阿伯塔巴德的一座豪宅里被美军海豹部队第六分队突袭击毙。其遗体于次日海葬于北阿拉伯海。

4. Patton　巴顿，1885 年巴顿出生在美国加利福尼亚州的一个军人世家，其曾祖父是美国独立战争时期的一位准将，祖父和父亲都毕业于弗吉尼亚军事学院。他从小爱出风头，立志要成为将军。 二战使许多美国将军声名显赫，巴顿是最引人注目的一位，他的名声主要来自于他作为战争指挥官的技巧和决策。巴顿作战勇猛顽强，重视坦克作用，强调快速进攻，有“热血铁胆”、“血胆老将”之称。巴顿一生经历了两次世界大战。1945 年二战结束，12 月 30 日巴顿因车祸结束一生，遗体被安葬在卢森堡哈姆的美军公墓。他的一生似乎是为战争而生，又为战争结束而死。

中文译文
Chinese Version

1　本周，我造访了阿富汗，去那里向我们远在他乡服役的官兵们致谢，并与当地政府签署一项有助于结束我们在当地的任务并结束那场战争的历史性协议。

2　作为总司令，能有机会与我们的官兵们在一起，我满怀谦卑并深受鼓舞。在巴格拉姆空军基地，我与部分优秀的士兵见面。我向他们做出的卓越贡献表示感谢，并代表全国向他们做出的牺牲表示敬意。

3　正由于他们的英勇善战和献身精神，阿富汗的战局才得以扭转。我们扼制了塔利班的进攻势头，为阿富汗建立起强大的安全部队，摧毁了基地组织的领导力量。一年前，我们的部队成功实施了击毙乌萨马•本•拉登的行动。我所设定的目标——击败基地组织，剥夺其东山再起的机会——的实现为期不远。

4　正由于我们取得的这些成就，我才能代表美国与阿富汗签署一项历史性的协议，重新定义两国关系——未来，阿富汗人民将担负起自己国家安全的责任，我们将在两个主权国家之间建立起平等的伙伴关系；未来，战争将结束，阿富汗将翻开新的篇章。

5　尽管我们的军人付出的巨大牺牲还未完全结束，但已有许多部队返回国内。去年，我们已从阿富汗撤回了1万名士兵。到今年夏季末，另有2.3万军人也将撤出。根据我们的联合声明，到2014年底，阿富汗人将完全担负起保卫自身安全的责任。

6　这一切本该如此。经历10多年的战争之后，现在是我们该关注国内建设的时候了。

7　当这杰出的新一代从国外凯旋，我们不禁要扪心自问，他们应该回到一个怎样的国度？应该是一个成功人士数量不断减少而勉强度日的人数不断增加的国度吗？或应该是一个人人都享有公平的机遇、人人都承担合理的义务、人人都按同样的游戏规则行事的国度，一个值得他们去保护的充满机遇的国度？

8　美国曾经很好地回答了这个问题。我的祖父，一名巴顿将军部队的老兵，得益于《退伍军人法》而有机会上大学。我的祖母，曾在轰炸机生产线上工作，她是生产全球最优秀的产品的劳动大军中的一员。他们的经历为构筑全体美国人都有机会分享的成功传奇添砖加瓦，并体现了只要你努力工作，你就能做得很好，能养家糊口，买得起房子，能将孩子送去大学，能为退休积攒一些积蓄这一国家对人民的基本承诺。

9　恪守这一承诺是关系我们如何定义这个时代的重大问题。这也意味着我们要做出负责任的选择。

10　我认为我们不应优先考虑为百万富翁们减税而同时削减为建立一个强大的中产阶级而进行的各类投资。

11　正是因为如此，我呼吁国会将因战事结束而留下来的资金中的一半来偿还我们的债务，用另一半来重建我们的国家。

12　因为我们还需要创造更多就业岗位，让更多的学生接受教育。生产更多清洁能源。让更多怀揣雄心壮志的企业家们能寻找到成功的机会。我们必须在教育和医疗研究方面进行投资。我们必须建设更新、更快的交通与通信网络。我们还必须保障我们的退伍军人所得的照料和福利，我们要像他们曾经为我们效力那样为他们服务。

13 每当我有机会与我们的官兵们会晤，我总是被他们英勇无畏、乐于奉献、无私和团结的精神而深深触动。他们是我们的良师益友。从大萧条以来的最严重的经济危机中复苏的工作还在进行中，但倘若我们以他们为楷模，那么，我坚信我们将继续秉承我们国家对人民的承诺，保护我们所珍视的自由理念，并为我们的后代留下一个可持续发展的美国。

14 上帝保佑大家，祝周末愉快！

第19周

Congress Must Act on "To-Do List"

May 12, 2012

国会必须按照"待办事项清单"行事

2012年5月12日

【摘要导读】

在本周的广播电视讲话中，巴拉克·奥巴马总统呼吁民主党人与共和党人齐心协力，按照他提出的国会"待办事项清单"行事，以创造就业机会并有助于恢复中产阶级的安全感。他表示：在这一对中产阶级而言成败的关键时刻，有着两党共同支持的这五项提议将帮助美国建立一种可持续发展的经济。虽然有人认为美国应重新执行那些导致这场自大萧条以来最为严重的经济危机的政策，但美国必须采取措施加快经济复苏，确保美国的经济能重新让勤劳和责任心得到回报，并使美国持续向前发展。

演讲再现 Original Text

1 We all know the past few years have been difficult for this country. After the worst recession of our lifetimes, it will take longer than any of us would like for the economy to fully recover. But there are plenty of steps we can take to speed up the recovery. There are things we can do — right now — to help create jobs and restore some of the financial security that so many families have lost.

2 Now, the other side isn't so optimistic. They think all we can do is cut taxes — especially for the wealthiest Americans — and go back to letting banks and corporations write their own rules again. That's their plan.

3 But I think they're wrong. We tried their ideas for

Words & Expressions

act on 对…起作用，按照…行事

to-do list 任务清单，工作安排，待办事项

optimistic [ˌɔptiˈmistik] *adj.* 乐观的，乐观主义的

nearly a decade, and it didn't work out so well. We can't go back to the same policies that got us into this mess. We've got to move forward. We need to build an economy where hard work and responsibility are rewarded — where you can find a good job, own your own home, maybe start a businesses, and give your kids the chance to do even better.

4 That's where we need to go. And I've been pushing Congress to help us get there by passing a few common-sense policies that would make a difference. Democrats and Republicans have already done some important work together — from passing tax cuts for workers, to opening up new markets for American products, to reforming our patent system. But now we need to do more.

5 That's why we made Congress a handy "To-Do" list — just like the kind I get from Michelle. It's short, but each of the ideas on this list will help create jobs and build a stronger economy right now.

6 First, Congress should stop giving tax breaks to companies that ship jobs overseas, and use that money to cover moving expenses for companies that bring jobs back to America.

7 Second, Congress should help the millions of Americans who have worked hard and made their mortgage payments on time refinance their mortgages at lower rates and save at least $3,000 a year.

8 Third, Congress should help small business owners by giving them a tax break for hiring more workers and paying them higher wages. Small businesses are the engine of economic growth in this country. We shouldn't be holding them back — we should be making it easier for them to succeed.

9 Fourth, if Congress fails to act soon, clean energy companies will see their taxes go up and could be forced to lay off employees. These companies are putting Americans to work and helping break our dependence on foreign oil. Congress should extend these tax credits.

10 And finally, Congress should help our veterans

get... into the mess 陷入困境，弄得一塌糊涂

patent ['peitənt] *n.* 专利，专利权，专利品，专利证

handy ['hændi] *adj.* 手边的，方便的，便利的，易于操纵的

hold... back 抑制，控制，阻止，阻碍，耽误，推迟

returning from Iraq and Afghanistan by creating a Veterans Job Corps. Our men and women in uniform have served this country with honor. Now it's our turn to serve them.

11 So that's Congress's "To-Do" List. But now we need them to start crossing things off. I need you to call your Members of Congress, write an email, tweet, and let them know we can't afford to wait any longer to get things done. Tell them now is the time to take steps we know will grow our economy and create jobs.

job corps 就业工作团

cross... off 划掉，删去，勾销

12 You're working harder. You're meeting your responsibilities. Your representatives in Washington should do the same. Let's push Congress to do the right thing. Let's keep moving this country forward together.

13 Thanks, and have a great weekend.

中文译文 Chinese Version

1 众所周知，过去几年对我们国家而言非常艰难。在我们今生遇到的最严重的经济危机之后，经济的完全复苏所需要的时间长度可能超出我们任何人的预期。但我们可以采取许多措施加速经济复苏的进度。眼下我们可以有所作为来帮助创造就业机会，恢复许多家庭失去的经济保障。

2 现在，对手们并不这么乐观。他们认为我们只能减税，尤其是为美国的富豪们减税，让银行和公司可以再次制定自己的游戏规则。这就是他们的计划。

3 但我认为他们错了。我们曾用将近十年的时间去尝试过这些想法，结果并不尽如人意。我们不能重新回到那些让我们走入困境的政策中去。我们必须向前挺进。我们应该建立一种这样的经济：辛勤劳动和责任心能得到回报，人们能够找到好工作，拥有自己的房子，还可能创办企业，并给自己的孩子提供更加成功的机会。

4 这才是我们要达到的目标。我一直在推动国会通过一系列合理的能起作用的政策来帮助我们实现这些目标。民主党人和共和党人共同做出了一些重大努力，包括通过对工薪阶层的减税政策，为美国产品打开新的市场、改革我们的专利体制等，但我们还需进一步的努力。

5 因此，我为国会提出了一份便利的“待办事项清单”，就像米歇尔给我列的清单一样。清单很短，但每项建议都将有助于我们当前创造就业机会并建立一种更加稳固的经济。

6 第一，国会应停止向海外输送就业机会的公司的税收优惠政策，而应用这笔钱为把

就业岗位带回国内的公司支付迁移成本。

7 第二，国会应该帮助数百万辛勤劳动并及时还清房贷的美国人，让他们以更低利率进行转按揭贷款，这样每年就至少能节约 3,000 美元。

8 第三，国会应该帮助小微企业主们，为他们提供税收优惠政策，让他们能雇用更多员工并提高他们的工资。小微企业是我国经济增长的引擎。我们不应该阻挡他们前进的步伐，而应为他们取得成功提供便利。

9 第四，倘若国会不尽快采取行动，那么清洁能源公司就将面临赋税上涨，并有可能被迫解雇员工。这些公司为美国带来了就业，并帮助我们降低对海外石油的依赖。国会应该把对他们的税收抵免政策进行延期。

10 最后，国会应该建立一个“退伍军人就业协会”来帮助从伊拉克和阿富汗战场回国的退伍军人。我们这些军人曾倍感荣耀地为国效力，而现在该轮到我们为他们服务了。

11 以上就是国会的“待办事项清单”。现在我们需要他们着手逐项完成。我请求大家给国会议员们打电话，给他们发邮件，发推特，让他们知道事情宜早不宜迟，我们等不及了也等不起了。告诫他们，现在就应该采取措施来促进经济增长并创造就业机会。

12 你们在辛勤工作，履行着自己的职责。你们在华盛顿的代表们也应该这么做。让我们共同推动国会为所应为。让我们共同推动国家向前发展。

13 谢谢大家，祝周末愉快！

第20周

Congress Must Move forward, Not Back on *Wall Street Reform*①

May 19, 2012

面对华尔街改革，国会要大胆前行而不是往后退缩

2012年5月19日

【摘要导读】

在本周的广播电视讲话中，巴拉克•奥巴马总统探讨了他所推动的《华尔街改革法案》，这一法案旨在保护消费者，使华尔街按与其他人相同的规则行事，确保纳税人再也不被华尔街不负责任的行为所绑架。奥巴马指出华尔街的所作所为几乎毁掉了美国整个金融系统并让美国失去了数百万个工作岗位。然而国会的共和党人依然试图拖延并废除这一关键的《华尔街改革方案》，奥巴马则继续敦促国会完成这一改革法案的实施，以便美国可以阻止那些放纵的冒险行径，并建立一种可持续发展的经济。

演讲再现 Original Text

Words & Expressions

breathtaking [ˈbreθˌteikiŋ] *adj.* 惊人的，惊险的，令人吃惊的，令人毛骨悚然的

casino [kəˈsiːnəu] *n.* 俱乐部，娱乐场，赌场

recover [riˈkʌvə] *vt.* 找回，恢复，康复，弥补

stabilize [ˈsteibilaiz] *vt.* 使稳定，使安定

1 For the past three and a half years, we've been fighting our way back from an historic economic crisis — one caused by breathtaking irresponsibility on the part of some on Wall Street who treated our financial system like a casino. Not only did that behavior nearly destroy the financial system — it cost our economy millions of jobs, hurt middle-class families, and left taxpayers holding the bag.

2 Since then, we've recovered taxpayer dollars that were used to stabilize troubled banks. And we've put in place Wall Street reform with smarter, tougher, commonsense rules that serve one primary purpose: to prevent a crisis like that

from ever happening again. And yet, for the past two years, too many Republicans in Congress and an army of financial industry lobbyists have actually been waging an all-out battle to delay, defund, and dismantle Wall Street reform.

3 Recently, we've seen why we can't let that happen. We found out that a big mistake at one of our biggest banks resulted in a two billion dollar loss. While that bank can handle a loss of that size, other banks may not have been able to. And without Wall Street reform, we could have found ourselves with the taxpayers once again on the hook for Wall Street's mistakes.

4 That's why it's so important that Members of Congress stand on the side of reform, not against it; because we can't afford to go back to an era of weak regulation and little oversight; where excessive risk-taking on Wall Street and a lack of basic oversight in Washington nearly destroyed our economy. We can't afford to go back to that brand of "you're-on-your-own" economics. Not after the American people have worked so hard to come back from this crisis.

5 We've got to keep moving forward.

6 We've got to finish the job of implementing this reform and putting these rules in place.

7 These new rules say that, if you're a big bank or financial institution, you now have to hold more cash on hand so that if you make a bad decision you pay for it, not the taxpayers.

8 You have to write out a "*living will*[②]" that details how you'll be wound down if you do fail.

9 The new law takes away big bonuses and paydays from failed CEOs, while giving shareholders a say on executive salaries.

10 And for the first time in our nation's history, we have in place a consumer watchdog whose sole job is to look out for working families by protecting them from deceptive and unfair practices.

11 So unless you run a financial institution whose business model is built on cheating consumers, or making

lobbyist [ˈlɔbiist] *n.* 说客

wage [weidʒ] *vt.* 进行（战争、战斗等），开展（运动等）

defund [diˈfʌnd] *vt.* 取消（或撤销）对…的资助，使政府丧失拨款（或支付利息）能力，使（资金）枯竭，使（财政）空虚，耗费…的金钱（或资金）

oversight [ˈəuvəsait] *n.* 疏忽，忽略，照管，监督

institution [ˌinstiˈtjuːʃən] *n.* 社会公共机构，事业机构，制度，习俗，惯例

wind down 平静下来，放松一下，（钟表等）慢下来

bonus [ˈbəunəs] *n.* 津贴，额外酬金，奖金，补助金，退役金

shareholder [ˈʃeəˌhəuldə] *n.* 股东，股票持有人[亦作shareowner]

deceptive [diˈseptiv] *adj.* 骗人的，虚伪的

business model 商业模式，经营模式，业务模式

risky bets that could damage the whole economy, you have nothing to fear from Wall Street reform. Yes, it discourages big banks and financial institutions from making risky bets with taxpayer-insured money. And it encourages them to do things that actually help the economy — like extending loans to entrepreneurs with good ideas, to middle-class families who want to buy a home, to students who want to pursue higher education.

12 That's what Wall Street reform is all about — making this economy stronger for you. And we're going to keep working — to recover every job lost to the recession; to build an economy where hard work and responsibility are once again rewarded; to restore an America where everyone has a fair shot, everyone does their fair share, and everyone plays by the same rules.

13 I believe the free market is one of the greatest forces for progress in human history; that businesses are the engine of growth; that risk-takers and innovators should be celebrated. But I also believe that at its best, the free market has never been a license to take whatever you want, however you can get it. Alongside our entrepreneurial spirit and rugged individualism, America only prospers when we meet our obligations to one another; and to future generations.

14 If you agree with me, let your Member of Congress know. Tell them to spend less time working to undermine rules that are there to protect the economy, and spend more time actually working to strengthen the economy. Thanks and have a great weekend.

discourage [dis'kʌridʒ] *vt.* 使失去勇气（或信心），使泄气，（试图）劝阻，使打消念头（与from 连用）

recession [ri'seʃən] *n.* 后退，撤回，（商业活动等的）衰退（现象）

license ['laisəns] *n.* 执照，许可证，特许

alongside [ə'lɔŋ'said] *prep.* 在…旁边，在…附近，和…并排，与…并存

rugged ['rʌgid] *adj.* 崎岖的，不平坦的，粗糙的，粗犷的，强健的，严峻的

undermine [ˌʌndə'main] *vt.* 在…下挖掘，削弱…的基础，逐渐损毁，暗中破坏

背景知识注释 Background Notes

1. *Wall Street reform* 华尔街改革。2009 年 12 月 11 日，美国第 111 届国会众议院以 223 比 202 通过《华尔街改革与消费者保护法案》(H.R.4173)。H.R.4173 号法案由众议院金融服务委员会主席弗兰克 (Barney Frank) 主持起草，全文长达 1279 页，被舆论和业界称为自 1930 年代美国罗斯福新政 (New Deal) 以来最重要的金融监管改革立法行动。该法案反映了奥巴马政府改革计划的绝大部分动议，其在众议院通过标志着奥巴马总统致力于推行的

金融监管改革计划取得突破性进展。H.R.4173 是一部综合性金融监管改革法案，包括 5 个独立的针对性法案 (Targeted Act)，即《金融稳定提升法案》、《公司和金融机构薪酬公平法案》、《OTC 衍生产品市场法案》、《消费者金融保护法案》、《资本市场系列法案》、《联邦保险办公室法案》。这些针对性法案此前已在众议院金融服务委员会逐一通过表决，并整合成综合性法案包，命名为《华尔街改革与消费者保护法案》。

2. living will 生前遗嘱，是一种对未来的医疗所做的事前书面声明，告诉医生和家人是否用积极的治疗方法延长生命。

中文译文
Chinese Version

1 过去三年半的时间里，我们一直在为摆脱一场历史性的经济危机而奋力前行。这一危机正是由华尔街的一小撮极端不负责任的人将我们的金融系统当成赌场所导致的。他们的行径不仅将我们的金融系统毁灭殆尽，还让我们付出了失去数百万工作岗位的沉重代价，伤害了中产阶级家庭，却把包袱甩给了我们的纳税人。

2 我们曾用纳税人的钱去救助陷入困境的银行，到现在为止，我们已经弥补上了这笔钱。但同时我们也对华尔街进行了改革，实施了更加严厉、更加强硬的合理规则，其主要目的就是要避免我们此类危机再次发生。然而，在过去的两年里，国会中太多的共和党人以及大量的金融业说客一直全力以赴地试图拖延、撤销、废除华尔街改革的方案。

3 最近，我们也已经目睹了不能让此事发生的原因所在。我们发现最大的银行之一（摩根大通）的一个严重错误就导致了 20 亿美元的损失。虽说这家银行有能力控制这样规模的损失，但其他银行可能就无能为力了。因此，倘若没有华尔街改革，我们可能又将处于用纳税人的钱为华尔街的错误埋单的地步了。

4 正是因为如此，所有的国会议员都应该支持改革而不是反对，这一点至关重要。因为我们无法承受重回措施无力、监管缺位的时代，华尔街不负责任的冒险行为和华盛顿缺乏最基本的监管导致我们的经济濒临崩溃。我们无法承受重回标榜“你只能依靠你自己”的经济时代。即使是在美国人民如此辛勤劳动从危机中走出来之际也是如此。

5 我们必须继续前行。

6 我们必须完成实施改革和落实这些规则的任务。

7 这些新规则规定：倘若你是一家大型银行或金融机构，你现在必须持有更多的现金，以便倘若你做出了错误的决策，你就得自己而不是纳税人来埋单。

8 你必须拟定出一份“生前遗嘱”，详细描述一旦遭遇失败如何缓解局面。

9 新法案规定，不成功的公司高层不能获得高额奖金和薪金，股东在管理层的薪酬上有话语权。

10 而且，在我国的历史上，我们第一次设立了消费者监督保护机构，其唯一的职责就是保护工薪家庭免受欺骗和不公平行为的侵害。

11 因此，除非你的金融机构的经营模式就是根基于要欺骗消费者，或者要做会危害整个经济的高风险投资，否则你就根本不必对华尔街改革担惊受怕。是的，该改革让大型银行和金融机构再也不能以纳税人的钱为担保进行赌博性的冒险。它鼓励他们去从事那些真正有助于我们经济的事情，例如扩大对有创意的企业家、想买房的中产阶级家庭以及想接受大学教育的学生的贷款。

12 这正是华尔街改革的实质所在——为你们创建一种更稳健的经济。我们将继续努力去恢复我们在经济衰退中失去的每一份工作，去建立一种通过勤劳和责任感能重新得到回报的经济，重建一个人人都享有公平的机遇、人人都承担公平的义务、人人都遵从同样规则行事的美国。

13 我深信，自由市场是人类历史进程中最伟大的推动力之一，而企业就是经济增长的引擎，探险家和创新人士都应该得到称颂。但同时我也深信，无论你取得的方式如何，最好的自由市场从来都不是你想为所欲为的通行证。伴随着我们的企业家精神和顽强的个体主义精神，美国只有在我们履行了对彼此之间以及对子孙后代的义务时才会更加繁荣昌盛。

14 倘若你们同意我的观点，请告知你们的国会议员们。告诫他们不要浪费时间去破坏那些旨在保护我们经济的规则，要将更多的时间放到夯实我们的经济基础的实际工作中。谢谢大家，祝周末愉快！

第21周

Honoring Our Fallen Heroes This *Memorial Day*①

May 26, 2012

阵亡将士纪念日之际，向我们逝去的英雄们致敬

2012 年 5 月 26 日

【摘要导读】

在本周的广播电视讲话中，巴拉克•奥巴马总统高度赞扬了为国捐躯的男女军人们。他重申了美国为退伍军人服务的决心，就如同他们曾经为美国人民效力一样，同时也就男女军人们对美国毫不动摇的献身精神深表谢意。他说："在阵亡将士纪念日我们聚集一堂，我们要让我们的军属和退伍军人们知道他们并不孤单，我们要向那些曾做出莫大牺牲，并帮助美国成为这个星球上最繁荣、最强大的国家的人们表示感激之情。"

演讲再现 Original Text

1 This weekend, folks across the country are opening up the pool, firing up the grill, and tanking a well-earned moment to relax. But Memorial Day is more than a three-day weekend. In town squares and national cemeteries, in public services and moments of quiet reflection, we will honor those who loved their country enough to sacrifice their own lives for it.

2 This Memorial Day, Michelle and I will join *Gold Star*② families, veterans, and their families at *Arlington National Cemetery*③. We'll pay tribute to patriots of every generation who gave the last full measure of devotion, from Lexington and Concord to Iraq and Afghanistan.

3 Later that day, we'll join Vietnam veterans and their

Words & Expressions

grill [gril] *n.*（烤炙肉、鱼等用的）烤架，铁丝格子，烧烤食品，烤炙

well-earned ['wel'ə:nd] *adj.* 当之无愧的，理应得到的，应得的

pay tribute to 称赞，歌颂，向…致敬，向…进贡

families at the Vietnam Veterans Memorial — the Wall. We'll begin to mark the 50th anniversary of the Vietnam War. It's another chance to honor those we lost at places like *Hue* ④, *Khe Sanh* ⑤, *Danang* ⑥ and *Hamburger Hill* ⑦. And we'll be calling on you — the American people — to join us in thanking our Vietnam veterans in your communities.

4 Even as we honor those who made the ultimate sacrifice, we reaffirm our commitment to care for those who served alongside them — the veterans who came home. This includes our newest generation of veterans, from Iraq and Afghanistan.

5 We have to serve them and their families as well as they have served us: By making sure that they get the healthcare and benefits they need; by caring for our wounded warriors and supporting our military families; and by giving veterans the chance to go to college, find a good job, and enjoy the freedom that they risked everything to protect.

6 Our men and women in uniform took an oath to defend our country at all costs, and today, as members of the finest military the world has ever known, they uphold that oath with dignity and courage. As President, I have no higher honor than serving as their Commander-in-Chief. But with that honor comes a solemn responsibility — one that gets driven home every time I sign a condolence letter, or meet a family member whose life has been turned upside down.

7 No words can ever bring back a loved one who has been lost. No ceremony can do justice to their memory. No honor will ever fill their absence.

8 But on Memorial Day, we come together as Americans to let these families and veterans know that they are not alone. We give thanks for those who sacrificed everything so that we could be free. And we commit ourselves to upholding the ideals for which so many patriots have fought and died.

9 Thank you, God bless you, and have a wonderful weekend.

warrior [ˈwɔriə] *n.* 勇士，武士，（老）战士，斗士

take an oath 宣誓，发誓，立誓

at all costs 不惜任何代价，无论如何

uphold [ʌpˈhəuld] *vt.* 举起，支撑，鼓励，赞成

condolence [kənˈdəuləns] *n.* 吊唁，哀悼，慰问，唁词

turn upside down 把…倒置，把…完全颠倒，把（屋子等）弄乱，搞乱

do justice to 公平对待，使…的价值充分发挥，适当处理

commit oneself to 承诺，致力于，使自己承担

背景知识注释
Background Notes

1. Memorial Day （美国）阵亡将士纪念日，美国人传统上在每年五月的最后一个星期一举行各种纪念活动，向为国捐躯的军人表达哀思和敬意。美国人最早开始举行阵亡将士纪念日的活动是在一百多年前的南北战争期间。当时各地教会和妇女组织等民间团体开始为战争中的阵亡士兵举行悼念活动。1868 年，指挥北方军队的洛根将军 (General Logan) 正式宣布那年的 5 月 30 号为阵亡将士纪念日，在那天在阿灵顿的国家公墓为南北双方的阵亡士兵献上鲜花。在第一次世界大战之后，这个节日从纪念南北战争中的阵亡将士演变为纪念任何战争中死亡的美国人。在每年的这个日子，美国政府大楼下半旗，人们通常在阵亡士兵的墓前插上国旗或者摆上鲜花，并且参观纪念馆，看望阵亡军人的家属。学校也举行活动，让学生记住那些为捍卫他们的自由生活而付出最大牺牲的人。在越南战争后的今天，阵亡将士纪念日在美国人心目中不再单单是纪念为荣誉和胜利献身的英雄的日子，它也是纪念历史的灰暗的一部分和反思的日子。同时，美国人修建的越南战争纪念墙等纪念性建筑也不再仅仅像过去为战争英雄修建的雕像和纪念碑那样仅代表荣誉和纪念的简单主题。

2. Gold Star （美）(纪念阵亡美军官兵的）金星奖章，象征性承认任何表示突出贡献或成就的纪念物。在美国，只要有家人在部队服役，就被认为是“蓝星”(Blue Star) 家庭，倘若有家人于服兵役期间牺牲，就被认为是“金星”(Gold Star) 家庭，这体现在一面旗帜的一颗蓝星上方再添一颗小金星。

3. Arlington National Cemetery 阿灵顿国家公墓。该公墓建于 1864 年，由美国陆军部管理，坐落于美国弗吉尼亚州阿灵顿郡。它是阿灵顿这个美国第四小郡境内为数不多的大型建筑之一。阿灵顿与华盛顿特区隔波多马克河相望，河上跨 5 座桥连接两地。内战期间（1861 年—1865 年)，联邦军队占领了该地，并在此建立了 20 处要塞作为华盛顿的防御设施。阿灵顿国家公墓规模庞大，占地达 170 公顷。陵园呈半圆形，周围树木蓊郁，园内芳草如茵，墓地绵延起伏，洁白的墓碑鳞次栉比，宛如逝者的庞大军阵，声威浩荡，蔚为壮观。公墓中央的山丘上，有一处占地 1.2 公顷的大宅，这就是柯蒂斯•李宅邸，也称“阿灵顿之屋”。在屋中凭窗而立，可俯瞰整个公墓以及波多马克河。这座公墓气氛庄严肃穆，环境静谧清幽。公墓内所有的墓碑都用白色大理石雕刻而成。只有美国荣誉奖章获得者、为国殉职的现役军人、长期服役的退伍老兵、在联邦政府担任过高级职务的退伍老兵以及他们的遗孤，才有资格在此安葬。所以，能够在阿灵顿国家公墓得到一处长眠之所是每一个美国人的荣耀。

4. Hue 顺化，越南城市。它是越南中部承天顺化省的省会，面积 150 平方公里，人口约 34 万，古称富春。顺化历史上曾先后为西山朝和阮朝 (1802 年—1945 年) 的京城，是越南的古都，以历史古迹著称。1993 年，顺化京城和顺化皇城（顺化历史建筑群）被联合国教科文组织列为世界文化遗产。

5. Khe Sanh　溪山，越南城市。1968 年初，越南人民军主力进入溪山地区，将驻守溪山要塞的美国海军陆战队 1 个团牢牢围困。该要塞位于一个四面环山的高原之上，长 1.6 公里、宽 0.8 公里，控制着通向老挝边境的九号公路。越南人民军仍旧采取围点打援的战术，打算借围困溪山要塞引诱美军大部队前来增援，通过伏击战把溪山守军和援军一起歼灭。为此，越南人民军指挥部投入了第 202 坦克团对守卫溪山的美国海军陆战队实施包围。溪山战役是越南战争中越南人民军首次大规模集中使用坦克部队，尽管最后未能达成战役预期目的。但越军由此获得了宝贵的坦克部队作战经验和教训，并且让越军司令部下定决心扩建坦克部队。到 1974 年为止，越军以中国和前苏联援助的大量坦克先后组建了 9 个坦克团。

6. Danang　[ˈdɑːˈnɑːŋ] 岘港，旧称 Tourane（土伦），位于越南中部，古都顺化的附近，区属中南沿海地区，是越南第四大城市，次于胡志明市、河内和海防。此地濒临南中国海、下辖五区两岛；距离北方的河内 764 公里、南方的胡志明市 964 公里。

7. Hamburger Hill　汉堡高地。越战中，围绕一座并没有实际战略意义的高地，美军与北越正规军打起了艰苦的拉锯战。在十天内美军战殁 110 人，越军战殁 500 人，战况激烈；尸体残缺不全，遍布山陵，形同 Hamburger 肉屑，因此名之。

中文译文 Chinese Version

1　本周末，来自全国各地的人们将开放泳池，点燃烧烤炉，享受这一应得的休闲时光。但阵亡将士纪念日的含义远超出这三天的周末。在城市广场上和国家公墓里，在公益服务的过程中和静心沉思的时刻，我们将向那些深爱着自己的国家并为之献身的人们致以崇高的敬意。

2　今年的阵亡将士纪念日，米歇尔和我将与那些荣获金星奖的家庭、退伍军人及其家人一道去阿灵顿国家公墓。我们将向从独立战争到伊拉克战争以及阿富汗战争中鞠躬尽力死而后已的每一代爱国者们致敬。

3　当天晚些时候，我们还将与越南老兵及其家人一起到越南老兵纪念碑——纪念墙前。我们将共同纪念越南战争 50 周年纪念日。这是我们再次向在顺化、溪山、岘港和汉堡高地等地牺牲的人们致敬的机会。同时我们也号召所有的美国人与我们一道向各社区的越战老兵们致谢。

4　甚至在向这些做出巨大牺牲的人们致敬的同时，我们也再次承诺要照顾好曾经与他们并肩作战的人们——这些回到家乡的退伍军人。这也包括从伊拉克和阿富汗回国的我们新一代的退伍军人。

5　我们一定要像他们曾经为我们效力一样为他们及其家人提供服务：保障他们获得所需的医疗保健和福利；照料那些受伤的勇士们并为军属提供援助；让退伍军人有机会上大

学，找到一份好工作，去享受他们冒着重重危险加以保护的自由。

6 我们的男女军人誓言要不惜一切代价保卫我们的国家。今天，作为当今世界上最优秀军队的成员，他们有尊严有勇气来捍卫这一誓言。作为总统，我为能担任他们的总司令而感到无上的荣耀。但是每当签署吊唁信或是看望正常生活被完全打乱的军属之时，我总是感到伴随荣耀而来的是庄严的职责——早日让他们回家的职责。

7 任何言语都无法带回我们失去的所爱的人。任何仪式都无法表达对他们的思念。任何崇敬之情都无法填满他们离去的空缺。

8 但在阵亡将士纪念日，我们美国人聚集一堂，让这些家庭和退伍军人感受到他们并不孤单。我们要向这些牺牲一切保护我们自由的人们深表谢意。我们一定要全力以赴地捍卫众多爱国志士为之奋斗牺牲的崇高理想。

9 谢谢大家，上帝保佑你们，祝周末愉快！

第22周

It's Time for Congress to Get to Work

June 2, 2012

国会该开始行动了!

2012年6月2日

【摘要导读】

在本周的广播电视讲话中，巴拉克•奥巴马总统在明尼苏达州霍尼韦尔公司的一个生产车间向全美人民发表演讲，谈及他提出的让企业更便捷地雇用退伍军人使其在适当的岗位发挥自身技能，帮助美国经济增长的提案。他呼吁国会就他的数项提案采取行动，其中包括促进经济增长和创造就业机会，让建筑工人重返工作岗位，向小微企业提供税收优惠以雇用更多人员，给有信用的房贷人抵押贷款再融资的机会，并确保妇女与男人同工同酬等。

演讲再现 Original Text

Words & Expressions

facility[fə'siliti] *n.* 容易，灵巧，便利，设备，设施

spouse[spaus] *n.* 配偶

1 Today I'm at one of *Honeywell's* ① manufacturing facilities in *Golden Valley* ②, Minnesota, where I just announced a step that will make it easier for companies to hire returning service members who have the skills our country needs right now. It's another part of our effort to make sure that no American who fights for this country abroad has to fight for a job when they come home. That's why businesses like Honeywell are answering our challenge to hire 100,000 post-9/11 veterans and their spouses by the end of next year. That's why I've directed the government to hire over 200,000 veterans so far — because our economy needs their tremendous talent, and because millions of Americans are still looking for a job.

2 Right now, this country is still fighting our way back from the worst economic crisis since the Great Depression. The economy is growing again, but it's not growing fast enough. Our businesses have created almost 4.3 million new jobs over the last twenty-seven months, but as we learned in this week's jobs report, we're not creating them fast enough. And just like last year at this time, our economy faces some serious headwinds. Gas prices are starting to come down again, but when they spiked over the last few months, it hit people's wallets pretty hard. The crisis in Europe's economy has cast a shadow on our own. And all of this makes it even more challenging to fully recover and lay the foundation for an economy that's built to last.

3 But from the moment we first took action to prevent another depression, we knew the road to recovery wouldn't be easy. We knew it would take time, that there would be ups and downs along the way. But we also knew that if we were willing to act wisely, and boldly, and together; if we were willing to keep at it, and never quit, we would come back stronger.

4 Nothing has shaken my faith in that belief. We will come back stronger. We do have better days ahead. And that's because of you. I would place my bet on American workers and American businesses any day of the week. You're the reason our auto industry has come roaring back. You're the reason manufacturing is hiring at its fastest pace since the 1990s. You work hard. You play by the rules. And what you deserve are leaders who will do the same; who will do whatever it takes to fight for the middle-class and grow this economy faster. Because while we can't fully control everything that happens in other parts of the world, there are plenty of things we can control here at home. There are plenty of steps we can take right now to continue to create jobs and grow this economy.

5 I sent Congress a jobs bill last September full of the kinds of bipartisan ideas that would have put our fellow Americans back to work and helped reinforce our economy against those outside shocks. I sent them a plan that would have reduced the deficit by $4 trillion in a way that's balanced —

headwind [ˈhedˌwind] *n.* 逆风，顶头风

cast a shadow on 给…投下阴影，给…带来影响

ups and downs 起伏，沉浮，盛衰

come roaring back 卷土重来，再次复苏，死灰复燃

deserve [diˈzəːv] *vt.* 应受，应得

bipartisan [ˌbaipɑːtiˈzæn] *adj.* 两党联立的，代表两党的

reinforce [ˌriːinˈfɔːs] *vt.* 加强，加固，强化，补充

that pays for the job-creating investments we need by cutting unnecessary spending and asking the wealthiest Americans to pay a little more in taxes.

6 Since then, Congress has only passed a few parts of that jobs bill, like a tax cut that's allowing working Americans to keep more of your paycheck every week. That was important. But Congress hasn't acted on enough of the other ideas in that bill that would make a difference and help create jobs right now. And there's no excuse for that. Not when so many people are looking for work. Not when so many people are struggling to pay the bills.

7 So my message to Congress is, let's get to work.

8 Right now, Congress should pass a bill to help states prevent more layoffs, so we can put thousands of teachers and firefighters and police officers back on the job. Congress should have passed a bill a long time ago to put thousands of construction workers back on the job rebuilding our roads and our bridges and our runways. Instead of just talking a good game about job creators, Congress should give small business owners a tax break for hiring more workers and paying them higher wages. Let's get that done.

9 Right now, Congress should give every responsible homeowner the opportunity to save an average of $3,000 a year by refinancing their mortgage. Next week, there's a vote in Congress on a bill that would give working women the tools they need to demand equal pay for equal work. Ensuring paycheck fairness for women should be a no brainer. And they need to pass that bill.

10 Right now, Congress also needs to extend the tax credits for clean energy manufacturers that are set to expire at the end of the year — so that we don't walk away from 40,000 good jobs that will be created. And it's long past time for Congress to end the tax breaks for companies that ship jobs overseas, and use that money to cover moving expenses for companies that are bringing jobs back to America.

11 It's not lost on anyone, least of all me, that this is an election year. But we've got responsibilities that are bigger than an election. We've got responsibilities to you. With so

runways ['rʌnwei] *n.* 机场跑道，河床，滑道

talk a good game about... 对…说得好听，就…滔滔不绝

no brainer 没有脑袋的人，不必花脑筋的事物，容易的事

expire [ik'spaiə] *vi.* 期满，终止，死亡，呼气

least of all 尤其，最不

many people struggling to get by, now is not the time to play politics. Now is not the time for Congress to sit on its hands. The American people expect their leaders to work hard, no matter what year it is. That's what I intend to do. And I expect Democrats and Republicans to join me.

play politics 玩弄权术，以不正当的手段达到政治目的

sit on its hands 袖手旁观，坐视不管，置之不理

背景知识注释 Background Notes

1. Honeywell 霍尼韦尔公司(全名为Honeywell International)。霍尼韦尔国际是美国一家营业额达380亿美元的多元化、高科技的先进制造企业。在全球，其业务涉及航空产品和服务，楼宇、家庭和工业控制技术、汽车产品、涡轮增压器以及特殊材料。霍尼韦尔公司总部位于美国新泽西州莫里斯镇，公司股票在纽约、伦敦和芝加哥股票交易所上市交易。霍尼韦尔在华的历史可以追溯到1935年。当时，霍尼韦尔在上海开设了第一个经销机构。目前，霍尼韦尔四大业务集团均已落户中国，旗下所辖的所有业务部门的亚太总部也都已迁至中国，并在中国的多个城市设有30多家分公司和合资企业。

2. Golden Valley 黄金谷，明尼苏达州亨内平县县治明尼阿波利斯西郊的一个城市。世界第六大食品公司通用磨坊和瑞典滨特尔集团美国总公司都位于黄金谷。

中文译文 Chinese Version

1 今天，我来到了霍尼韦尔公司(Honeywell)位于明尼苏达州黄金谷镇的一个生产车间。在此，我刚刚宣布了一项措施让企业更便捷地雇用退伍军人为国所需发挥其技能才智。这也是我们为确保那些曾在海外为国而战的美国人回国后不必为工作而战所做出的努力的一部分。正是因为如此，一些诸如霍尼韦尔那样的公司响应了我们的挑战，截至明年末将雇用10万名后9•11时期的退伍军人及其配偶。迄今为止我也指示联邦政府雇用20万退伍军人，因为我们的经济需要他们的聪明才智，而且还有数百万美国人仍然在寻找工作。

2 目前，我们国家依然在奋力从自大萧条以来最为严重的经济危机中摆脱出来。经济正再次增长，但增速还不够快。在过去27个月里，我们的企业已经创造了将近430万个新的工作岗位。但从本周的就业报告里我们获悉，就业增长的速度还不够快。正如去年这个时候，我们的经济面临一些严重的冲击。油价又开始下跌，但过去几个月里油价的飙升使人们的钱袋子蒙受了巨大损失。欧债危机也对我们的经济产生了影响。所有这些都使我们完全复苏并为建设可持续发展的经济奠定良好基础要面临更多的挑战。

3 但从我们开始采取措施避免陷入另一场大萧条的时刻起，我们就知道复苏的道路不

会平坦。我们懂得这需要时间，而且一路上也会充满起伏。但我们也明白，只要我们愿意采取明智、大胆并一致的行动，只要我们愿意坚持不懈并永不放弃，我们就会变得更为强大。

4 任何事物都无法动摇我对此的信念。我们一定会变得更为强大。我们的明天会更美好。正因为有你们做后盾，任何时候我都敢将赌注押到美国的劳工和美国企业身上。是你们让汽车工业得以复兴，是你们让制造业雇用员工的速度达到20世纪90年代以来的最高水平。你们辛勤工作，遵规行事。你们理应拥有像你们一样行事的领导人，这些领导人们应该竭尽全力地为中产阶级和更快地发展经济而奋斗。尽管我们无法完全控制世界上其他地方所发生的事情，但在国内，我们有许多事情是可以驾驭的。目前，我们可以采取众多措施来帮助创造就业和发展经济。

5 去年9月，我向国会递交了一份就业法案，该法案完全体现了两党达成的共识，这些共识本来会让美国人重返工作岗位并帮助巩固我们的经济免受外来冲击。我还向他们提交了一份本可以削减4万亿赤字实现财政平衡的计划，通过削减不必要的支出，并要美国的大富豪们多缴一点税来向我们所需要的创造就业的领域进行投资。

6 自那时起，国会仅通过了就业法案的几个部分，例如减税，让工薪阶层的美国人每周可以保留更多的收入。这当然很重要。但在该法案中其他具有重大影响并有助于创造就业的提议上，国会却做得不尽如人意。这是毫无理由的。当这么多人还在寻找工作，这么多人还在为支付账单而挣扎的时候，这是毫无道理的！

7 因此，我向国会表达的意图就是：立即行动起来！

8 目前，国会应该通过一项法案帮助各州避免更多的解雇事件发生，这样我们才能让成千上万的教师、消防队员和警察重返工作岗位。国会早就该通过一项法案让成千上万的建筑工人重返工作岗位，重建我们的道路、桥梁和机场。有关创造就业，国会不要在嘴上说得动听，应该给小微企业主提供税收优惠，让他们可以雇用更多的工人，为工人提供更高的薪水。让我们共同将此事妥善完成。

9 目前，国会还应给有信用的房贷人一个抵押贷款再融资的机会，这样他们每年均能节约3,000美元。下周，国会将对妇女与男性同工同酬的法案进行投票。让妇女得到公平的工资待遇应该是毫无疑问的事情。国会理应通过这一法案。

10 目前，国会还需要为清洁能源企业延长年末到期的税收优惠政策，这样我们才不会失去4万个优秀的工作岗位。而且国会早就该终止那些将就业输送到海外的公司的税收优惠，该将这些钱用于把就业岗位带回国内的公司支付转移成本。

11 今年是大选年，谁都不想竞选失败，我本人尤其如此。但我们肩负着比选举更重要的责任。我们必须对大家负责。有这么多人还在勉强度日，现在不是玩弄权术的时候。现在不是国会袖手旁观的时候。美国人民期待着他们的领导人努力工作，无论今年是个什么年头。这是我的打算，我也期望民主党人和共和党人与我共同行动。

第23周

Congress Must Act to Keep Our Teachers on the Job

June 9, 2012

国会必须采取行动让教师们留在教学岗位上

2012年6月9日

【摘要导读】

在本周的广播电视讲话中，巴拉克·奥巴马总统敦促国会采取行动让教师重返教学岗位，他指出：在目前的经济环境下无论是个人还是美国的成功都取决于良好的教育基础；在2009年和2010年，美国政府帮助数十万教师保住了工作岗位，但还需要进一步努力。

演讲再现
Original Text

1 This week, I spent some time talking with college students about how we can make higher education more affordable. And one of the things I told them was how proud I was that they were making that investment in themselves — because in today's economy, the best predictor of success is a good education.

2 That's not just true for our individual success; it's also true for America's success. New jobs and new businesses will take root wherever they can find the most highly-educated, highly-skilled workers. And I want those workers to be American workers. I want those good-paying, middle-class jobs to take root right here.

3 So it should concern everyone that right now — all across America — tens of thousands of teachers are getting laid off. In Pennsylvania alone, there are 9,000 fewer

Words & Expressions

the best predictor 最好的预测，最佳预测值，最好的指示器

be true for 对…适用，符合于

educators in our schools today than just a year ago. In Ohio, the number is close to 7,000. And nationwide, over the past three years, school districts have lost over 250,000 educators. Think about what that means for our country. When there are fewer teachers in our schools, class sizes start climbing up. Our students start falling behind. And our economy takes a hit.

4 The point is: teachers matter. One study found that a good teacher can increase the lifetime income of a classroom by over $250,000. A great teacher can change the course of a child's life. So the last thing our country needs is to have fewer teachers in our schools.

5 Now, I know states are still going through some tough times. I realize that every Governor is dealing with limited resources and many face stark choices when it comes to their budgets.

6 But that doesn't mean we should just stand by and do nothing. When states struggle, it's up to Congress to step in and help out. In 2009 and in 2010, we provided aid to states to help keep hundreds of thousands of teachers in the classroom. But we need to do more. That's why a critical part of the jobs bill that I sent to Congress back in September was to help states prevent even more layoffs and rehire even more teachers who had lost their jobs.

7 But months later, we're still waiting on Congress to act.

8 When it comes to this recovery, we can't fully control everything that happens in other parts of the world. But there are plenty of things we can control. There are plenty of steps we can take, right now, to strengthen our economy. Putting teachers back in our kids' classrooms is one of those steps. And there's no excuse for inaction. You work hard. Your leaders should, too. Especially at this make-or-break moment for the middle-class.

9 I know this is an election year. But some things are bigger than an election. Some things are bigger than politics. So I hope you'll join me in telling Congress to do the right thing; to get to work and to help get our teachers back in the classroom. We can't afford to wait any longer.

class size 班级规模，班级人数，班级大小

fall behind 拖欠，落后，失利，掉队

stark [stɑːk] *adj.* 完全的，荒凉的，刻板的，光秃秃的，（对比）鲜明的，严酷的

stand by 站在旁边，准备，支持，袖手旁观，

inaction [inˈækʃən] *n.* 不活动，迟钝

10 Thanks and have a great weekend.

中文译文
Chinese Version

1 本周，我与一些大学生一起谈论了我们如何让高等教育更能让人负担得起的话题。我告诉他们，我为他们来到大学为自己的未来投资感到非常自豪——因为在当今的经济环境下，成功将完全取决于是否具有良好的教育基础。

2 这不仅符合于我们个人的成功，也符合于我们国家的成功。新的工作岗位和新兴企业将扎根于任何拥有受过最好教育和具有最优秀技能的员工的地方。我希望这些员工都是美国人。我也希望这些高薪酬的中产阶级工作岗位就扎根于美国。

3 因此，目前全国各地数万教师正在遭遇解聘，这件事与我们每个人应该都休戚相关。仅在宾夕法尼亚一州，现在学校的教育工作者就比一年前少了 9,000 人。而在俄亥俄州，这一数字接近 7,000。全国范围内，在过去三年中，各学区的教育工作者减少了 25 万多。设想一下这对我们国家意味着什么。一旦学校的老师减少，班级的人数就会攀升。我们的学生就会掉队，我们的经济也将遭受打击。

4 问题的关键就在于教师。一项研究表明，一名优秀的教师能让他所教班级学生的一生至少多挣 25 万美元。一名伟大的教师能改变一个孩子的生命历程。因此，我们绝不允许学校老师不断减少的境况发生在我们国家。

5 现在，我知道各州还在经历艰难时期。我也知道各位州长能利用的资源有限，在面对预算时需要做许多严酷的选择。

6 但这并不意味着我们就该袖手旁观并无所事事。当各州处于困境的时候，国会就该挺身而出伸出援手。2009 年和 2010 年，我们向各州提供援助保住了数十万教师的教学岗位。但我们还需要进一步努力。正是因为如此，帮助各州避免更多的解雇事件发生并重新招聘更多的教师让他们重返工作岗位，这是我去年 9 月向国会递交的就业法案的重要组成部分。

7 但数月已过，我们仍然在等待国会的行动。

8 至于我们的经济复苏，世界上其他地方发生的事情我们无法全面控制。但国内大量的事情还是在我们的掌控中。当前，我们可以采取许多措施来夯实我们的经济基础。让老师重返教学岗位就是这些措施之一。国会没有借口不作为。大家要努力工作，而你们的领导人们也应如此。尤其是在这一关系中产阶级成败的关键时刻。

9 我知道今年是大选年。但有些事情要比选举更加重要。有些事情比政治也更重要。因此，我希望大家与我一道呼吁国会要为所应为，采取行动让我们的教师们重返教学岗位。我们实在是等不及了。

10 谢谢大家，祝周末愉快！

第24周

Ending the Stalemate in Washington June 16, 2012

华盛顿的僵局该结束了

2012年6月16日

【摘要导读】

在本周的广播电视讲话中，巴拉克·奥巴马总统告诫美国民众，在目前关系中产阶级成败的关键时刻，华盛顿的政治僵局阻碍了美国的经济发展。他认为：对于他提出的就业法案，倘若国会在一些常识性的构想上愿意放弃其对立立场，例如给小微企业减税使其雇用更多员工，帮助各州留住成千上万的教师、消防员和警察的工作岗位，让成千上万的建筑工人重返工地，那么美国将能新增100多万个就业岗位。他说，现在，国会应该终结党派之争，为了美国人民的利益与他精诚合作，以促进经济不断增长并创造新的就业岗位。

演讲再现 Original Text

1 Over the last few weeks, I've been talking a lot about America's economic future. I've told you how I believe we should go about creating strong, sustained growth; how we should pay down our long-term debt in a balanced way; and most of all, what we should do right now to create good, middle-class jobs, so people who work hard can get ahead.

2 This isn't some abstract debate or trivial argument. I've said that this is the defining issue of our time, and I mean it. I've said that this is a make-or-break moment for the middle-class, and I believe it. The decisions we make over the next few years will have an enormous impact on the country we live in, and the one we pass on to our children.

Words & Expressions

sustained[sə'steind] *adj.* 持续的，经久不衰的

abstract['æbstrækt] *adj.* 抽象的，难解的

trivial['triviəl] *adj.* 琐碎的，不重要的

defining issue 定义问题，决定性问题，最重要的议题

3 Right now, we're still fighting our way back from the worst economic crisis since the Great Depression. The economy is growing again, but it's not growing fast enough. Our businesses have created 4.3 million new jobs over the last 27 months, but we're not creating them fast enough. And we're facing some pretty serious headwinds — from the effects of the recent spike in gas prices, to the financial crisis in Europe.

4 But here's the thing. We have the answers to these problems. We have plenty of big ideas and technical solutions from both sides of the aisle. That's not what's holding us back. What's holding us back is a stalemate in Washington.

5 Last September, I sent Congress a jobs bill full of the kinds of bipartisan ideas that could have put over a million Americans back to work and helped bolster our economy against outside shocks. I sent them a plan that would have reduced our deficit by $4 trillion in a balanced way that pays for the investments we need by cutting unnecessary spending and asking the wealthiest Americans to pay a little bit more in taxes.

6 Since then, Congress has passed a few parts of that jobs bill, like a tax cut that's allowing working Americans to keep more of your paycheck every week. But on most of the ideas that would create jobs and grow our economy, Republicans in Congress haven't lifted a finger. They'd rather wait until after the election in November. Just this past week, one of them said, "Why not wait for the reinforcements?" That's a quote. And you can bet plenty of his colleagues are thinking the same thing.

7 I think that's wrong. This isn't about who wins or loses in Washington. This is about your jobs, and your paychecks, and your children's future. There's no excuse for Congress to stand by and do nothing while so many families are struggling. None.

8 Right now, Congress should pass a bill to help states put thousands of teachers, firefighters and police officers back on the job. They should have passed a bill a long time ago to put thousands of construction workers back to work rebuilding

stalemate ['steilmeit] *n.* 僵局，陷于困境

bolster ['bəulstə] *n.* 垫子，衬垫，坐垫，靠垫 *vt.* 支撑，加固，加强，鼓励

lift a finger 尽举手之劳，做出努力，帮忙，采取行动[常用于否定，亦作 lift（或 raise）a hand]

reinforcement [ˌriːin-'fɔːsmənt] *n.* 增援，加强，援军，增援部队，加固物

our roads and bridges and runways. And instead of just talking about job creators, they should give small-business owners a tax break for hiring more workers and paying them higher wages.

9 Right now, Congress should give every responsible homeowner the opportunity to save an average of $3,000 a year by refinancing their mortgage. They should extend tax credits for clean energy manufacturers so we don't walk away from 40,000 good jobs. And instead of giving tax breaks to companies who ship jobs overseas, Congress should take that money and use it to cover moving expenses for companies that are bringing jobs back to America. There's no reason to wait.

independent [ˌindiˈpendənt] *adj*. 独立的，单独的 *n*. 独立自主者，无党派者

10 Every problem we face is within our power to solve. What's lacking is our politics. Remind your Members of Congress why you sent them to Washington in the first place. Tell them to stop worrying about the next election and start worrying about the next generation. I'm ready to work with anyone — Republican, Democrat, or Independent — who is serious about moving this country forward. And I hope Members of Congress will join me.

11 Thanks, and have a great weekend.

中文译文 Chinese Version

1 在过去数周中，我一直在谈论美国经济的未来前景。我将自己的看法告诉过你们：如何实现稳健的可持续的经济增长，如何通过平衡的方式清偿长期债务，最重要的是，目前如何采取适当的措施创造优质的中产阶级工作岗位，让勤奋工作的人们能获得成功。

2 这并不是什么抽象的辩论或是琐碎的争吵。我说过，这是我们这个时代最重要的议题，我是字字当真的。我说过，对中产阶级而言现在是关乎成败的关键时刻，这的确是我的看法。在今后数年中我们所做出的决定将对我们所生存的这个国家产生重大影响，并延续至我们的下一代。

3 目前，我们还在为摆脱自大萧条以来最严重的经济危机而拼搏。虽然经济开始恢复增长，但增速依然缓慢。我们的企业在过去的两年零三个月里新增了 430 万个就业岗位，但数量还远远不够。而且我们当前还面临着包括油价的飙升和欧洲的金融危机在内的一些相当严重的不利因素。

4 但事实是：对于这些问题我们是有解决办法的。两党都有大量的精明的策略和具体的解决方案。因此，这并不是掣肘我们的所在，掣肘我们的是当下华盛顿的政治僵局。

5 去年9月，我向国会提交了一份就业法案，包括两党各种的共识，该就业法案可以让上百万美国人重返工作岗位，并增强我们的经济免受外来冲击。我还向他们提交了一项平衡削减4万亿财政赤字的方案：通过减少不必要的支出并让富豪们稍微多缴一点税，向我们急需的领域投资。

6 自那时起，国会通过了该就业法案的部分内容，包括一项减税政策，让美国工薪阶层每周能够留住更多的薪水。但对于大多数可以创造就业和促进经济增长的方案，国会的共和党人却无动于衷。他们宁愿等到11月份的大选过后再说。就在这个星期，他们当中有人说："为什么不静待援军呢？"这可是他的原话啊。我敢打赌他的许多同僚当中有很多都持同样的想法。

7 我认为这是错误的。这并不关乎谁将是否赢得华盛顿竞选的事宜。这是关乎大家的工作、薪水和孩子们未来的事宜。这么多的家庭还在挣扎着度日，国会没有借口袖手旁观和无所事事。绝对没有！

8 目前，国会应该通过一项法案协助各州使成千上万的教师、消防员和警察重返工作岗位。而且他们早就该通过一项法案让成千上万的建筑工人回到工地，重建我们的公路、桥梁和机场。不要只是把创造就业岗位挂在嘴边，国会应该给小微企业提供税收优惠，使他们能够雇用更多的员工并提高员工薪资待遇。

9 目前，国会应该给每个有信用的业主一个抵押贷款再融资的机会，这样每年均能节省3,000美元。国会应该延长对清洁能源生产商的税收抵免政策，这样我们才不会失去4万个优秀的工作岗位。而且国会不要将减税政策再提供给那些把就业岗位输送到海外的公司，而应该用这些钱来补偿那些将就业岗位带回美国的公司的成本支出。所有这些都没有理由再等下去了。

10 我们有能力解决我们所面临的每个问题，所缺乏的只是政治策略。请大家提醒国会议员们，你们选送他们到华盛顿来的首要原因是什么。告诫他们不要再为下届的选举担心，还是为我们的下一代操操心吧。我已经准备好与任何人合作，无论他是共和党人、民主党人还是无党派人士，只要他真心想要推动国家向前发展。我希望国会议员们能与我同行。

11 谢谢大家，祝周末愉快！

第25周

Congress Must Act on Transportation Bill and Student Loans

June 23, 2012

国会必须通过交通和助学贷款两项法案

2012年6月23日

【摘要导读】

在本周的广播电视讲话中，巴拉克·奥巴马总统谈到了迫切需要国会通过两项基本措施来帮助辛勤的中产阶级家庭。他说：倘若下周国会还不采取行动，成千上万的员工将被迫离开工作岗位回家，数百万学子也将眼睁睁地看着他们的助学贷款利率翻番；正当数十万建筑工人急盼着重返工作岗位的时刻，交通基金到期停摆是毫无道理的；正当大学教育对找到一份好工作空前重要的时候，让740万学子受到相当于平均多缴纳1,000元税的打击也是毫无道理的；共和党和民主党理应就这些基本措施一起达成共识，以帮助国家度过自大萧条以来最严重的经济危机。

演讲再现
Original Text

Words & Expressions

claw one's way... 奋力爬…，艰难行进

1 Over the past three years, we've been clawing our wayback from the worst economic crisis of our lifetimes. And we know it will take longer than any of us would like to fully recover all the jobs and savings that have been lost. But there are things we can do — right now — to help put people back to work and make life a little easier for middle-class families.

2 For months, I've been pushing Congress to help us along by passing common-sense policies that would make a difference. Democrats and Republicans have already done some important work together — like passing a tax cut that's allowing working Americans to keep more of their paycheck

every week. But Congress has refused to act on most of the other ideas in my jobs plan that economists say could put a million more Americans back to work.

3 There's no excuse for inaction. Right now, we are seven days away from thousands of American workers having to walk off the job because Congress hasn't passed a transportation bill. We are eight days away from nearly seven and a half million students seeing their loan rates double because Congress hasn't acted to stop it.

4 This makes no sense. We know that one of the most important things we can do for our economy is to make sure that all Americans get the best education possible. Right now, the unemployment rate for Americans with a college degree or more is about half the national average. Their incomes are twice as high as those who don't have a high school diploma. So, if we know that a higher education is the clearest path to the middle-class, why would we make it harder to achieve?

5 So much of America needs to be repaired right now. Bridges are deteriorating after years of neglect. Highways are choked with congestion. Transportation delays cost Americans and businesses billions of dollars every year. And there are hundreds of thousands of construction workers who have never been more eager to get back on the job. So why would we let our transportation funding run out? This is a time when we should be doing everything in our power — Democrats and Republicans — to keep this recovery moving forward.

6 My Administration is doing its part. On Friday, *Secretary of Transportation*① *Ray LaHood*② announced $500 million in competitive grants for states and communities that will create construction jobs on projects like road repair and port renovation. And that's an important step, but we can't do it all on our own.

7 The Senate did their part. They passed a bipartisan transportation bill back in March. It had the support of 52 Democrats and 22 Republicans.

8 Now, it's up to the House to follow suit; to put aside partisan posturing, end the gridlock, and do what's right for

deteriorate [di'tiəriəreit] *vi.* 变质，恶化，败坏，堕落

choke [tʃəuk] *vt.* 使窒息，阻塞，堵塞，阻止

congestion [kən'dʒestʃ(ə)n] *n.* 拥挤，拥塞，充血

renovation [ˌrenəu'veiʃən] *n.* 革新，更新，整修，修理

follow suit 学样，照别人的方式去做

the American people.

9 It's not lost on any of us that this is an election year. But we've got responsibilities that are bigger than an election. We answer to the American people, and they are demanding action. Let's make it easier for students to stay in college. Let's keep construction workers rebuilding our roads and bridges. And let's tell Congress to do their job. Tell them it's time to take steps that we know will create jobs now and help sustain our economy for years to come.

answer to 对…有反应，响应，对…负责，向…负责说明

背景知识注释 Background Notes

1. Secretary of Transportation （美国）交通部部长，是美国运输部的主管，在美国内阁排名第14位。1966年10月15日，林登·约翰逊签署法律条文，这个职位正式诞生。该部门的使命是"制定和调整政策，提供一个高效运作和有经济效益的国家运输系统，在适当的情况下辅助国防。"运输部长负责11个机构，包括美国联邦航空管理局、联邦高速公路管理局、美国国家公路交通安全管理局等。首任美国运输部长是艾伦·斯蒂芬森·博伊德，他是由民主党总统林登·约翰逊提名的。现任运输部长是安东尼·福克斯。

2. Ray LaHood 雷·拉胡德（1945.12.6—），来自于伊利诺伊州的共和党人，母亲为德裔美国人，父亲乃黎巴嫩裔。2009年1月至2013年7月担任美国第16任运输部长。此前他曾连续七次当选代表伊利诺伊州第18选区的联邦众议员（1995—2009）。

中文译文 Chinese Version

1 在过去的三年中，我们一直在为摆脱此生所遇的最严重的经济危机而艰难前行。我们也知道完全恢复我们所失去的就业岗位和储蓄所需要的时间将超出我们任何人的想象。但现在我们能有所作为——帮助人们重返工作岗位，并使中产阶级家庭的生活过得更安逸一些。

2 数月以来，我一直在推动国会并敦促国会助我们一臂之力，通过一些能起到重要影响的基本政策。民主党和共和党也共同完成了一些重要的工作，例如通过了一项减税法案，让美国工薪阶层每周能够留住更多的薪水。但国会对我就业计划中的大部分建议都无动于衷，尽管经济学家们认为该计划的实施将让一百多万人重返工作岗位。

3 国会不作为没有任何理由。目前，由于国会未能通过交通法案，距成千上万员工不得不离开现在的工作岗位仅剩下7天。由于国会未采取制止措施，离750万学子眼睁睁看着

他们的助学贷款利率翻倍也只剩 8 天了。

4　这样做简直不可理喻。众所周知，我们能为我们的经济所做的最重要的一件事情就是确保所有美国人都尽可能接受最好的教育。当前，拥有大学及以上学历的美国人的失业率是全国平均水平的一半左右。而且他们的收入也是没有高中学历人群的两倍多。因此，既然我们知道高等教育是通往中产阶级的康庄大道，那我们为什么要让这条路变得难于企及呢？

5　当前美国许多地方百废待兴。桥梁因多年疏于维护而日益破损。高速公路也拥挤不堪。交通运输的延误让美国人及其企业每年蒙受着数十亿美元的损失。而当数十万建筑工人正迫切地要重返工作岗位，我们为什么还要让交通基金到期停摆呢？现在民主党和共和党应该尽一切所能来共同推动复苏大业继续前进。

6　本届政府正在履行其职责。上周五，交通部部长雷•拉胡德 (Ray LaHood) 宣布在紧张的经费中向各州和社区拨款 5 亿美元用于道路修缮和港口改造等项目上创建工作机会。这是一项重要举措，但这一切仅靠政府是无法完成的。

7　参议院也履行了其职责。他们在 3 月份通过了一项两党联合提出的交通法案。该法案获得了 52 名民主党参议员和 22 名共和党参议员的支持。

8　现在，众议院该效仿跟进，结束党派之争与僵局，并做对美国人民有益的事情了。

9　今年是大选年，这对我们任何人来说都不无影响。但我们肩负着比选举更重大的职责。我们要对美国人民负责，他们正期待着我们的行动。让学子们能更轻松地留在学校学习。让建筑工人能继续重建我们的道路和桥梁。让我们呼吁国会履行其职责。告诉他们，现在该采取众所周知的措施，创造就业机会，并保持我们的经济在未来的岁月中能持续发展。

第26周

An All-Hands-On-Deck Approach to Fighting the Colorado Wildfires

June 30, 2012

全民动员扑灭科罗拉多州山林大火

2012 年 6 月 30 日

【摘要导读】

在本周的广播电视讲话中，巴拉克•奥巴马总统在科罗拉多州向美国民众发表讲话，他刚刚结束了对遭受沃尔多峡谷严重山林大火损毁地区的探访，在那里他会见了应急人员和受到大火影响的家庭。奥巴马对英勇的消防队员以及为他们提供所需的食物、水和休息场所的志愿者们深表谢意，并表示美国政府将继续调用一切资源来协助扑灭这场大火。

演讲再现 Original Text

1 Hi, everybody. I'm here in *Colorado Springs* ①, visiting some of the devastating fires that have been taking place over the last several days. As many of you have been watching on television, entire communities are under threat. And we had a chance to tour some of the devastation that has been taking place in some of the subdivisions here.

2 Firefighters are working 18 hours a day, around the clock, trying to make sure that they get this blaze under control. We've got volunteers who are out here who are making sure that these firefighters have the food and the water and all the resources that they need. And we've been engaging in some unprecedented coordination between federal, state, and local communities to try to bring this fire under control.

Words & Expressions

all hands on deck 全员参与

devastate ['devəsteit] *vt.* 毁坏，蹂躏，使荒芜

under threat 受到威胁

subdivision ['sʌbdiˌviʒən] *n.* 再分，分成小块的建筑地皮

around the clock 夜以继日

blaze [bleiz] *n.* 火光，火灾

unprecedented [ʌn'presidəntid] *adj.* 空前的

3 And one of the things I've done here, in addition to saying thank you to these firefighters, is to let them know that all of America has their back. One of the things that happens, whether it's a fire here in Colorado, or a tornado in Alabama or Missouri, or a flood or a hurricane in Florida, one of the things that happens here in America is when we see our fellow citizens in trouble and having difficulty, we come together as one American family, as one community. And you see that spirit and you see that strength here in Colorado Springs, where people are working together, promising each other to rebuild. We've got to make sure that we are there with them every step of the way, even after this fire is put out.

4 So for those of you who can provide some help, you should get on the online site of *the American Red Cross* ②. They're very active in this community and you can make your contributions there. We're going to continue to make sure that *the Federal Emergency Management Agency* ③, *the Forest Service* ④, our military and *National Guard* ⑤ and all the resources that we have available at the federal level are brought to bear in fighting this fire.

5 But this is a good reminder of what makes us Americans. We don't just look out for ourselves; we look out for each other. And one of the things that I told these firefighters is that we can provide them all the resources they need, but only they provide the courage and the discipline to be able to actually fight these fires. And it's important that we appreciate what they do not just when our own communities are struck by disaster. It's important that we remember what they do each and every single day, and that we continue to provide support to our first responders, our emergency management folks, our firefighters, our military — everybody who helps secure our liberty and our security each and every day.

6 So, America, I hope you guys remember the folks during these times of need. I know this is a little bit unusual — we don't usually do weekly addresses like this, but I thought it was a good opportunity for us to actually focus attention on a problem that's going on here in Colorado Springs. We never

tornado [tɔː'neidəu] *n.* 龙卷风，旋风，飓风

hurricane ['hʌrikən] *n.* 暴风，暴风雨，飓风，风暴

discipline ['disiplin] *n.* 训导，磨炼，遵守纪律，纪律，惩戒，学科

know when it might be our community that's threatened, and it's important that we're there for them.

7 All right. Thank you very much.

背景知识注释 Background Notes

1. Colorado Springs 科罗拉多科泉市，又译科罗拉多斯普林斯，美国科罗拉多州中部城市，是美国空军学院所在地。

2. the American Red Cross 美国红十字会，1881 年 5 月由克拉尔•巴顿 (Clara Barton) 创建，是美国从事紧急救援和救灾防灾等人道主义工作的社会救助团体，国际红十字运动的成员。

3. the Federal Emergency Management Agency （缩写为 FEMA)(美国）联邦紧急事务管理局，是美国防灾部，总部设在华盛顿哥伦比亚特区，负责减轻自然灾害的影响。2003 年 3 月 1 日 FEMA 并入美国国土安全部。

4. the Forest Service （美国）森林服务局，是管理美国森林与草地的联邦机构，也是世界上最大的林业研究组织，它向美国国有或私有林业机构提供财政与技术支持。1905 年美国森林服务局成立，开始专职保护美国联邦政府拥有的近两亿英亩森林。森林保护的首要责任自然是防火，重要手段是公共教育和宣传，号召人们防御森林火灾。

5. National Guard （美国）国民警卫队，常简称为国民兵，是美国军队的重要后备力量。美军的预备役部队分为国民警卫队和联邦后备役部队两大部分。美国国民警卫队创建于 1636 年 12 月 13 日，当时是为保卫殖民地而在波士顿建立的一支民兵队伍，1824 年 8 月 25 日改名为国民警卫队。国民警卫队是美军整体力量的重要组成部分，也是隶属于各州政府的地方部队。

中文译文 Chinese Version

1 嗨，大家好！我正在科罗拉多斯普林斯市，视察多日来受到严重大火损毁的地区。正如你们许多人已经从电视上所看到的，我们整个社会都受到了威胁。大家都可以看到部分地区遭受火灾严重损毁的惨状。

2 消防队员们每天都连续工作 18 小时，为的就是确保火势得到控制。我们还有大量志愿者来到这里，保证消防员们得到所需的事物、水和各种他们所需的物力。而我们一直在联邦政府、州政府以及当地社区进行前所未有的协调，力图将大火控制住。

3 我来此地除了感谢这些消防队员们之外，还要做的一件事情就是要让他们知道所有美国人民都是他们的后盾。任何事情的发生，无论是科罗拉多的大火，还是阿拉巴马或密苏里的龙卷风，或者是佛罗里达的洪水或飓风，当这些事情发生在美国大地上的时候，当我们看见我们的公民遭受艰难困苦的时候，我们团结起来就如同一个家庭、一个社区。大家可以看见科罗拉多斯普林斯这里所展现出来的精神和力量，人们团结协作，相互许诺重建家园。我们必须确保我们要在一路上与他们相伴，即使在大火扑灭之后也是如此。

4 因此，倘若你能提供一些帮助，你可以访问美国红十字会的网站。他们在这个领域表现得非常活跃，你可以通过他们捐款捐物。我们要继续确保联邦紧急事务管理局、森林服务局、军队、国民警卫队以及所有我们联邦层面可以调动的资源都投入到扑灭这场大火的工作中。

5 这也很好地见证了到底是什么让我们成为美国人。我们并不是只顾照料自己，我们相互关心。我告诉这些消防队员们的一件事就是，我们可以为他们提供一切他们所需要的物力，但只有他们所表现的勇气和纪律才能真正扑灭这场大火。重要的是，我们不仅要感激他们在我们社区遭受灾难袭击时所做的一切，我们也要牢记他们每天为我们所做的一切，我们要继续为我们的应急反应人员、紧急事务管理人员、消防人员、军队提供支持，是他们每天让我们的自由和安全得到保障。

6 因此，我希望美国民众在这样的艰难时刻能铭记这些人。我知道今天有些不同寻常，我们的每周讲话并不经常如此，但我认为这为我们提供了一个良好的机会，让我们真切地关注在科罗拉多斯普林斯市出现的问题。我们从不知道我们的社区何时会受到威胁，但重要的是我们随时为他们提供服务。

7 就这样吧。谢谢大家！

第27周

Pushing Congress to Create Jobs, Keep College in Reach for Middle-Class

July 7, 2012

推动国会创造就业机会，构筑中产阶级大学之梦

2012年7月7日

【摘要导读】

在本周的广播电视讲话中，巴拉克•奥巴马总统在俄亥俄州与民众谈论他周五签署的一项法案。该法案成就了两件重要的事情：首先，保住了成千上万建筑工人的工作岗位，让美国的基础设施能够得以重新修缮；其次，让700万学子摆脱了联邦助学贷款今年利率翻番的压力。在讲话中，奥巴马还敦促国会做出更多的努力以帮助经济复苏和创造就业岗位，包括将因战争结束节省下来的军费的一半用于国内公路、桥梁和无线网络的建设，以及在创造机会让200万学子学习眼下企业所需各项技能的同时，延长对他们的财政资助。

演讲再现 Original Text

1 Hi, everybody. I'm here in Ohio, where I've spent the past couple days talking with folks about our central challenge as a country — not just reclaiming all the jobs lost to the recession, but reclaiming the economic security that so many Americans have lost over the last decade.

2 Our mission isn't just to put people back to work — it's to rebuild an economy where that work pays; an economy in which everyone who works hard has the chance to get ahead.

3 For months, we've been pushing Congress to pass several common-sense ideas that will help us do that. And on

Words & Expressions

reclaim [ri'kleim] *vt.* 开拓，回收再利用，改造某人

recession [ri'seʃən] *n.* 后退，（经济）不景气

get ahead 获得成功，取得进步，走在前面

Friday, I signed into law a bill that will do two things for the American people.

4 First, it will keep thousands of construction workers on the job rebuilding our nation's infrastructure.

5 Second, it will keep interest rates on federal student loans from doubling this year — which would have hit more than seven million students with about a thousand dollars more on their loan payments.

6 Those steps will make a real difference in the lives of millions of Americans. But make no mistake: we've got more to do.

7 The construction industry was hit brutally hard when the housing bubble burst. So it's not enough to just keep construction workers on the job doing projects that were already underway.

8 For months, I've been calling on Congress to take half the money we're no longer spending on war and use it to do some nation-building here at home. There's work to be done building roads and bridges and wireless networks. And there are hundreds of thousands of construction workers ready to do it.

9 The same thing is true for our students. The bill I'm about to sign is vital for millions of students and their families. But it's not enough to just keep their student loan rates from doubling.

10 For months, I've been calling on Congress to reform and expand the financial aid that's offered to students. I've been asking them to help us give two million Americans the opportunity to learn the skills that businesses in their area are looking for — right now — through partnerships between community colleges and employers. In America, a higher education cannot be a luxury reserved for just a privileged few. It's an economic necessity that every American family should be able to afford.

11 Finally, I want to thank every American who took the time to sit down and write a letter, type out an e-mail, make a phone call or send a tweet hoping your voice would

infrastructure [ˈinfrəˌstrʌktʃə] *n.* 基础设施，公共建设，下部构造

make no mistake 不要搞错，毫无疑问，不要误会

brutally [ˈbru:təli] *adv.* 残忍地，野蛮地，兽性地

the housing bubble 房地产泡沫

underway [ˈʌndəˈwei] *adj.* 正在进行中的

luxury [ˈlʌkʃəri] *n.* 奢侈品，奢侈，豪华

make a difference. I promise you — your voice made all the difference. And as long as I have the privilege of being your President, your voice will be heard in the White House.

12 So thanks and have a great weekend.

中文译文
Chinese Version

1 嗨，大家好。我现在在俄亥俄州。过去几天里我一直在此与人们探讨我们国家所面临的最重要的挑战：不仅仅是要找回在此次衰退中所失去的所有工作岗位；更是要重获过去十年里大量民众所失去的经济安全保障。

2 我们的任务不仅仅是让民众重返工作岗位——而是要重建一个付出就能得到回报、任何辛勤劳动的人都有机会获得成功的经济体系。

3 几个月以来，我一直在推动国会通过数项基本政策以帮助我们实现这些目标。周五，我签署批准了一项法案。这项法案将有助于美国民众成就两件事情。

4 首先，该法案将使数以万计的建筑工人通过修缮我国的基础设施，保住自己的工作岗位。

5 其次，该法案避免了今年的联邦助学贷款利率翻番，否则700多万名学子将受到影响，为此多还1,000美元贷款。

6 这些措施将对数百万美国民众的生活带来确实的改变。但不要忘了，我们任重而道远。

7 建筑行业随着房地产市场泡沫的破灭受到了沉重打击。因此仅仅保住在建工程建筑工人的工作岗位是远远不够的。

8 几个月以来，我一直在呼吁国会将因战争结束节省下来的军费的一半用于国内的基础设施建设。在国内修路架桥、建设无线网络，这些都是需要做的事情。而数十万建筑工人们已经为此做好了准备。

9 此次努力也惠及我们的学子。我即将签署的法案对数百万学子及其家庭而言至关重要。但仅仅避免助学贷款利率翻番是不够的。

10 几个月以来，我一直在呼吁国会改革并扩大对学生的财政资助。我一直在要求他们给200万学子一个机会，通过社区大学和雇主之间的合作计划，让他们可以学到当地企业所需要的各项技能。在美国，高等教育绝不能是少数人的奢侈品。它是一种必需品，每个美国家庭在经济上都应当负担得起才对。

11 最后，我要感谢所有花些时间坐下来写信、发电子邮件、打电话以及发送推文希望自己的意见能带来改变的美国民众。我向你们大家保证：一切变革源自你们的呼声。只要我还在总统的任上，白宫一定会听取大家的意见。

12 谢谢大家，周末愉快！

It's Time for Congress to Pass the *Middle-Class Tax Cut Extension*[①]

July 14, 2012

国会应尽快通过《中产阶级减税展期法案》

2012年7月14日

【摘要导读】

在本周的广播电视讲话中，巴拉克•奥巴马总统呼吁国会尽快采取行动，对占全美总人数98%、年收入低于25万美元的人的减税政策进行延期。他指出：倘若国会按兵不动，2013年元旦，数百万中产阶级家庭以及国家的经济将因税赋上涨受到冲击。奥巴马认为现在正是国会有所作为的时候，这样美国政府才能给中产阶级和小微企业信心，而这正是创造一个可持续发展的经济体系所必需的。

演讲再现 Original Text

1 Over the past couple weeks I've been talking with folks across the country about how we're going to rebuild an economy where if you work hard, you and your family can get ahead.

2 And right now, there's a big debate going on in Washington over two **fundamentally** different paths we can take as a country to do that.

3 One path — pushed by Republicans in Congress and their nominee for President — says that the best way to create prosperity is to let it *trickle down from the top*[②]. They believe that if we spend trillions more on tax cuts for the wealthy, it'll somehow create jobs — even if we have to pay for it by cutting education and training and by raising middle-class

Words & Expressions

fundamentally [ˌfʌndəˈmentəli] *adv.* 根本地，从根本上，基础地

taxes.

4 I think they're wrong. We already tried it that way for most of the last decade, and it didn't work. We're still paying for trillions of dollars in tax cuts that benefitted the wealthiest Americans more than anyone else; tax cuts that didn't lead to the rise in wages and middle-class jobs that we were promised; and that helped take us from record surpluses to record deficits.

5 The last thing we need right now is more top-down economics. What we need are policies that will grow and strengthen the middle-class; that will help create jobs, make education and training more affordable, and encourage businesses to start up and stay right here in the United States.

6 Soon, we'll face a choice between these two different approaches. On January 1st, taxes are set to go up for tens of millions of Americans. I think that would be a huge financial hit for middle-class families. That's why I've cut middle-class taxes every year that I've been President — by $3,600 for the typical family. And that's why, this week, I called on Congress to immediately stop the January 1st tax hike from hitting any American on the first $250,000 of their income.

7 Under my plan, 98% of American families won't see their income taxes go up at all. But the other 2% of Americans will have to pay a little more in taxes on anything they make over $250,000. In other words, the wealthiest few Americans will go back to the income tax rates they were paying under *Bill Clinton* ③. And if you remember, that was when our economy created nearly 23 million new jobs, the biggest budget surplus in history, and millionaires were doing pretty well.

8 The folks in Congress and on the campaign trail who oppose this plan warn that it would somehow hurt small businesses and job creators. Well, they're completely ignoring the facts.

9 Under my plan, 97% of small business owners would avoid getting hit with any income tax hike whatsoever. In fact, I've cut taxes for small businesses eighteen times since I've

record [ˈrekɔːd] *adj.* 创纪录的

surplus [ˈsəːpləs] *n.* 过剩，顺差，盈余 *adj.* 过剩的，多余的

deficit [ˈdefisit] *n.* 赤字，逆差，亏损，亏空，不足

top-down economics 涓滴经济学

affordable [əˈfɔːdəbl] *adj.* 负担得起的

start up *v.* 开始，发动，突然站起，突然出现

tax hike 加税

on the campaign trail 在竞选过程中

get hit 被击中，遭受打击

been President. And just this week, I ordered a series of new steps to help our small businesses grow and hire.

10 The only place we disagree is whether we keep giving tax cuts to the wealthiest 2% of Americans. Republicans in Washington want more of those tax cuts. With the deficit we have, I don't think we can afford them.

11 But even if we disagree on the tax cuts for the wealthiest Americans, we all agree that no American should pay more taxes on the first $250,000 of their income. So let's at least agree to do what we all agree on. That's what compromise is all about. Let's not hold the vast majority of Americans and our entire economy hostage while we debate the merits of another tax cut for the wealthy. Let's skip the unnecessary drama, the needless delays and all the partisan posturing and let's just do the right thing for the people who sent us here to serve.

12 And I'm going to keep fighting to make sure we rebuild an economy that rewards work, grows the middle-class, and gives new opportunity to those trying to earn their way into the middle-class.

13 Thanks, and have a great weekend.

compromise [ˈkɔmprəmaiz] *n.* 妥协，折中 *vt.* 妥协处理，危害 *vi.* 妥协，让步

hold sb. hostage 劫持作人质

partisan [ˈpɑːtizən] *adj.* 党派的

posture [ˈpɔstʃə] *n.* 姿势，态度，情形 *vi.* 摆姿势 *vt.* 作…的姿势

背景知识注释 Background Notes

1. *Middle-Class Tax Cut Extension* 《中产阶级减税展期法案》。
2. trickle down from the top 涓滴模式，即主张将政府财政津贴交由大企业，然后陆续流入小企业和消费者，从而促进经济增长的一种经济学理论。
3. Bill Clinton （即William Jefferson "Bill" Clinton）威廉•杰斐逊•"比尔"•克林顿（1946.8.19—），美国律师、政治家，美国民主党成员，曾任阿肯色州州长（1979年—1981年、1983年—1992年）和第42任美国总统（1993年—2001年）。

中文译文
Chinese Version

1 过去的几个星期里，我一直在与全美各地民众一起谈论我们将要如何重建一个这样的经济体系：那就是只要你努力工作，你以及你的家人就一定能够获得成功。

2 眼下，摆在我们眼前的是两条迥然不同的道路，华盛顿正在就我们国家该走哪条道路进行着激烈的辩论。

3 其中一条——是由国会中的共和党成员及其总统候选人所推崇的——即涓滴模式是打造繁荣社会的最佳方式。他们认为，假如我们为富人减税过万亿，在某种程度上就是在创造岗位——即便我们必须为此削减教育和培训的支出、提高中产阶级的税负也在所不惜。

4 我认为他们是在抱薪救火。过去十年里的大多数时间我们一直在尝试走这条道路，根本就不管用！我们现在依旧对富人减免税负数万亿美元，而他们获得的利益却比其他任何人都多！所以说，对富人减税不仅不能实现我们所承诺的提高薪酬及增加中产阶层就业岗位，而且还可以"帮助"我们实现从创纪录盈余到破天荒赤字的蜕变。

5 因此，眼下我们并不需要这种从上而下的涓滴经济学理论。我们现在需要的是那些可以壮大和巩固中产阶级，可以创造就业岗位，可以使教育和培训的负担更易承受，以及鼓励企业增资扩产并留在美国本土的政策。

6 关于这两种不同的道路，不久我们就将面临抉择。1 月 1 日，数千万美国人民的税负眼见就要增加。我想这在经济上是对中产阶级家庭的重大打击。正是因为如此，我担任总统以来，每年都会为中产家庭减税，一个普通家庭就达到 3,600 美元。亦正是因为如此，这个星期，我号召国会尽快行动，避免任何一个年收入第一次达到 25 万美元的人在 1 月 1 日因税负上涨而受到冲击。

7 按照我的方案，98% 的美国家庭全然不用面对所得税上涨的压力。但另外那收入超过 25 万美元的 2% 的美国人则需要多承担一点赋税。换言之，极少数最富裕的人的税负率将回到克林顿时代的水平。倘若你们还记得的话，那个时期，我们创造了将近 2,300 万个岗位和历史上最多的财政盈余，而且富翁们亦顺风顺水。

8 而反对这项计划的国会议员以及参与竞选的人则警告说，我这项计划在某种程度上会损害小微企业，对创造就业岗位亦不利。显然，他们这是完全罔顾事实！

9 按照我的方案，97% 的小微企业主都可以完全避免任何因所得税上涨而受到冲击的风险。事实上，我自从担任总统以来，已经对小微企业减税 18 次了。而就在本周，我就制定了一系列新的措施，以帮助小微企业成长壮大及招聘员工。

10 我们唯一的分歧就在于是否要继续为全美 2% 的最富裕的人减少税赋。华盛顿的共和党人希望这一减税幅度更一大些。但在面对现有的赤字水平，我认为我们再也无力承担。

11 不过，即便我们无法在是否为最富裕人群减税的问题上达成共识，我们在首次获得 25 万美元收入的美国人不应当提高税负的问题上是一致的；那么我们至少应该对双方都认同的事情进行落实。这就是妥协的意义之所在。与其绑架大多数国民和我们整个的经济来对富人减税的好处进行辩论，倒不如跳过那些无谓的闹剧、无聊的拖延和无尽的党派之争，为选送我们到这里来工作的民众做些有益的事情。

12 我们将重建一个这样的经济体系，在这里有付出就有回报、中产阶级不断成长壮大、有志于靠自己的努力跻身于中产阶级的人们将获得新的机会，我也将继续为确保这一目标的实现而不懈努力。

13 谢谢，祝周末愉快！

第29周

Remembering the Victims of the *Aurora*①, Colorado Shooting

July 21, 2012.

悼念科罗拉多州奥罗拉市枪击案遇难者

2012年7月21日

【摘要导读】

在本周的广播电视讲话中，巴拉克•奥巴马总统悼念科罗拉多州悲剧中的遇难者，慰问那些与他们相知相爱以及那些受伤后尚在恢复之中的人们。

演讲再现 Original Text

Words & Expressions

suspect ['sʌspekt] *n.* 嫌疑犯 *adj.* 可疑的，不可信的 *v.* 怀疑，猜想

custody ['kʌstədi] *n.* 保管，监护，拘留，抚养权

bring... to justice 绳之以法，把…交付审判，使归案受审

heinous ['hainəs] *adj.* 可憎的，极凶恶的

terrorize ['terəˌraiz] *v.* 令人恐怖，实施恐怖统治

1 As many of you know, early on Friday, at least twelve people were killed when a gunman opened fire at a movie theater in Aurora, Colorado. Dozens more are being treated for injuries at local hospitals. Some of the victims are being treated at a children's hospital.

2 We are still gathering all the facts about what happened, but we do know that the police have one **suspect** in **custody**. And the federal government stands ready to do everything necessary to **bring** whoever's responsible for this **heinous** crime **to justice**. We will take every step possible to ensure the safety of all our people. And we will stand by our neighbors in Colorado during this extraordinarily difficult time.

3 Even as we come to learn how this happened and who's responsible, we may never understand what leads anyone to **terrorize** their fellow human beings. Such evil is senseless — beyond reason. But while we will never know

fully what causes someone to take the life of another, we do know what makes that life worth living.

4 The people we lost in Aurora loved, and were loved. They were mothers and fathers; husbands and wives; sisters and brothers; sons and daughters; friends and neighbors. They had hopes for the future and dreams that were not yet fulfilled. And if there's anything to take away from this tragedy, it's a reminder that life is fragile. Our time here is limited and it is precious. And what matters in the end are not the small and trivial things which often consume our lives. It's how we choose to treat one another, and love one another. It's what we do on a daily basis to give our lives meaning and to give our lives purpose. That's what matters. That's why we're here.

5 I'm sure many of you who are parents had the same reaction I did when you first heard this news: what if it had been my daughters at the theater, doing what young children enjoy doing every day? Michelle and I will be fortunate enough to hug our girls a little tighter this weekend, as I'm sure you will do with your children. But for those parents who may not be so fortunate, we need to embrace them and let them know we will be there for them as a nation.

6 This weekend I hope everyone takes some time for prayer and reflection — for the victims of this terrible tragedy, for the people who knew them and loved them, for those who are still struggling to recover, and for all the victims of the less publicized acts of violence that plague our communities on a daily basis. Let us keep all these Americans in our prayers. And to the people of Aurora, may the Lord bring you comfort and healing in the hard days to come.

fragile [ˈfrædʒail] *adj.* 易碎的，脆的，精细的，虚弱的

precious [ˈpreʃəs] *adj.* 宝贵的，珍贵的，矫揉造作的

trivial [ˈtriviəl] *adj.* 不重要的，琐碎的，琐细的

embrace [imˈbreis] *vt.* 拥抱，信奉，皈依，包含

reflection [riˈflekʃ(ə)n] *n.* 反射，沉思，映象

publicize [ˈpʌblisaiz] *vt.* 宣传，公布

plague [pleig] *n.* 瘟疫，灾祸 *vt.* 折磨，使苦恼

背景知识注释
Background Notes

1. Aurora 奥罗拉，美国科罗拉多州第三大城市、阿拉帕霍县最大的城市。

中文译文
Chinese Version

1 你们中许多人都知道了，星期五凌晨，在科罗拉多州奥罗拉市 (Aurora) 的一家电影院，一名持枪男子开枪杀死了至少 12 人。还有数十名伤者在当地医院接受医治。部分伤者则在一家儿童医院进行治疗。

2 我们依旧还在搜寻所有与这起案件如何发生有关的证据，但我们可以确定的是警方已经拘留了一名嫌疑犯。联邦政府也做好准备，将竭尽全力把这名十恶不赦的罪犯绳之以法，无论他是谁。我们将采取一切可能的措施来确保所有民众的安全。在科罗拉多州的同胞们经受这一异乎寻常的艰难时刻，我们将始终与你们站在一起。

3 即便是我们在调查该案件何以发生以及谁是肇事者的时候，我们始终也无法理解是什么样的事情导致一个人如此残忍地对待自己同是人类的同胞。这种邪恶行径简直是毫无道理——完全不可理喻。但即便我们永远无法完全弄清某些人夺走他人生命的缘由，我们都知道这一生命有着活着的价值。

4 我们在奥罗拉 (Aurora) 失去的那些同胞曾经爱着别人，也被别人所爱着。他们曾经是母亲或父亲、丈夫或妻子、姐妹或兄弟、儿子或女儿、朋友或邻居。他们曾对未来充满希望，他们还有许多梦想尚未实现。倘若说从这场悲剧中能够吸取什么教训的话，那就是它提醒我们生命是如此脆弱。我们此生的时光是如此的短暂有限而弥足珍贵。最最重要的事情不是那些时常消耗我们生命时光的鸡毛蒜皮的小事儿，而是我们选择如何对待其他人，如何爱其他人，是我们如何去珍视每一天的时光，使得我们的生活有意义、有目标。这才是最重要的。这才是我们来到这个世界上的原因。

5 我相信很多父母在听到这则消息的第一时间会跟我有着相同的反应：倘若我的女儿们当时就在这家电影院里会发生什么？小孩子们每天都有类似的娱乐活动。米歇尔和我倘若足够幸运，这个周末我们会紧紧地把姑娘们搂在怀里，我知道你们也会这样对待自己的孩子们的。但对于这些没有这么幸运的父母们而言，我们应该拥抱他们，让他们知道我们整个国家和民族将永远与他们在一起。

6 这个周末，我希望每个人都花些时间进行祈祷和反思，为在这起可怕的惨剧中遇难的同胞们，为那些与他们相知相爱的人们，为那些受伤后依旧在恢复之中的人们，也为那些每天困扰着我们国家而没有引起这么大的公众关注的暴力事件中遇难的人们。让我们为所有这些同胞们祈祷。愿万能的主给奥罗拉 (Aurora) 的人民带去安慰，并抚平他们在未来艰难日子里的伤痛。

第30周

The House of Representatives Must Act on *Middle-Class Tax Cut Extension*

July 28, 2012

众议院必须就《中产阶级减税展期法案》进行表决

2012 年 7 月 28 日

【摘要导读】

在本周的广播电视讲话中，巴拉克•奥巴马总统敦促众议院的共和党人行动起来，就他所提出的保护中产阶级家庭和小微企业在2013年到来之时免受税金上涨冲击的议案进行表决。他表示：每个人都认为美国应该对中产阶级的减税进行展期，而参议院已经通过了他的这项提案——这可以避免一个普通家庭的税金上涨2,200美元。但国会的共和党人却依然以这一减税方案为要挟，要美国为富豪们减税之后再通过这一方案。奥巴马呼吁国会通过《中产阶级减税展期法案》，这样才能继续促进经济增长，创造更多的就业机会。

演讲再现
Original Text

1 This week, the Senate passed a plan that I proposed a few weeks ago to protect middle-class Americans and virtually every small business owner from getting hit with a big tax hike next year — a tax hike of $2,200 for the typical family.

2 Now it comes down to this: If 218 Members of the House vote the right way, 98% of American families and 97% of small business owners will have the certainty of knowing that that their income taxes will not go up next year.

3 That certainty means something to a middle-class family who's already stretched the budget as far as it can go. It means something to a small business owner who's trying to

Words & Expressions

virtually [ˈvəːtʃuəli] *adv.* 实际上，几乎

come down 下来，降落，流传下来，倒塌，落魄，失势

stretch the budget 精打细算

plan ahead. That's security at a time when folks could use some.

4 And here's the thing: everyone in Washington says they agree on this. Everyone says they agree that we should extend the tax cuts for the middle-class. When Democrats and Republicans agree on something, it should be pretty easy to get it done.

5 But right now, that's not the case. Instead of doing what's right for middle-class families and small business owners, Republicans in Congress are holding these tax cuts hostage until we extend tax cuts for the wealthiest Americans.

6 You see, Republicans in Congress and their nominee for President believe that the best way to create prosperity in America is to let it trickle down from the top. They believe that if our country spends trillions more on tax cuts for the wealthy, we'll somehow create jobs — even if we have to pay for it by gutting things like education and training and by raising middle-class taxes.

trickle down from the top 从上细细地流下

gut [gʌt] *vt.* 取出内脏，摧毁内部装置

7 They're wrong. And I know they're wrong because we already tried it that way for most of the last decade. It didn't work. We're still paying for trillions of dollars of tax cuts that benefitted the wealthiest Americans more than anyone else; tax cuts that didn't lead to the middle-class jobs or higher wages we were promised and that helped take us from record surpluses to record deficits.

8 We can't afford more top-down economics. What we need are policies that will grow and strengthen the middle-class; that will help create jobs, make education and training more affordable, and encourage businesses to start up and stay right here in the United States.

9 That's why I've cut middle-class taxes every year that I've been President — by $3,600 for the typical family. That's why I've cut taxes for small businesses eighteen times. And that's why I'm calling on 218 Members of the House to do their jobs and not raise taxes on the middle-class.

10 As soon as they pass that bill, I'll sign it right away. And in the meantime, I'm going to keep fighting for an economy where we're not just putting folks back to work,

but making sure that work pays off — an economy where every American, no matter who you are, what you look like, or where you come from, can have the confidence that if you work hard, you can get ahead.

pay off 付清，取得成功，贿赂，报复

11 Thanks, and have a great weekend.

中文译文
Chinese Version

1 本周，参议院通过了我几周前提出的一项提案。该提案将保护中产阶级和几乎每一个小微企业主在明年免受税金大幅上涨带来的冲击。这一上涨幅度对普通家庭而言可达2,200 美元。

2 现在的问题是：倘若众议院有 218 位议员投票赞成这一提案，98% 的美国家庭以及97% 的小微企业主就可以确切地知道明年他们的收入所得税将不会上涨。

3 这一份保障对已经开始准备过紧日子的中产阶级家庭而言意义重大。这对于正在想方设法提前筹划和布局的小微企业主而言亦意义重大。拥有更多收入可供支配在这一时刻带给人们的是安全感。

4 但现在我们面临的情况是：华盛顿的每个人都说同意这一提案。每个人都同意我们为中产阶级减税进行展期。当民主党和共和党在某件事情上达成共识时，这件事情应该很容易办好。

5 但现在事实并非如此。国会的共和党人不但不为中产家庭和小微企业主减税，相反，他们竟以此为要挟，要我们先为富翁们的减税延期之后再做这件事。

6 你们瞧，国会的共和党人以及他们的总统提名候选人都相信，创造美国经济繁荣的最好方式就是采用自上而下的消滴式经济。他们认为，倘若国家用几万亿给富翁们减税，我们应当能创造就业岗位，即便我们不得不为此减少教育和培训的投资、提高中产阶级税负来支付这一成本。

7 他们大错特错了。他们之所以错是因为我们曾经在过去十年的大部分时间尝试走这条道路，但压根儿就不管用。到现在，我们依旧为减税花费数万亿美元，美国的富翁们因此受益要远大于其他任何人；减税并没有因此带来我们承诺的中产阶级的就业或更高的薪酬，却把我们从史上最高的财政盈余带入最大的财政赤字中。

8 我们不能继续实行这种自上而下的经济模式。我们需要巩固和壮大中产阶级的经济政策；需要创造就业，让教育培训成本更加容易担负得起、鼓励企业增资扩产并留在美国本土的经济政策。

9 正是因为如此，我担任总统以来每年都为中产阶级减税，对普通家庭而言这一金额多达 3,600 美元。正是因为如此，我 18 次为小微企业减税。亦正是因为如此，我号召 218 位

众议院议员为避免中产阶级的税负上涨履行自己的职责。

10 只要他们通过这项法案，我就立马签署。同时，我也将继续为创造这样一个经济体系而不懈奋斗。在这里，人们不仅能重返工作岗位，更要让他们得到应有的回报；在这里，无论你为何方人士，外貌长相如何，或来自何处，只要努力付出就能获得成功。每一个美国人都应对此充满信心。

11 谢谢，祝大家周末愉快！

第31周

Celebrating the Summer Olympics and *Paralympics*[1]

August 4, 2012

欢呼夏季奥运会和残奥会的召开

2012 年 8 月 4 日

【摘要导读】

在本周的广播电视讲话中，巴拉克•奥巴马总统对参加夏季奥运会和残奥会的全体美国运动员表示祝贺。他说这些男女运动员刻苦训练、顽强拼搏、不屈不挠，向全世界展示美国最好的一面，使大家深受鼓舞；他还告诉美国的奥运会和残奥会参与者，美国人民为他们感到无比自豪，感谢他们提醒美国人民："我们乃一家人，通过共同努力一定能成就伟大事业。"

演讲再现
Original Text

1 Hi, everybody. Today, I want to take a break from the back-and-forth of campaign season, and talk about something that's brought us all together this week — the Summer Olympics.

2 These games remind us that for all our differences, we're Americans first. And we could not be prouder of the men and women representing our country in London, in both the Olympics and in the Paralympics.

3 Last weekend, Michelle led the American delegation to London and reaffirmed the special relationship we share with our strongest ally, Great Britain. She met with *the Queen*[2], and with Prime Minister *Cameron's*[3] wife, *Samantha*[4]. She spent some time thanking our brave service

Words & Expressions

back-and-forth *adj.* 前后移动的，来回的，往返的，反复的

members and military families. And, of course, she took in as many events as she could to cheer on our athletes.

4 I've got to admit I was a little jealous she got to go. But like many of you, I caught as many events as I could, jumping off the couch for a close race, or a perfect vault. I watched the wonderful young women of our gymnastics team recapture the team gold for America, and I was filled with pride watching *Gabby Douglas* ⑤ win the all-around gold with incredible poise and grace. I watched our swimmers win a haul of medals, and *Michael Phelps* ⑥ become the most decorated Olympic athlete of all time. I saw our women's soccer team power through the competition.

5 And I'm just as proud of all our athletes in sports that don't always get as much attention. The U.S. women's eight continued its rowing dominance with another gold medal. *Kayla Harrison* ⑦ won America's first-ever gold medal in *Judo* ⑧, and *Marti Malloy* ⑨ won a bronze. *Kim Rhode* ⑩ became the first American to win individual medals in five straight Olympics with her gold in skeet shooting; and her teammate, Army Sergeant *Vincent Hancock* ⑪, won his second skeet gold.

6 I also thought of the truly difficult journeys that many of our athletes have made. Some have faced personal loss, or beaten cancer. Some have worked long shifts at multiple jobs to feed their Olympic dream. And some have done the impossible. Less than four years ago, *Bryshon Nellum* ⑫ was shot three times in his legs. But this week, he'll run the 400 meters. And as a boy, *Lopez Lomong* ⑬ fled war and persecution and life as a refugee — one of the *"Lost Boys" of Sudan* ⑭. Today's he's an American — and representing his country at the Olympics for the second time.

7 So it's no surprise America is vying for the top of the medal count. But it's not the medal count alone that inspires us — most of our athletes won't claim a medal at all. It's the character of the men and women who compete for those medals. It's their hard work and sacrifice — the countless hours in the gym, in the pool, on the track. It's their dogged perseverance and unyielding determination, through

take in 吸收，领会，欺骗，接待，接受，理解，拘留，欺骗，改短
cheer on 鼓励，为某人打气
gymnastics [dʒim'næstiks] *n.* 体操，体育，体操运动
recapture [ri'kæptʃə] *vt.* 夺回，拿回，再体验
a haul of 大量的
power ['pauə] *vi.* 快速前进
dominance ['dɔminəns] *n.* 优势，统治，支配
bronze [brɔnz] *n.* 青铜，青铜制品，铜牌，铜质奖章
skeet shooting 双向飞碟射击
personal loss 个人损失
beaten cancer 治愈的癌症
persecution [ˌpəsi'kjuʃən] *n.* 迫害，烦扰
vie [vai] *vt.* 使针锋相对，提出…来竞争，以…作较量 *vi.* 争，竞争
dogged ['dɔgid] *adj.* 顽强的，顽固的
perseverance [ˌpəsə'viərəns] *n.* 坚持不懈，不屈不挠，耐性，毅力

disappointment and triumph alike.

8 It's that unconquerable spirit — that American spirit — that says even though we may have very different stories to tell; even though we may not look alike or talk alike or *be dealt the same hand*⑮ in life — if we work hard, we can achieve our dreams. We can make it if we try. We are one people, with common values and ideals; we celebrate individual excellence, but recognize that only together can we accomplish great and important things we cannot accomplish alone.

9 That's why we watch. That's why we cheer. That's why we come together, for two weeks in summer, and swell with pride at the incredible things our fellow citizens can do.

10 So to all our Olympic and Paralympic athletes — whether you've already competed or have yet to compete — your country could not be prouder of you. Thank you for presenting the best of America to the rest of the world. And, thank you for becoming new role models to our children — mine included — and inspiring them to believe that if they work hard and do their best, they can achieve great things, too.

11 Go get 'em this week, Team USA. We can't wait to welcome you home.

12 God bless you, and God bless America.

triumph [ˈtraiəmf] *n.* 胜利，凯旋，欢欣

celebrate [ˈselibreit] *vt.* 庆祝，举行，赞美，祝贺

swell [swel] *vi.* 膨胀，鼓胀

背景知识注释 Background Notes

1. Paralympics 即 Paralympic Games 残疾人奥林匹克运动会。它始办于 1960 年，是由国际奥委会和国际残疾人奥林匹克委员会主办的、专为残疾人举行的世界大型综合性运动会，每四年于夏季奥运会后举办一届。

2. the Queen 即 Queen Elizabeth II 伊丽莎白二世（1926.4.21—），全名：伊丽莎白·亚历山德拉·玛丽·温莎 (Elizabeth Alexandra Mary Windsor)，为现任英国君主，即大不列颠及北爱尔兰联合王国女王，同时是英国及英联邦 16 个成员国的元首，于 1952 年 2 月 6 日登基，1953 年 6 月 2 日加冕。伊丽莎白二世是目前在世的在位时间第 2 长的国家元首，同时也是英国在位时间第二长的君主，仅次于维多利亚女王，是英国、英联邦及 15 个成员国的

国家元首，同时也是英国国教会的最高首领，以她为国家元首的英联邦国家中大约生活着1.25亿人。

3. Cameron　即 David William Donald Cameron 戴维•威廉•唐纳德•卡梅伦（1966.10.9—），现任英国联合政府首相、第一财政大臣、公务员事务部部长和保守党党魁，也是英国国会下院威特尼选区的现任议员，而且是英国近两百年来最年轻的首相。

4. Samantha　即 Samantha Gwendoline Cameron 萨曼莎•卡梅伦（1971.4.18—），英国现任首相戴维•卡梅伦的妻子，英国精品的创意总监，教养良好、学识丰富，既把家打理得井井有条，又能为卡梅伦的工作提出建议。她的大儿子伊万患有脑瘫和大田原综合征（癫痫性脑病），2009年2月，仅7岁便早夭。卡梅伦与妻子萨曼莎现有二女一子，分别是9岁的南希（Nancy）、7岁的阿瑟（Arthur）和3岁的弗洛伦斯（Florence）。

5. Gabby Douglas　嘉比尔•杜格拉斯（1995.12.31—），绰号"飞翔的松鼠"，美国女子竞技体操运动员、奥运金牌得主。

6. Michael Phelps　即Michael Fred Phelps II 迈克尔•弗雷德•菲尔普斯二世（1985.6.30—），出生于美国马里兰州巴尔的摩市，是美国游泳运动员，绰号"巴尔的摩子弹"、"水怪"、"飞鱼"、"水神"，男子个人混合泳、蝶泳三项世界纪录的保持者。他在2004年的雅典奥运会上一人拿下游泳项目上的六枚金牌，成为雅典奥运会上得到金牌数最多的运动员。2008年北京奥运，他以八枚金牌的成绩打破了马克•施皮茨在1972年慕尼黑奥运会所创下的七金纪录，成为在同一届奥林匹克运动会中获得最多金牌的运动员。2012年伦敦奥运会后，又成为奥运会历史上获得金牌数（18枚）及总奖牌数（18金2银2铜，共22枚）最多的运动员。

7. Kayla Harrison　凯拉•哈里森（1990.7.2—），美国柔道运动员。2008年赢得世界青年锦标赛冠军；2009年获得亚军；2010年赢得世界锦标赛冠军；2011年世锦赛铜牌。2012年在伦敦奥运会柔道女子78公斤以下级比赛中，为美国队夺得了史上首枚柔道金牌。

8. Judo　柔道，在日语中是"柔之道"的意思，就是"温柔的方式"。它是发源于日本的一项武道，1882年由日本人嘉纳治五郎创立。其原型为日本传统武术之一的柔术。柔道通过把对手摔倒在地而赢得比赛，它是奥运会比赛中唯一的允许使用窒息或扭脱关节等手段来制服对手的项目。柔道是一种对抗性很强的竞技运动，它强调选手对技巧掌握的娴熟程度，而非力量的对比。目前，柔道是奥运会比赛项目之一。

9. Marti Malloy　马蒂•马洛伊（1986.6.23—），美国柔道运动员，在2012年在伦敦奥运会柔道女子57公斤以下级比赛中获得铜牌。

10. Kim Rhode　即 Kimberly "Kim" Susan Rhode 金伯利•"金"•苏珊•罗德（1979.7.16 —），美国加利福尼亚人，射击运动员，主攻飞碟双向与飞碟多向。她在奥运会中先后赢得5枚奖牌（3金1银1铜），她曾是美国射击代表队中最年轻的成员，在2012年伦敦奥运会中射击女子飞碟双向中再次夺得冠军宝座。

11. Vincent Hancock　文森特•汉考克（1989.3.19—），美国运动员，是美国双向飞碟的小明星，五岁时他射中了自己运动生涯中的第一个碟靶。文森特•汉考克出生于美国佛罗里达州的夏洛特，现居住在佐治亚州的伊屯顿，是奥科尼湖射击俱乐部的成员。2005年，他在昌原国际射联世界杯(ISSF)上首次参加国际比赛，就取得了最好成绩，获得了金牌。同年参加了七项国际比赛，每次都获得了奖牌，成为取得这样优异成绩的第一位射击选手。凭借这些成绩，他被授予了2005年度国际运动射击联合会最佳射击运动员奖。

12. Bryshon Nellum　布莱森•内拉姆（1989.5.1—），美国田径选手。伦敦奥运会上参加男子400米比赛，虽然他在400米跑中甚至没能进入决赛，但仍然获得了400米接力的银牌。布莱申在伦敦奥运会四年前的万圣节那天，因为被歹徒误认为仇家，腿部中了三枪。当时走路困难的他，被医生断言不会再有机会回归赛场，可是他不顾医生的忠告，又坚强地回来了。因此，在伦敦奥运会闭幕式上经美国运动员们投票推选他为美国代表团的旗手。

13. Lopez Lomong　洛佩兹•卢蒙洛（1985.1.5—），美国中长跑运动场上的实力不凡的田径运动员。2008年北京奥运会上，扛着美国国旗出现在入场式上。他出生在南苏丹一个不起眼的小村庄。在苏丹第二次内战中6岁的他作为战俘被关押，差点死在狱中。偶然的机会，他与另外3名一同入狱的小伙伴通过栅栏下面的洞逃出来，跑了三天三夜，最后到达肯尼亚。他在一个难民营一待就是10年——“洛佩兹”就是他住的帐篷的名字。2001年通过天主教慈善机构，洛佩兹才被送到美国接受教育。到达美国后，洛佩兹顺利进入纽约塔利中学(Tully High School)就读，展现出非凡的中长跑天赋。高中时他帮助学校横扫全美、领跑各个级别的径赛。

14. “Lost Boys” of Sudan　苏丹迷失的孩子。第二次苏丹内战始于1983年，是1955年至1972年之间第一次苏丹内战的延续。这场战争主要地点是苏丹南部，是第二次世界大战以后平民死亡人数最多的一场战争——大约有190万名南苏丹平民死亡，以及超过400万人被迫离开家园。其中包括了一群年龄大多在15岁以下的孤儿。他们成群结队穿越沙漠以逃避北方政府军的追杀。这群孩子又被国际救援组织称呼为“苏丹的迷失男孩”。

15. be dealt the same hand　典出 when life deals you a bad hand，而此语源自扑克牌游戏，指生活中的坎坷。

中文译文
Chinese Version

1　嗨，大家好。今天，我想在你争我夺的选战时期稍事休息，谈谈本周我们大家都在关注的事情——夏季奥林匹克运动会。

2　这一盛会告诉我们，尽管我们彼此之间存在着这样或那样的分歧，但首先我们是美国人。我们为在伦敦代表我们参加奥运会和残奥会的所有男女运动员感到无比自豪。

3 上周末，米歇尔带领美国代表团抵达伦敦，与我们最强有力的盟友——大不列颠王国再次确认了我们特殊的关系。她在卡梅伦 (Cameron) 首相夫人萨曼塔 (Samantha) 的陪同下谒见了英国女王。她还抽空去探望了我们英勇的部队指战员和军人家庭。当然，她还尽可能观看了一些比赛，为我们的运动员们助威呐喊。

4 说实话，她能去伦敦，我有点儿嫉妒。但是和你们许多人一样，我也尽可能多地关注些比赛，一旦看到旗鼓相当的赛事或完整无缺的一跳，我也会从沙发上跳起来。我观看了我们优秀的年轻女子体操队再次为美国夺得团体金牌；我充满自豪地观看了戈比•道格拉斯 (Gabby Douglas) 以难以置信的稳健发挥和优雅姿势获得了女子个人全能金牌。我看到了我们的游泳运动员们赢得一大堆奖牌，迈克尔•菲尔普斯 (Michael Phelps) 成为奥运历史上最辉煌的运动员。我还看到了我们的女子足球队在激烈竞争中的强势晋级。

5 同时，我也为那些鲜为外人瞩目的项目的运动员感到骄傲。美国队在女子八人单桨赛艇中保持了传统优势再次获得金牌。凯拉•哈里森 (Kayla Harrison) 获得美国柔道项目历史上首枚金牌，马蒂•马洛伊 (Marti Malloy) 获得铜牌。金•罗德 (Kim Rhode) 再次获得女子飞碟双向射击金牌，成为美国历史上首个在该项目获得 5 枚个人奖牌的运动员，她的队友，陆军中士文森特•汉考克 (Vincent Hancock) 获得男子飞碟双向金牌。

6 我还想起了许多运动员的坎坷经历。有些人得面对个人缺失，或力克癌症。有些人为了实现自己的奥运梦想在多个工时颇长的工作岗位上来回奔波。还有些人完成了原本不可企及的事情。不到四年以前，布莱森•内拉姆 (Bryshon Nellum) 腿部连中三枪，但在本周，他将参加男子 400 米的比赛。洛佩兹•罗蒙 (Lopez Lomong) 作为一个孩子经历了战乱、迫害和难民生活，是苏丹众多“迷失的男孩”中的一位。但今天的他是一名美国人，代表着他的国家第二次参加奥运会。

7 毫无疑问，美国将力争荣登奖牌榜的第一。但激励我们的不仅仅是奖牌的数量，因为大多数的运动员将不会获得任何奖牌。激励我们的是参与争夺这些奖牌的男女运动员的人格品质，是他们刻苦训练和自我牺牲的精神——在体育馆中、游泳池里和田径场上数不清的日日夜夜，是他们经历失望与荣耀之后坚忍不拔的毅力以及永不言弃的决心。

8 正是这种坚不可摧的精神——这种美国精神——证明了即便我们的经历千差万别，即便我们长相各不相同、说话方式存在差异、或者即便我们生活中的坎坷林林总总，只要我们肯努力，就能梦想成真。只要努力，就能成功。我们是一个民族，有着共同的价值观和理想，我们推崇个人的优秀与杰出，却也深知只有团结一致才能取得我们个人所不能企及的伟大而重要的成就。

9 正是因为如此，我们观看奥运比赛。正是因为如此，我们为之摇旗呐喊。正是因为如此，在这个盛夏的两个星期里，我们齐聚一堂，为我们的同胞所创造的这些不可思议的成就而激情澎湃。

10 因此，对于我们所有的奥运会和残奥会运动员们——无论你们已经完成赛程或尚未参赛——祖国都为你们感到无比自豪。感谢你们向世界上其他国家展示美国最好的一面。同时也感谢你们为我们的孩子们——当然也包括我的孩子——树立了新的榜样，并激励这些孩子，让他们认识到只要努力拼搏，尽自己最大努力，他们也能实现伟大的目标。

11 加油，美国队！我们迫切期待着你们凯旋。

12 愿上帝保佑你们，愿上帝保佑美国。

第32周

All-Hands-On-Deck Response to the Drought

August 11, 2012

全民动员抗旱救灾

2012年8月11日

【摘要导读】

在本周的广播电视讲话中，巴拉克•奥巴马总统谈论了政府全力应对50年不遇的严重干旱的救灾措施。他说：这次旱情对农牧民影响尤甚，他们不得不面对农作物减产和饲养牲畜的艰辛；正是因为如此，政府正在尽一切可能为他们提供援助帮助他们抗旱救灾和恢复生产。政府已经采取了数项措施，其中包括开放更多联邦用地提供草料和放牧场地，准许农牧民以及小微企业获得低息紧急贷款，为受干旱影响的牲畜和恢复地力提供更多水源。另外，奥巴马再一次号召国会与他一起采取行动，通过一项农场法案，进行必要的改革，以便在遭遇这种自然灾害的时候为农牧民提供帮助，给予他们应有的信心。

演讲再现 Original Text

Words & Expressions

all-hand-on-deck 全力的

on record 记录在案的，公开发表的

1 Hi, everybody. Today, I want to talk about something that most of you already know — it's hot outside. It's really hot. And if this feels worse than normal, that's because it is. We just found out that the month of July was the warmest month on record — warmer than any other month since we began keeping track more than a century ago.

2 But the heat is just half the story. We're also suffering through one of the worst droughts in over 50 years. More than a fifth of this country is experiencing what we call "extreme" or "exceptional" drought — with states like Nebraska, Kansas,

Missouri, Oklahoma and Arkansas getting hit harder than most.

3 That's bad news for a lot of people, but it's especially tough on our farmers. Right now, half of the corn crop in America is in poor or very poor condition. Cattle farmers are struggling to feed their animals. Many folks are seeing their livelihoods dry up in front of their eyes. And if we don't get relief soon, Americans everywhere will start feeling the pinch, with higher prices on grocery store shelves all across the country.

4 We can't let that happen. That's why, at my direction, the Department of Agriculture, led by *Secretary Vilsack* ①, has been working with other agencies across the federal government to make sure we're doing everything we can to help farmers and ranchers fight back and recover from this disaster. Already, we've given farmers across 32 states access to low-interest emergency loans.

5 We've opened up more federal land for grazing. And we're working with crop insurance companies to give farmers a short grace period on their premiums, since some families will be struggling to make ends meet at the end of the year.

6 This past week, we went even further — announcing an additional $30 million to help get more water to livestock and restore land affected by the drought. We're making it easier for even more farmers, ranchers and businesses to get emergency loans. And *the Department of Transportation* ② is helping more truck drivers deliver supplies to states that need them the most.

7 This is an all-hands-on-deck response, and we'll be doing even more in the coming weeks to help families and communities that are suffering right now.

8 But my Administration can't do it alone. Congress needs to do its part, too. They need to pass a farm bill that not only helps farmers and ranchers respond to these kinds of disasters, but also makes necessary reforms and gives them some certainty year-round. That's the single best way we can help rural communities right now, and also in the long-term.

9 So call your Members of Congress, write them an

feel the pinch 感到经济拮据

a grace period 宽限期

premium [ˈpriːmiəm] *n.* 保险费，额外费用，奖金

year-round 整年的，一年到头的

look out for 留心，提防，留意找，设法得到

email, and tell them that now is the time to come together and get this done. Too many Americans are suffering right now to let politics get in the way. Let's help farmers, ranchers and business owners recover. Let's make sure that families who already stretch their budgets to the limit don't have to pay more for groceries this fall.

10 In the meantime, I'll keep doing everything I can to help respond to this disaster. Because at times like these, it doesn't matter if you live in *Des Moines* ③ or *Detroit* ④ — we're Americans first. And if we look out for each other, we'll come out of this stronger than before.

11 Have a great weekend, everybody. And stay cool.

背景知识注释 Background Notes

1. Secretary Vilsack　维尔萨克部长。Thomas James Vilsack 托马斯•詹姆斯•维尔萨克（1950.12.13—），美国律师、政治家，美国民主党人，曾任艾奥瓦州州长（1999 年—2007 年），现任美国农业部长（2009 年至今）。
2. the Department of Transportation　美国运输部，是美国联邦政府的交通部门，1966 年 10 月 15 日美国国会通过设立运输部法案，1967 年 4 月 1 日正式办公。负责管理航空、铁路、联邦公路、海事、公共运输等方面。
3. Des Moines　得梅因，美国艾奥瓦州的首府、波尔克县县治。35 号和 80 号州际公路通过该城。市内有得梅因国际机场。
4. Detroit　底特律，美国密歇根州最大的城市，也是韦恩县的县治所在。1701 年由法国毛皮商建立，是位于美国中西部，加拿大温莎以北、底特律河沿岸的一座重要的港口城市、世界传统汽车中心和音乐之都。城市得名于连接圣克莱尔湖和伊利湖的底特律河，它源自法语“Rivière du Détroit”，意为“海峡之河 (River of the Strait)”。

中文译文 Chinese Version

1　嗨，大家好。今天，我想谈谈你们大多数人都已经知道的情况——外面很热，确实热极了！倘若你觉得比平常时候要难受，那就是因为热。气象记录显示 7 月是最热的一个月，要比我们有记录以来的一个多世纪里的任何一个七月都要热。

2　但是天气很热还只是事情的一部分。我们还遭遇着 50 多年来最严重的干旱。全国有超过五分之一的地方受到级别为“极度严重”甚至“异常严重”干旱的影响：包括内布拉

斯、加州、堪萨斯州、密苏里州、俄克拉荷马州、阿肯色州在内的一些州受灾尤为严重。

3 对许多人来说，这样的消息极为不幸；但对我们的农民来说，这尤为艰难。当下，全国有一半的玉米生长条件不佳甚至极其不佳。奶牛养殖户们正在为饲养牲畜而苦苦地挣扎着。很多人眼睁睁地看着自己的牲口在他们面前渴死。倘若这一情况不能尽快得到救援，全国上下食杂商店货架上的货物价格将水涨船高，全美各地的人都将掐着手指头过日子。

4 我们不能让这一情况发生。根据我的指示，农业部在维尔萨克部长 (Secretary Vilsack) 带领下，已经与联邦政府其他部门一起尽我们最大的努力去帮助农牧民，帮助他们抗旱和恢复生产。我们也已经让 32 个州的农民取得了获取低息紧急贷款的许可。

5 我们已经开放更多联邦用地用于放牧，并正在与农作物保险公司商谈，让他们给予农民一个短暂的保险金缴纳宽限期，因为到年底的时候部分家庭要实现收支平衡将非常困难。

6 在过去一个星期里，我们做出了更进一步努力——宣布提供 3,000 万美元的追加资金，为受干旱影响的牲畜和恢复地力提供更多的水源。我们正在努力让更多的农牧民以及企业获得紧急贷款。交通运输部也正在帮助更多的卡车司机将补给品运送到急需的一些州。

7 这是真正的全民行动，而我们也将继续在未来数周做更多事情，帮助依然遭受灾害影响的家庭和街区。

8 但做这些事情不能仅靠政府。国会也应该做出自己的努力。他们应该通过一项农场法案，这样不仅仅能为遭受这类灾害的农牧民提供应急支持，更能进行必要的改革，给他们提供全年的信心保障。这才是从眼下以及长远来看，我们帮助农村地区唯一最佳的方式。

9 因此，请大家打电话给你们的国会议员们，给他们发邮件，告诉他们现在需要团结一心把这件事情办好。眼下尚有许许多多的人正在遭受痛苦，我们不能让政治成见挡道。让我们一道帮助农牧民以及企业主恢复生产。让我们确保收支预算原本就已达到极限的家庭不要在今年秋天吃饭的问题上花销增多。

10 同时，我也将继续恪尽职守以应对这场灾难。因为在这样的时刻，你生活在德梅因 (Des Moines) 还是底特律 (Detroit) 并不重要——毕竟我们首先都是美国人。倘若我们能彼此照料，我们必将战胜灾害并变得比以往更为强大。

11 祝大家周末愉快！谨防中暑。

第33周

Congress Should Back Plan to Hire Teachers

August 18, 2012

国会应当支持招募教师的计划

2012年8月18日

【摘要导读】

随着学生重返学校，奥巴马总统利用这次的每周讲话与大家讨论了教育在美国未来所发挥的关键作用。他认为：对于一个孩子的教育而言，没有什么比一个好老师更为重要了。奥巴马还指出他已经提出了一项就业法案来帮助各州防止更多的教师下岗并重新招募教师，但国会却拒绝通过；相反，每一个共和党人要投票支持的预算法案都将进一步削减教育支出，这样做只是为了要给富豪们提供减税。对此，白宫已经采取了多项措施，包括加大科学和数学教学的投入，给各州在实施《不让一个孩子掉队》计划上更多灵活性，为数百万年轻学子提供更多资金援助。

演讲再现 Original Text

1 Hi, everybody. This week, I spent some time traveling across Iowa talking with folks about rebuilding an economy where if you work hard, you and your family can get ahead.

2 And along the way, I stopped in at *Cascade High School*① to thank the teachers there for doing such a great job — and wish them luck as they head back to the classroom for this school year.

3 There's nothing more important to our country's future than the education we give our kids. And there's no one more important to that education than the person at the front of the classroom.

4 Teachers matter. Most work tirelessly, with modest pay, sometimes digging into their own pocket for school supplies — just to make a difference. They give everything for our kids — and **in return**, we should invest in them.

5 But here's the thing: this year, several thousand fewer educators will be going back to school. Since 2009, we've lost more than 300,000 education jobs, in part, because of budget cuts at the state and local level.

6 Think about what that means for our country. At a time when the rest of the world is racing to out-educate America; these cuts force our kids into crowded classrooms, cancel programs for preschoolers and kindergarteners, and shorten the school week and the school year.

7 That's the opposite of what we should be doing as a country. States should be making education a priority in their budgets, even in tough **fiscal** times. And Congress should be willing to help out — because this affects all of us.

8 That's why part of the jobs bill that I sent to Congress last September included support for states to prevent further layoffs and to rehire teachers who'd lost their jobs. But here we are — a year later with tens of thousands more educators laid off — and Congress still hasn't done anything about it.

9 In fact, the economic plan that almost every Republican in Congress voted for would make the situation even worse. It would actually cut funding for education — which means fewer kids in ***Head Start*** ②, fewer teachers in our classrooms, and fewer college students with **access** to financial aid — all to pay for a **massive** new tax cut for millionaires and billionaires.

10 That's backwards. That's wrong. That plan doesn't invest in our future; it **undercuts** our future.

11 If we want America to lead in the 21st century, nothing is more important than giving everyone the best education possible — from the day they start preschool to the day they start their career.

12 That's why we launched a national competition to improve our schools. And for less than one percent of what

Words & Expressions

in return 作为报答

fiscal [ˈfiskl] *adj.* 会计的，财政的，国库的

access [ˈækses] *n.* 进入，使用权，通路 *vt.* 使用，存取，接近

massive [ˈmæsiv] *adj.* 大量的，巨大的，厚重的，魁伟的

undercut [ˈʌndəkʌt] *vt.* 廉价出售，削弱…的地位，削减…的力量

our nation spends on education each year, we've encouraged almost every state to raise their standards — the first time that's happened in a generation.

13 That's why we've invested in math and science education, and given states more flexibility on *No Child Left Behind*[3].

14 And that's why we've reformed the student loan program to put students before big banks, and increased financial aid for millions of young people — because in America, higher education cannot be a luxury; it's an economic necessity every family should be able to afford.

flexibility [ˌfleksəˈbiliti] *n.* 灵活性，柔韧性，适应性

15 This is a country where no matter what you look like or where you come from, if you're willing to study and work hard, you can go as far as your talents will take you. You can make it if you try. I am only the President of the United States today because of the chance my education gave me. I want every child in America to have that chance. That's what I'm fighting for. And as long as I have the privilege of being your President, that's what I'm going to keep fighting for.

16 Thanks, have a great weekend.

背景知识注释 Background Notes

1. Cascade High School 喀斯喀特高中，位于爱荷华州东南部迪比克县和琼斯县的喀斯喀特市。该校美术和体育两个科目甚强。
2. *Head Start* 《启蒙计划》/《领先计划》，美国卫生及公共服务部的一项计划，旨在为低收入的孩子及其家庭提供全面的教育、健康、营养和家长参与的服务。1965年由朱尔•休格曼发起。
3. *No Child Left Behind* 《不让一个孩子掉队》法案，由布什总统于2002年初签署实施。作为1965年以来美国最重要的中小学改革法，内容包括：（1）建立中小学教育责任制；（2）给地方和学校更大的自主权；（3）给孩子父母更多的选择；（4）保证每一个孩子都能阅读；（5）提高教师质量；（6）检查各州学生的学习成绩；（7）提高移民儿童的英语水平。

中文译文
Chinese Version

1 嗨，大家好。本周我花些时间走访了爱荷华州，和大家探讨如何重建我们的经济，让辛勤工作能为你和你的家人带来更加美好的生活。

2 途中，我在喀斯喀特高中 (Cascade High School) 驻足，感谢那里的教师们成就如此出色的工作，并希望他们在本学年能有幸重回讲台。

3 对我们国家的未来而言，没有什么比给孩子们提供良好的教育更为重要了。在教育方面也没有任何人比站在教室前的那个人更加关键了。

4 教师事关重大。他们大多数都废寝忘食地工作着，而所得薪酬却十分微薄，有时候还不得不自己掏腰包购买教学用品——为的只是要给孩子们带来些许改变。他们为了我们的孩子们付出了一切——而反过来，我们对他们也应当有所投入。

5 但事实却并非如此：今年，有数千名教育工作者将无法重返校园。自 2009 年以来，我们总共失去了 30 万个教育工作岗位，其部分原因在于全国和地方的预算削减。

6 想一想，这对于我们国家意味着什么？眼下世界其他国家都在加快步伐，要在教育上赶超美国；而这些预算削减却迫使我们孩子的教室更加拥挤，一些学前教育和幼儿教育项目被迫被取消，每周学习时间和学年被缩短。

7 这绝非是我们作为一个国家应有的行为。即使是在财政紧张时期，各州应该将教育列为预算中的头等重要位置。而国会应当伸出援助之手……因为此事关乎我们所有人。

8 正是因为如此，在去年 9 月我提交国会的一份就业法案中就包括为各州提供支持以避免更多的教师被裁员并重新招募已经失业的教师。但事实却是——一年以后，又有成千上万的教育工作者下岗——而国会却依旧无动于衷。

9 实际上，几乎每个共和党议员投票支持的经济计划都将使形势更加恶化。它事实上将削减我们的教育经费——这意味着受《领先计划》资助的孩子更少了，教室里的教师更少了，能获得经济援助的大学生更少了——这一切都将为给百万富翁、亿万富豪们的新的大规模减税政策埋单。

10 这显然是开倒车，且大错特错。那样的计划不是要为我们的未来投资，而是扼杀我们的未来。

11 倘若我们希望美国在 21 世纪引领全球，没有什么比给予每个人最好的接受教育的机会更为重要——从开始接受学前教育的那一天直到开启职业生涯的那一天为止。

12 正是因为如此，我们实施了一项改善学校教学环境的全国性竞争计划。由于每年教育支出仅占全国支出的不到 1%，我们呼吁几乎每一个州都提高自己的标准。这在这一代人中是头一次。

13 正是因为如此，我们在数学和科学教育上加大投入，并给予各州在《不让一个孩子掉队》法案实施上更多的灵活性。

14 正是因为如此，我们改革助学贷款计划，让大银行为学生提供贷款，增加对数百万年轻学子的财政补助——因为在美国，高等教育不应该是奢侈品，而应当成为每个家庭在经济上都能承担得起的必需品。

15 在这个国家里，无论长相如何，无论来自何方，只要你肯努力学习与工作，就能发挥自己所有的天赋。只要努力就一定能成功。我之所以成为当今的美国总统，就是由于我所受到的教育给予我机会。我希望每位美国孩子都有这样的机会。这也是我为之奋斗的目标。而且只要我还在总统的任上，我就要继续为此奋斗不息。

16 谢谢，祝周末愉快。

第34周

Preserving and Strengthening *Medicare*[1]

August 25, 2012

保留和巩固医疗保险法案

2012年8月25日

【摘要导读】

在本周的广播电视讲话中，巴拉克•奥巴马总统与美国民众谈论了为老年人及其子孙后代保留和巩固医疗保险法案的迫切必要性。这些人一生辛劳不应因为一场大病就被迫失去自己的住房或毕生的积蓄。奥巴马认为他们理应获得更好的照料，他表示他将继续与任何一个希望持续改进当前这一医保体系的人合作，为老人们提供他们应得的保障与安宁。

演讲再现 Original Text

1 Over the last few weeks, there's been a lot of talk about Medicare, with a lot of accusations and misinformation flying around. So today I want to step back for a minute and share with you some actual facts and news about the program.

2 This week, we found out that, thanks to the health care law we passed, nearly 5.4 million seniors with Medicare have saved over $4.1 billion on prescription drugs. That's an average of more than $700 per person. And this year alone, 18 million seniors with Medicare have taken advantage of preventive care benefits like mammograms or other cancer screenings that now come at no extra cost.

3 That's progress. It means that seniors everywhere are getting the care they need for less. And if you have questions about what benefits you're entitled to, you can go to www.

Words & Expressions

step back 抽身出来

prescription drugs 凭处方供应的药品

mammograms ['mæməgræm] *n.* 乳房X线照片

cancer screenings 癌症筛检

be entitled to 有权，有…的资格

medicare.gov to find out.

4 This news is also a reminder of what's really **at stake** when we talk about the future of Medicare. It's not about overheated **rhetoric** at election time. It's about a promise this country made to our seniors that says if you **put in** a lifetime of hard work, you shouldn't lose your home or your life savings just because you get sick.

5 Over the last 47 years, millions of Americans have worked for that promise.

They've earned it. And for many seniors, the care they've gotten through Medicare has made all the difference in the world.

6 Growing up as the son of a single mother, I was raised with the help of my grandparents. I saw how important things like Medicare and ***Social Security***[2] were in their lives. And I saw **the peace of mind** it gave them.

7 That's why, as President, my goal has been to strengthen these programs now, and preserve them for future generations. Because today's seniors deserve that same peace of mind. And the millions of Americans who are working hard right now deserve to know that the care they need will be available when they need it.

8 That's why, as part of the ***Affordable Care Act***[3], we gave seniors deeper discounts on prescription drugs, and made sure preventive care like mammograms are free without a **co-pay**. We've extended the life of Medicare by almost a decade. And I've proposed reforms that will save Medicare money by getting rid of wasteful spending in the health care system and **reining in** insurance companies — reforms that won't touch your guaranteed Medicare benefits. Not by a single dime.

9 Republicans in Congress have put forward a very different plan. They want to turn Medicare into a **voucher** program. That means that instead of being guaranteed Medicare, seniors would get a voucher to buy insurance, but it wouldn't keep up with costs. As a result, one plan would force seniors to pay an extra $6,400 a year for the same benefits they get right now. And it would effectively end Medicare as

at stake 危如累卵，处于危险中，在紧要关头

rhetoric [ˈretərik] *n.* 修辞，修辞学，华丽虚饰的语言 *adj.* 花言巧语的

put in 提出，提交，放入，种植，使就职

the peace of mind 心灵的平静

co-pay 付费，自付率

rein in 控制，放慢，止住

voucher [ˈvautʃə] *n.* 收据，证人，保证人，证明者，代金券

we know it.

10 I think our seniors deserve better. I'm willing to work with anyone to keep improving the current system, but I refuse to do anything that undermines the basic idea of Medicare as a guarantee for seniors who get sick.

undermine [ˌʌndəˈmain] *vt.* 破坏，渐渐破坏，挖掘地基

11 Here in America, we believe in keeping our promises — especially to our seniors who have put in a lifetime of hard work and deserve to enjoy their golden years. That's what Medicare is all about. That's why we need to strengthen and preserve it for future generations. And as long as I have the honor of serving as your President, that's exactly what I'll do.

12 Thanks, and have a great weekend.

背景知识注释 Background Notes

1. Medicare 医疗保险（制度）。西方国家社会保险制度的建立，大多是从医疗保险起步的。医疗保险始于1883年德国颁布的《劳工疾病保险法》，其中规定某些行业中工资少于限额的工人应强制加入医疗保险基金会，基金会强制性征收工人和雇主应缴纳的基金。这一法令标志着医疗保险作为一种强制性社会保险制度的产生。目前，所有发达国家和许多发展中国家都建立了医疗保险制度。

2. Social Security 社会保险制度或社会保障体系，指国家和社会通过立法对国民收入进行分配和再分配，对社会成员特别是生活有特殊困难的人们的基本生活权利给予保障的社会安全制度。社会保障的本质是维护社会公平进而促进社会稳定发展。

3. *Affordable Care Act* 即*Patient Protection and Affordable Care Act* (PPACA)《平价医疗法案》，为奥巴马总统2010年3月23日签署的一项联邦法律。该法令和2010年3月30日签署的《2010医疗与教育和解法》构成了2010年的医疗改革。这些法律着力改革私人医疗保险市场，为既往病史的人们提供更多的赔付，提高医疗保险处方药覆盖面并延长医疗保险信托基金（至少为12年）。

中文译文 Chinese Version

1 在过去的几个星期里，医保法案成了人们争相谈论的话题，而夹杂其间的各种指责声音和误导信息甚嚣尘上。因此，今天我想花点时间在这里与大家分享关于这一计划的确切信息。

2 本周，我们发现，由于医疗保险法案的通过，将近540万拥有医保的老年人在处方药上节省了共计41亿元。每个人均摊就是700多美元。仅今年一年，1,800万拥有医保的老年人享受到预防保健服务所带来的便利，比如乳腺X光检查以及其他的癌症筛查现在就不需要额外付费了。

3 这就是进展。这说明各地的老人都能以比以往较小的代价得到他们所需的医疗服务。倘若你对你应得的医疗福利尚有疑问，请登录www.medicare.gov这个网站获取相关信息。

4 这则消息也提醒着我们，当我们谈及医疗保险的未来时什么才是真正需要关注的事情。这不是总统选战期间盛行的花言巧语。这是我们国家对于老年人的承诺：倘若你的一生都是在辛勤地工作，你就不会只因一场大病而失去自己的住所或毕生的积蓄。

5 在过去的47年里，数以百万计的美国民众为这一承诺而奋斗并得到了兑现。而对于很多老年人而言，通过医保得到的医疗服务使他们的生活全然不同。

6 作为一位由单身母亲抚养成人的孩子，我的成长得益于祖父祖母的帮助。我也曾看到像医疗保障及社会保障这些福利对于老年人的生活是多么的重要。而且我也看到了这些福利能够使他们的心灵得到慰藉。

7 正是因为如此，身为总统，当下我的目标就是要巩固这些计划并为我们的子孙后代传承下去。因为今天的老人们也应该得到同样的心灵上的慰藉。现在正在努力拼搏的无数美国人应该知道，他们所应得到的关照在他们需要的时候是可以得到的。

8 正是因为如此，作为《平价医疗法案》的一部分，我们在处方药上给老年人们提供更大的折扣，让乳房X线检查等预防性保健服务再也不需额外支付固定费用。我们将医保法案的生命周期延长了将近10年。我还提出了数项改革措施，通过打击医疗保险体系中的铺张浪费以及严格管理保险公司节约了医保资金，而这些改革肯定不会触及你们医保法案的福利。一个子儿都不会碰。

9 国会的共和党人提出了一套截然不同的方案。他们想把医保法改成医疗代金券计划。这将意味着老年人得不到有保障的医疗服务，而要通过获得的代金券去购买保险，但这些代金券是跟不上医疗支出增长的步伐的。因此，这一计划将迫使老年人每年多花6,400美元来获得他们现在已经享受到的同等福利待遇。而结果正如我们所知道的那样，这实际上就是废除了医保法案。

10 我认为老年人们应该获得更为悉心的照料。我真心希望与任何致力于改进这一现有体系的人合作，但拒绝做任何有损医保基本理念的事情。医保应是老年人生病时的有力保障。

11 在美国，恪守承诺才能赢得信赖——尤其是对老人们而言，他们一生辛勤劳作，理应安享晚年的黄金岁月。这就是医疗保险的本意。正是因为如此，我们需要巩固并为我们的子孙后代保留这一医疗保险。只要我还在总统的任上，我将继续为之不懈努力。

12 谢谢大家，祝你们周末愉快。

第35周

Honoring Our Nation's Service Members and Military Families

September 01, 2012

向为国服役的军人及其家人致敬

2012 年 9 月 1 日

【摘要导读】

本周，巴拉克•奥巴马总统在其广播电视讲话中，纪念美国在伊拉克作战任务结束两周年并对男女军人为国家所做的奉献表示感谢。

演讲再现 Original Text

1 Hi, everybody. On Friday, I visited *Fort Bliss* ① in Texas, where I met with some of our extraordinary men and women in uniform to mark the second anniversary of the end of major combat in Iraq.

2 It was a chance to thank our troops for the outstanding work they've done over the last decade. Fort Bliss is home to soldiers who took part in every major phase of *the Iraq War* ② — from the initial assault on *Baghdad* ③; to the years of fighting block by block; to the partnership with the Iraqi people that helped give them a chance to forge their own destiny.

3 And while the war itself remains a source of controversy here at home, one thing will never be in doubt — the members of our armed forces are patriots in every sense of the word. They met every mission and performed every task

Words & Expressions

assault [əˈsɔːlt] *n.* 攻击，突袭，抨击 *vt.* 袭击，突袭

controversy [ˈkɔntrəˌvəːsi] *n.* 争论，论战，辩论

that was asked of them with precision, commitment and skill. And now, with no Americans fighting in Iraq, it's my privilege on behalf of a grateful nation to once again congratulate these men and women on a job well done.

4 This anniversary is a chance to appreciate how far we've come. But it's also a reminder that there is still difficult work ahead of us in *Afghanistan*④. Some of the soldiers I met at Fort Bliss had just come home from the battlefield, and others are getting ready to ship out.

5 We've broken the *Taliban*⑤'s momentum in Afghanistan, and begun the transition to an Afghan lead. Next month, the last of the troops I ordered as part of the surge against the Taliban will come home, and by 2014, the transition to Afghan lead will be complete.

6 But as long as we have a single American in harm's way, we will continue to do everything in our power to keep them safe and help them succeed. That means giving them a clear mission and the equipment they need on the front lines. But it also means taking care of our veterans and their families. Because no one who fights for this country should have to fight for a job or a roof over their head when they come home.

7 I also told our soldiers at Bliss that part of honoring their service means strengthening the nation they fought so hard to protect. As we turn the page on a decade of war, it's time to do some nation-building here at home.

8 My grandfather's generation came back from World War II and helped form the backbone of the greatest middle-class in history. They helped this country come back stronger than before. Today's veterans have the skills, the discipline, and the leadership skills to do the exact same thing — and it's our job to give them that chance.

9 It's time to build a nation that lives up to the ideals that so many Americans have fought for — a nation where they can realize the dream they sacrificed to protect. We need to rebuild our roads and runways and ports. We need to lay broadband lines across this country and put our veterans back

precision [pri'siʒən] *n.* 精度，精密度，精确 *adj.* 精密的，精确的

momentum [məu'mentəm] *n.* 势头，动力

surge [sə:dʒ] *n.* 大浪，汹涌澎湃 *v.* 激增，汹涌，使颠簸

in harm's way 处于危险中，在战场上

broadband ['brɔ:d'bænd] *adj.* 宽频带的，宽波段的，宽频通讯的 *n.* 宽频，宽波段

to work as cops and firefighters in communities that need them. And we need to come together to make America a place where hard work is rewarded and anyone willing to put in the effort can make it if they try.

10 That's how we can honor our troops. That's the welcome home they've earned.

11 Thanks, and have a great weekend

背景知识注释 Background Notes

1. Fort Bliss 布里斯堡基地，位于新墨西哥州和得克萨斯州，但司令部设在得克萨斯州艾尔帕索城北，正门在10号州际公路和54号公路旁，建于1848年，占地110万英亩，为全美仅次于白沙导弹靶场的第二大军事设施。

2. the Iraq War 伊拉克战争，又称美伊战争，是以英美军队为主的联合部队在2003年3月20日对伊拉克发动的军事行动，美国以伊拉克藏有大规模杀伤性武器并暗中支持恐怖分子为由，绕开联合国安理会，单方面对伊拉克实施军事打击。到2010年8月美国战斗部队撤出伊拉克为止，历时7年多，美方最终没有找到所谓的大规模杀伤性武器，反而找到萨达姆政权早已将其销毁的文件和人证。2011年12月18日，美军全部撤出。

3. Baghdad 巴格达，伊拉克首都，巴格达省省会，伊斯兰世界历史文化名城。巴格达跨底格里斯河两岸，距幼发拉底河仅30多公里，处于东西方的交通要道，铁路、公路和航空构成陆地和空中的立体运输，十分便捷。铁路向北通往叙利亚和土耳其，向南延伸至波斯湾，也是国际东方快车的必经之地。在中东地区位于开罗、德黑兰和伊斯坦布尔之后列第四位。

4. Afghanistan 阿富汗伊斯兰共和国，是一个位于亚洲中南部的内陆国家，坐落在亚洲的心脏地区。它的位置有着不同的定义，有时候会被认为处在中亚或者南亚，甚至被归类于中东地区（西亚）。它与大部分比邻的国家有着宗教上、语言上、地理上相当程度的关联，领土的五分之三交通不便。农业是主要的经济支柱，但可耕地还不足农用地的三分之二，是世界上最贫穷的国家之一。时至今日，阿富汗仍呈现极度贫穷与派别割据的现象，久经战乱而破坏的基础设施、大量未爆地雷，还有大量非法鸦片与海洛因毒品贸易充斥其中。

5. Taliban 塔利班，发源于阿富汗的坎大哈地区的宗教激进主义运动组织。塔利班，在波斯语中是“学生”的意思，它的大部分成员是阿富汗难民营伊斯兰学校的学生，故又称伊斯兰学生军。其领导人是穆尔维·奥马尔。拉登被击毙后，塔利班2011年5月初称巴基斯坦将成为头号报复目标。

中文译文
Chinese Version

1 嗨，大家好！本周五，我视察了位于得克萨斯州的布里斯堡基地 (Fort Bliss)。在那里我会见了我们无与伦比的男女军人们，与他们一道纪念伊拉克战争结束两周年。

2 值此机会，我对我们的部队在过去十年里出色地完成各项任务表示诚挚的谢意。布里斯堡 (Fort Bliss) 是伊拉克战争期间每一个重要阶段战士们的家园——从开始对巴格达的突袭，到接下来数年间街区里的巷战，再到与伊拉克人民携手并进，帮助给予他们掌握自己命运的机会。

3 尽管在国内对这场战争本身还存在着诸多的争议，但有一点是不容置疑的：我们武装力量的成员无论在何种意义上来说都是爱国主义者。他们所经历的每一次战斗，执行的每一次任务，都要求他们严谨精准、勇于奉献和技能娴熟。现在，我们在伊拉克已经没有作战人员，我谨代表一个感恩的国家向他们优异的表现再次表示祝贺。

4 这个周年纪念日，给了我们一个机会回味我们所走过的历程，但也提醒我们，在阿富汗，仍然有许多艰巨的工作有待我们去完成。我在布里斯堡 (Fort Bliss) 见到的士兵，有些刚刚从战场班师回朝，另一些则正整装待发。

5 我们已经粉碎了阿富汗塔利班的进攻势头，开始向由阿富汗发挥主导作用的阶段过渡。下个月，我下令增兵打击塔利班的最后一批部队将启程回国，到 2014 年，将完成向由阿富汗发挥主导作用的阶段过渡。

6 然而，只要我们的同胞还受到威胁，我们都会继续竭尽全力保障他们的安全并且帮助他们脱离险境。这就需要给部队明确的任务，并向他们提供前线所需的装备。这也意味着，要照顾好我们的退伍军人及其家属。因为，任何为我们国家而浴血奋战的人，都不应该在回国之后再为寻找一份工作或是寻求一个栖身之所而继续“战斗”。

7 在布里斯堡 (Fort Bliss)，我还告诉我们的战士们：我们要把他们不辞辛劳奋力保护的国家建设得更加强盛，这才是对他们为国奉献崇敬之情的内涵。当我们翻开十年战争之后的崭新篇章，现在到了美国本土搞好国内建设的时候了。

8 我外祖父那一代人从二战战场回国。他们成了帮助构建我国历史上最伟大的中产阶级的中坚力量。在他们的帮助下，我们的国家变得比以往更加强大了。今天的退伍军人拥有的娴熟技艺、严明纪律和领导才能足以让他们成就同样辉煌的事业——而我们义不容辞的责任就是给他们一个机会。

9 现在到了建设我们国家的时候了，这样才能不辜负诸多美国人为之奋斗的理想——这是一个他们牺牲自己生命保护、要让大家都能实现自己梦想的国度。我们需要重建我们的道路、机场和港口。我们需要铺设遍布全国的宽带网络，让我们的退伍军人像警察、消防队员一样在社会上需要他们的地方重回工作岗位。我们需要团结起来让美国成为只要辛勤工作就能得到回报，任何愿意付出的人都能获得成功的国度。

10 唯有如此，才是我们对自己军队所应表示的敬意。唯有如此，才是他们荣归故里时实至名归的欢迎。

11 谢谢，祝大家周末愉快！

第36周

Coming Together to Remember September 11th

September 8, 2012

一同纪念 9·11

2012 年 9 月 8 日

【摘要导读】

在本周的广播电视讲话中，巴拉克·奥巴马总统强调在9·11袭击11周年纪念日，美国人民要怀念那些失去的无辜的亲人们，并向那些紧急救援人员和为国服役甚至牺牲自己生命来保护美国安宁的男女指战员们致敬。他说：经历袭击之后的艰难岁月，美国又重新变得比以往更加强大；美国摧毁了基地组织的领导机构，并巩固了与世界各地盟友间的关系，让乌萨马·本·拉登再也没有机会袭击美国；展望未来，美国将继续向世人展示9·11留下的精神遗产：那就是任何敌人或恐怖袭击都不能改变美国人的本色，而美国人民永远都会团结一致来呵护和保卫美国。

演讲再现 Original Text

1 This week, we mark the eleventh anniversary of *the September 11th attacks*[①]. It's a time to remember the nearly 3,000 innocent men, women and children we lost, and the families they left behind. It's a chance to honor the courage of the first responders who risked their lives — on that day, and every day since. And it's an opportunity to give thanks for our men and women in uniform who have served and sacrificed, sometimes far from home, to keep our country safe.

2 This anniversary is about them. It's also a time to reflect on just how far we've come as a nation these past eleven years.

Words & Expressions

the first responders 紧急救援人员

3 On that clear September morning, as America watched the towers fall, and *the Pentagon* ② burn, and the wreckage smoldering in a Pennsylvania field, we were filled with questions. Where had the attacks come from, and how would America respond? Would they fundamentally weaken the country we love? Would they change who we are?

4 The last decade has been a difficult one, but together, we have answered those questions and come back stronger as a nation.

5 We took the fight to al Qaeda, decimated their leadership, and put them on a path to defeat. And thanks to the courage and skill of our intelligence personnel and armed forces, Osama bin Laden will never threaten America again.

6 Instead of pulling back from the world, we've strengthened our alliances while improving our security here at home. As Americans, we refuse to live in fear. Today, a new tower rises above the New York skyline. And our country is stronger, safer and more respected in the world.

7 Instead of turning on each other, we've resisted the temptation to give in to mistrust and suspicion. I have always said that America is at war with al Qaeda and its affiliates — and we will never be at war with Islam or any other religion. We are the United States of America. Our freedom and diversity make us unique, and they will always be central to who we are as a nation.

8 Instead of changing who we are, the attacks have brought out the best in the American people. More than 5 million members of *the 9/11 Generation* ③ have worn America's uniform over the past decade, and we've seen an outpouring of goodwill towards our military, veterans, and their families. Together, they've done everything we've asked of them. We've ended the war in Iraq and brought our troops home. We brought an end to the Taliban regime. We've trained Afghan Security Forces, and forged a partnership with a new Afghan Government. And by the end 2014, the transition in Afghanistan will be complete and our war there will be over.

wreckage [ˈrekidʒ] *n.*（失事船或飞机等的）残骸，（船只等的）失事

decimate [ˈdesimeit] *vt.* 十中抽一，取十分之一，大批杀害，毁掉

pull back from 撤出，撤回

diversity [daiˈvəːsiti] *n.* 多样性，差异

forge [fɔːdʒ] *vt.* 锻造，伪造，建立 *vi.* 伪造，做铁匠

9 And finally, instead of turning inward with grief, we've honored the memory of those we lost by giving back to our communities, serving those in need, and reaffirming the values at the heart of who we are as a people. That's why we mark September 11th as a National Day of Service and Remembrance. Because we are one American family. And we look out for each other — not just on the difficult days, but every day.

10 Eleven years later, that's the legacy of 9/11 — the ability to say with confidence that no adversary and no act of terrorism can change who we are. We are Americans, and we will protect and preserve this country we love. On this solemn anniversary, let's remember those we lost, let us reaffirm the values they stood for, and let us keep moving forward as one nation and one people.

adversary ['ædvəsəri] *n.* 对手，敌手

背景知识注释 Background Notes

1. the September 11th attacks　9•11 恐怖袭击事件，简称 9•11。
2. the Pentagon　五角大楼，美国国防部。它于 1941 年 9 月 11 日破土动工，1943 年 1 月 15 日完成，位于美国华盛顿特区西南方的弗吉尼亚州阿灵顿县，是美国国防部办公地，美国最高军事指挥机关所在地。由于其特殊的职能，所以有时“五角大楼”一词不仅仅代表这座建筑本身，也常常用做美国国防部的代名词。
3. the 9/11 Generation　9•11 一代人，指的是美国被 9•11 事件激发的新一代爱国主义者。

中文译文 Chinese Version

1　本周，我们纪念 9•11 遇袭事件 11 周年。在这个时刻，我们追念在袭击中逝去的将近 3,000 名无辜的男女老少，并向他们的亲属表示亲切的慰问。在这个时刻，我们向紧急救援人员表示崇高的敬意。他们在那一天以及此后的日日夜夜里，英勇无畏地冒着危险舍己救人。我们向身着戎装为国服役并做出牺牲的男女军人们表达诚挚的谢意。为了保家卫国他们有时得远离故土。

2　这是个向他们表示敬意的纪念日。这也是反思过去 11 年我们作为一个国家风雨路程的时刻。

3 在那年9月一个晴朗的早晨，美国目睹了双子大楼轰然倒塌，五角大楼起火燃烧，飞机残骸在宾夕法尼亚田野中焚毁殆尽，心中不禁充满了疑问。这些袭击来自何方，美国应该如何应对，我们所深爱的国家是否从此一蹶不振？我们是否会因此丧失自己的本色？

4 过去的十年荆棘载途，但我们共克时艰，回应了这些难题，再次重振国之雄风。

5 我们打击了基地组织，摧毁了他们的领导机构，使他们走上了不归之路。由于我们的情报人员和武装力量大智大勇，乌萨马·本·拉登再也无法对美国造成威胁。

6 我们没有在世界上退守一隅。相反，我们加强了联盟的力量，同时改善了国内的安全形势。作为美国人，我们拒绝生活在恐惧之中。今天，一座崭新的高楼在纽约直冲云霄。我们的国家也变得更加强盛，更为安全，并受到全世界更多的尊重。

7 我们没有相互指责，而是抵挡住了各种诱惑，避免陷入不可自拔的猜忌和怀疑中。我经常表示，美国正在与基地组织及其附庸作战，但是我们永远都不会与伊斯兰教或其他任何宗教信仰为敌。我们是美利坚合众国。正是崇尚自由和包容多元使我们独树一帜。自由与多元始终是我们的立国之本。

8 袭击非但没有改变美国人民的本色，反之，让我们展示了自己最优秀的品质。十年来，500多万"9·11一代人"投身军旅。我们看到了军人、老兵及其家人处处受到了应有的尊重和热情的欢迎。他们同心协力完成了我们要求他们做的每一件工作。我们结束了在伊拉克的战争，回撤了我们的军队。我们推翻了塔利班政权。我们为阿富汗安全部队提供训练，与阿富汗新政府建立了伙伴关系。到2014年底，阿富汗将完成过渡，而我们在那里的战事将宣告结束。

9 最后，我们化悲痛为力量，用回馈社会的方式来缅怀那些我们所失去的人们，为需要的人提供服务，再次树立我们作为一个民族的核心价值观。正是因为如此，我们将9月11日确定为"全国奉献和纪念日"。因为我们同属美国这一大家庭。我们不仅在艰难的日子里相互守望，而且每一天都互相搀扶。

10 11年以后的今天，我们有能力满怀自信地说，任何敌人或任何恐怖袭击都无法改变我们的本色，这就是9·11为我们留下的精神遗产。我们是美国人，我们将永远呵护和保卫我们深爱着的国家。在这一庄严的纪念日里，让我们铭记那些失去的生命，重申他们所坚守的价值观，作为一个民族与一个国家，团结起来共同前进。

第37周

Carrying on the Work of Our Fallen Heroes

September 15, 2012

继承先烈的遗志

2012 年 9 月 15 日

【摘要导读】

在本周的广播电视讲话中，巴拉克•奥巴马总统谈到了在利比亚班加西从事外交工作的四名美国同胞不幸遇害。他表示：这些美国人是美国最优秀的代表，倘若没有像他们这样的人，美国就不可能保持如今所享有的自由，不可能拥有所需要的安全，更不会具备世界各国所倚重的领导力。另外，他还强调绝对不能容忍任何伤害美国人民的行径。他保证将把那些袭击民众的人绳之以法。

演讲再现 Original Text

1 This week in Libya, we lost four of our fellow Americans. *Glen Doherty*①, *Tyrone Woods*②, *Sean Smith*③, and *Chris Stevens*④ were all killed in an outrageous attack on our diplomatic post in *Benghazi*⑤.

2 These four Americans represented the very best of our country.

3 Glen and Tyrone had each served America as *Navy SEALs*⑥ for many years, before continuing their service providing security for our diplomats in Libya. They died as they lived their lives — defending their fellow Americans, and advancing the values that all of us hold dear.

4 Sean also started his service in uniform, in the Air Force. He then spent years at the State Department, on several continents, always answering his country's call. And

Words & Expressions

outrageous [aut'reidʒəs] *adj.* 粗暴的，可恶的，令人吃惊的

Ambassador Chris Stevens died a hero in two countries — here in the United States, where he inspired those of us who knew him; and in Libya, a country that he helped to save, where he ultimately laid down his life.

5 On Friday, I was able to tell their families how much the American people appreciated their service. Without people like them, America could not sustain the freedoms we enjoy, the security we demand, and the leadership that the entire world counts on.

6 As we mourn their loss, we must also send a clear and resolute message to the world: those who attack our people will find no escape from justice. We will not waver in their pursuit. And we will never allow anyone to shake the resolve of the United States of America.

7 This tragic attack takes place at a time of turmoil and protest in many different countries. I have made it clear that the United States has a profound respect for people of all faiths. We stand for religious freedom. And we reject the denigration of any religion — including Islam.

8 But there is never any justification for violence. There is no religion that condones the targeting of innocent men and women. There is no excuse for attacks on our Embassies and Consulates. And so long as I am Commander-in-Chief, the United States will never tolerate efforts to harm our fellow Americans.

9 Right now, we are doing whatever we can to protect Americans who are serving abroad. We are in contact with governments around the globe, to strengthen our cooperation, and underscore that every nation has a responsibility to help us protect our people. We have moved forward with an effort to see that justice is done for those we lost, and we will not rest until that work is done.

10 Most of all, we must reaff irm that we will carry on the work of our fallen heroes.

11 I know the images on our televisions are disturbing. But let us never forget that for every angry mob, there are millions who yearn for the freedom, and dignity, and hope that

sustain [sə'stein] *vt.* 支持，承受，维持，认可，经受

waver ['weivə] *v.* 动摇，摇曳，犹豫，颤抖 *n.* 动摇，踌躇

denigration [ˌdeni'greiʃən] *n.* 诋毁

justification [ˌdʒʌstifi'keiʃən] *n.* 理由，辩护，认为有理，认为正当，释罪

condone [kən'dəun] *vt.* 宽恕，赦免

underscore ['ʌndə'skɔː] *vt.* 画线于，强调

mob [mɔb] *n.* 暴徒，民众，乌合之众

yearn for 极想，渴望

our flag represents. That is the cause of America — the ideals that took root in our founding; the opportunity that drew so many to our shores; and the awesome progress that we have promoted all across the globe.

12 We are Americans. We know that our spirit cannot be broken, and the foundation of our leadership cannot be shaken. That is the legacy of the four Americans we lost — men who will live on in the hearts of those they loved, and the strength of the country they served.

13 So with their memory to guide us, we will carry forward the work of making our country stronger, our citizens safer, and the world a better and more hopeful place. Thanks.

take root 生根，建立，确立

shores [ʃɔːz] *n.* 国家

awesome [ˈɔːsəm] *adj.* 可怕的，表示敬畏的，了不起的，精彩的，绝妙的

legacy [ˈlegəsi] *n.* 遗赠，遗产

背景知识注释 Background Notes

1. Glen Doherty 盖伦·多尔蒂（1970—2012.9.11），前“海豹”突击队员。

2. Tyrone Woods 蒂龙·伍兹（1971.1.15—2012.9.11），前“海豹”突击队员。

3. Sean Smith 肖恩·史密斯（1978—2012.9.11），早年曾在空军服役六年，是美国外交服务处信息管理官员、在网络游戏世界颇具知名度的电脑专家。

4. Chris Stevens 即 Christopher Stevens 克里斯·斯蒂文森（1960.4.18—2012.9.11），1982年毕业于柏克莱加州大学。1983至1985年，他作为美国和平队的一名志愿者在摩洛哥教授英语。1989年，他取得加州大学法学院的法律博士学位。2010年取得国家战争学院(National War College) 理学硕士。他能讲阿拉伯语和法语。在进入美国外交部门工作以前，他在华盛顿特区是一名国际贸易领域的律师。1990年代，他曾在沙特阿拉伯、埃及、叙利亚和以色列等中东国家工作，分别于2007年和2011年派驻利比亚。2012年6月到9月担任美国驻利比亚第10任大使。2012年9月11日，他在利比亚班加西遭到袭击身亡。他也因此成为自1979年美国驻阿富汗大使阿道夫·达布斯 (Adolph Dubs) 在喀布尔遭绑架遇害33年以来，首位遇袭殉职的在任美国大使。

5. Benghazi 班加西，利比亚第二大城和重要海港，班加西区首府。它是古代重镇，为通往非洲内陆的商贸中心；有纺织、鱼类加工、水泥等工业；交通枢纽，有国际航空站，建有巨大的海水淡化厂，冬季旅游、疗养胜地。

6. Navy SEALs 即 SEALs 或 United States Navy Sea, Air and Land Teams 美国海军三栖特种部队，一般称做海豹部队，是直属美国海军的一支特种部队，亦是世界知名的特种三栖部队，主要任务包括：非常规战争、国内外防御、直接行动、反恐怖主义行动、特殊侦查

任务五项。要成为一个三栖特战队成员并不容易，甄选者必须先通过基础水下爆破训练 (Basic Underwater Demolition/SEAL，BUD/S) 以及专业的三栖资格训练 (SEAL Qualification Training，SQT)，最后才能佩带显示三栖特战队的佩章。这枚佩章已经不仅仅是代表整个三栖特战队，间接也成为被广泛辨识的美国特战部队的佩章之一。

中文译文

Chinese Version

1　本周我们在利比亚失去了我们的四位同胞。盖伦•多尔蒂 (Glen Doherty)、蒂龙•伍兹 (Tyrone Woods)、肖恩•史密斯 (Sean Smith) 和克里斯•斯蒂文森 (Chris Stevens) 在我们驻班加西 (Benghazi) 领事馆遭受的一次极其卑劣的袭击中被害身亡。

2　这四位美国人是我们国家最为优秀的代表。

3　盖伦 (Glen) 和蒂龙 (Tyrone) 曾在海军海豹突击队效力多年，后来到利比亚担任保卫我国外交官员的任务，继续为国家服务。他们用生命诠释了自己的一生：永远保护自己的美国同胞，并弘扬我们所珍视的价值观。

4　肖恩 (Sean) 的奉献也始于军队，他曾在空军服役。后来在国务院工作多年，他总是听从国家的召唤，足迹遍及几大洲。美国驻利比亚大使——克里斯•史蒂文斯 (Chris Stevens) 的死使他成为两个国家的英雄——在这里，即在美国，他激励了我们这些认识他的人；在利比亚，他把生命最终献给了这个他帮助拯救的国家。

5　本周五，我终于能告诉他们的家人：我们的国民们是多么感激他们所付出的一切。倘若没有像他们这样的人，我们的国家就不可能享有我们所喜爱的自由，不可能拥有我们所需要的安全，更不会具备世界各国所倚重的领导力。

6　在哀悼逝去的英灵之际，我们必须向全世界发出明确且坚定的信息：袭击我国公民的人绝不会逃脱法律的制裁。我们对这些人的追捕绝不动摇。我们也绝不会允许任何人动摇我们美利坚合众国的意志。

7　这次不幸的袭击发生在许多国家出现动荡骚乱和示威抗议之中。我已经很明确地表示：我们绝对地尊重所有人的宗教信仰。我们倡导宗教信仰自由。我们反对对任何宗教的诋毁——这其中包括伊斯兰教。

8　然而，暴力行径从来就没有任何正当的理由。任何宗教也绝不会宽恕以无辜男女作为袭击目标的人。袭击我们的大使馆和领事馆更是毫无道理。只要我还在总司令的任上，美国就绝不容忍任何伤害我国同胞的行径。

9　现在，我们将尽一切努力来保护那些在海外工作的美国人。我们与世界各国的政府保持着联系，加强我们之间的合作，并强调每个国家都有帮助保护我国国民的义务。我们会不断努力，等待着见证为那些我们失去的人伸张正义。不达目的，誓不罢休。

10　最重要的是，我们必须重申：我们将继承先烈的遗志。

11 我深知这几天电视上的画面让人揪心。但我们永远都不要忘记：我们看到的只是一群愤怒的暴民，千百万人向往我们的国旗所代表的自由、尊严和希望。这就是美国的事业——那些根植于我们立国之初的追求，那些吸引千千万万移民来到我们国家的机遇，以及我们在世界各地所推动的令人瞩目的进步。

12 我们是美国人。我们知道我们的精神坚不可摧，我们的领导地位的基石牢不可破。这就是我们失去的四位美国同胞留给我们的遗产——他们将永远活在那些他们所热爱的人们心中，并化做他们为之效力的国家所具有的力量。

13 因此，在缅怀之情的激励之下，我们将推进他们未竟的事业，把我们的国家建设得更为强盛，让我们的公民享有更多的安全，使世界变得更加美好且充满更多的希望。谢谢大家。

第38周

Congress Must Act to Create Jobs and Grow the Economy

September 22, 2012

国会必须采取行动以创造就业机会并促进经济增长

2012年9月22日

【摘要导读】

在本周的广播电视讲话中，巴拉克•奥巴马总统告诉美国民众，众议院上周休会放假时，并未完成创造就业机会和巩固国家经济等重要工作；国会把诸如有关组建退伍军人就业协会以帮助荣归故里的英雄们找到像警察或消防员这样的工作的法案，以及帮助农牧民应对像今年夏天干旱这样的自然灾害的农业法案等全都留在办公桌上了。他还指出国会原本也应给信用良好的房屋贷款人一个机会，让他们通过有史以来最低的利率重新转按揭贷款，这样他们每年在抵押贷款上可以节省3,000美元；并向98%的美国民众和97%的小微企业主做出一个明年的税收不会上涨的保证。他进一步强调这些提案是两党共同支持的，没有理由不通过。他号召国会在11月份复会后采取措施，以一个强大和稳固的中产阶级作为工作的出发点，促进经济增长，把国家推向前进。

演讲再现

Original Text

1 Hi, everybody. Last week, without much fanfare, Members of the House of Representatives banged a gavel, turned out the lights, and rushed home, declaring their work finished for now.

2 If that frustrates you, it should — because their work isn't finished.

3 See, when they skipped town, Members of Congress left a whole bunch of proposals sitting on the table — actions

Words & Expressions

fanfare ['fænfeə] *n.* 夸耀

gavel ['gævəl] *n.* 议事槌

for now 目前，暂时

frustrate [frʌs'treit] *vt.* 挫败，阻挠，使感到灰心

skip town 离开，溜走

that would create jobs, boost our economy, and strengthen middle-class security. These ideas have been around for months. The American people want to see them passed. But apparently, some Members of Congress are more worried about their jobs and their paychecks this campaign season than they are about yours.

4 Right now, if Congress had done the right thing, we could be on our way to having a *veterans' jobs corps*① that helps returning heroes find work as cops and firefighters in communities all across the country. These men and women have made incredible sacrifices for our country. They shouldn't have to worry about finding a job when they get home. But last week, Republicans in Congress voted it down. And then they left.

5 Right now, if Congress had gotten its act together, we would have a farm bill to help farmers and ranchers respond to natural disasters like the drought we had this summer. And we'd have made necessary reforms to give our rural communities some long-term certainty. But so far, Republicans in Congress have dragged their feet. And now they're gone.

6 Right now, if Congress had acted, thousands of responsible homeowners could be saving an extra $3,000 a year on their mortgages by refinancing at historically low rates. But instead, Republicans in Congress decided that working families could wait. And now they'll have to wait a little longer.

7 And finally, if Congress had listened to you, they could have given 98% of Americans and 97% of small business owners a guarantee that your taxes won't go up next year by a single dime. This is something we all agree on. It should have gotten done a long time ago. But Republicans in Congress have refused to budge. They're holding tax cuts for 98% of Americans hostage until we pass tax cuts for the wealthiest 2% of Americans. And now middle-class families and small business owners are left wondering what their tax bill will look like next year.

8 All of these ideas would strengthen our economy and

around [ə'raund] *adv.* 大约，到处，在附近 *adj.* 存在着的，流通着，可得到的

vote... down 否决，罢免

drag one's feet 拖拉，拖着脚走，不合作

help the middle-class right now. All of them are supported by Democrats, Republicans and Independents. There's no reason to wait.

9 That's why, after going home and listening to their constituents for a few weeks, Members of Congress should come back in November and do this work. They should do the right thing for veterans and farmers; for responsible homeowners and small businesses; for Americans everywhere who are just trying to get ahead.

an answering machine 录音电话

10 And if you agree with me, I need your help. Tell your Members of Congress you can't afford to wait any longer. If you get an answering machine, leave a message. If you see them campaigning back home, tell them in person. Because there's been enough talk. It's time for action. That's what you deserve, and that's what it's going to take to move this country forward.

11 Thanks, and have a wonderful weekend.

背景知识注释 Background Notes

1. veterans' jobs corps 退伍军人就业协会。

中文译文 Chinese Version

1 嗨，大家好。上周，众议院的议员们落槌定音，关灯拉闸，悄无声息地匆匆回家，并宣布他们的工作暂告一个段落。

2 倘若这让你感到沮丧的话，那么事实上也的确如此——因为他们的工作远未完成。

3 瞧，当国会议员们匆匆离开这个城市时，桌子上留下的是厚厚一叠提案——包括创造就业、提振经济以及增强中产阶级安全感等等。这些想法已经提出来好几个月了。美国人民希望通过这些议案。但很显然，一些国会议员在这个选季更关心的是他们自己的饭碗和腰包，而非你们的问题。

4 倘若国会已经采取的行动正确的话，我们现在就能组建一个促进退伍军人就业的团体来帮助凯旋的英雄们在全国各地社区找到诸如警察和消防队员这样的工作了。这些男女士兵为我们的国家做出了巨大牺牲。他们不应该在归国返乡之后还要为找到一份工作而担忧。但是上周，国会中的共和党人却投票否决了这个提案，然后扬长而去。

5 倘若国会同心协力采取行动的话，我们现在应该已经通过了一个农场法案来帮助农牧民们应对我们今年夏天遭遇的这类自然灾害。而且我们还可以进行必要的改革来为农村社区提供一些长期的保障。但是迄今为止，共和党国会议员一直踟蹰不前。现在倒好，他们溜了。

6 倘若国会有所作为的话，那么现在成千上万的信用良好的房屋贷款人可能已经通过有史以来最低的利率重新转按揭贷款，这样他们每年在抵押贷款上可以节省3,000美元。但是，相反地，国会的共和党人决定让这些工薪家庭等待下去。现在他们可能要等上更长的时间了。

7 最后，倘若国会能够倾听你们的心声，那么他们可能已经给予98%的美国民众和97%的小微企业主一个保证——即他们明年的税赋一个子也不涨。这是我们大家都认同的事情，早就应该这样做了。而国会中的共和党人拒绝调整预算，他们以此为要挟要为2%美国最富有的群体减税。结果现在中产家庭和小微企业主被弄得一头雾水，不知道下一年他们的税单会是什么样子的。

8 所有这些提议在当下可以巩固我们的经济，并帮助中产阶级。所有这些提议都得到民主党人、共和党或无党派人士的支持。没有理由再等下去了。

9 正是因为如此，在回家休假并听取他们的选民的心声几个星期之后，国会议员们将在11月重返岗位着手这一工作。他们应该为退伍军人、农民、诚实守信的房主、小微企业以及在各地努力奋斗希望获得成功的美国人做些正确的抉择。

10 倘若你同意我的观点，我急需你们的帮助。告诉你们的国会议员们，你们不能再等下去了。倘若是录音电话，请留言。倘若你们看到他们回家拉选票了，请亲口告诉他们。因为已经讨论得差不多了。该是行动的时候了。这是你们应有的权利，而也是为推动国家前进所应该采取的措施。

11 谢谢，祝大家周末愉快！

第39周

It's Time for Congress to Help Responsible Homeowners

September 29, 2012

该是国会出手帮助信誉良好的房屋贷款人的时候了

2012 年 9 月 29 日

【摘要导读】

在本周的广播电视讲话中，巴拉克•奥巴马总统告诉美国民众，四年前的今天，一场很大程度上由房地产市场不负责任的行为引发的金融危机几乎摧毁了整个美国经济。四年后，房地产市场缓慢复苏，但远未达到目标。正是因为如此，政府采取了数项激进措施来帮助人们保住自己的房子。这些措施包括给诚实守信的房主重新转按揭贷款的机会，这样他们每年可以节省数千美元。但这需要国会的帮助来做更多的事情。

演讲再现 Original Text

Words & Expressions

free-fall 突然大幅下跌

make payroll 开工资，做工资单

likes [laiks] *n.* 相似的人（或物），相对物，相配物

reckless ['reklis] *adj.* 不在意的，粗心的，鲁莽的

secure [si'kjuə] *vt.* 使安全，获得，固定 *vi.* 停泊，（海上工作人员）停止工作，抛锚 *adj.* 安全的，牢靠的，稳妥的

1 Hi, everybody. Four years ago this month, a crisis that started out on *Wall Street* ① almost brought down our entire economy. The nation's biggest banks were days away from failing. The stock market — and millions of American retirement accounts — were in free-fall. Credit froze. Lending stopped. And businesses large and small didn't even know if they'd be able to make payroll. It was a moment the likes of which few Americans had ever seen.

2 Today, we know the biggest cause of that crisis was reckless behavior in the housing market.

3 Millions of Americans who did the right and responsible thing — who shopped for a home, secured a mortgage they could afford, and made their payments on time

— were badly hurt by the irresponsible actions of others. By lenders who sold loans to families who couldn't afford them — and buyers who knew they couldn't afford them. By speculators who were looking to make a quick buck. And by banks that packaged and sold those risky mortgages for phony profits.

4 When the party stopped, and the housing bubble burst, it pushed our entire economy into a historic recession — and left middle-class families holding the bag.

5 Four years later, the housing market is healing. Home sales and construction are up. Prices are beginning to rise. And more than a million families who began this year owing more on their mortgages than their homes are worth, are now back above water.

6 We're moving in the right direction. But we're not there yet. There are still millions of Americans who are struggling with their mortgages, even at a time of historically low rates.

7 Now, I know there are some who think that the only option for homeowners is to just stand by and hope that the market has hit bottom. I don't agree with that.

8 That's why my Administration teamed up with state attorneys general to investigate the terrible way many homeowners were treated, and secured a settlement from the nation's biggest banks — banks that were bailed out with taxpayer dollars — to help families stay in their homes.

9 And that's why we announced new steps to help responsible homeowners refinance their mortgages. Already, hundreds of thousands of Americans who were stuck in high-interest loans have been able to take advantage of lower rates and save thousands of dollars every year.

10 That's not only good for those families; it's also good for our economy. When folks are spending less on mortgage payments, they're spending more at local businesses. And when those businesses have more customers, they start hiring more workers.

11 But we can do even more if Congress is willing to

speculator [ˈspekjuleitə] *n.* 投机者，思索者

buck [bʌk] *n.* 一笔钱，（一）美元

package [ˈpækidʒ] *vt.* 打包，将…包装 *n.* 包，包裹 *adj.* 一揽子的

phony [ˈfəuni] *adj.* [口]假的，欺骗的 *n.* 假冒者，赝品

hold the bag 独自承担责任，背别人摔掉的包袱，背黑锅，代人受过

back above water 回到水面上，解套

state attorneys general 州大法官

bail out 帮助摆脱

do their part.

12 Back in February I sent Congress a plan to give every responsible homeowner the chance to save about $3,000 a year on their mortgages by refinancing at lower rates. It's a plan that has the support of independent, nonpartisan economists and leaders across the housing industry. But Republicans in Congress worked to keep it from even getting to a vote. And here we are — seven months later — still waiting on Congress to act.

13 This makes no sense. Last week, mortgage rates were at historic lows. But instead of helping more and more hardworking families take advantage of those rates, Congress was away on break. Instead of worrying about you, they'd already gone home to worry about their campaigns.

nonpartisan [ˌnɒnpɑːtiˈzæn] *adj.* 无党派的，超党派的 *n.* 无党派的人

14 The truth is, it's going to take a while for our housing market to fully recover. But it's going to take a lot more time — and cause a lot more hurt — if Congress keeps standing in the way. If you agree with me, I hope you'll make your voices heard. Call your Representative. Send them an email. Show up at their town hall and tell them that when Congress comes back to Washington, they better come back ready to work. All of you are doing everything you can to meet your responsibilities. It's time Congress did the same.

15 Thanks and have a great weekend.

背景知识注释 Background Notes

1. Wall Street 华尔街，是纽约市曼哈顿区南部从百老汇路延伸到东河的一条大街道的名字，全长仅三分之一英里，宽仅 11 米，是英文"墙街"的音译。街道狭窄而短，从百老汇到东河仅有 7 个街段，却以"美国的金融中心"闻名于世。美国摩根财阀、洛克菲勒石油大王和杜邦财团等开设的银行、保险、航运、铁路等公司的经理处集中于此。著名的纽约证券交易所也在这里，至今仍是几个主要交易所的总部：如纳斯达克、美国证券交易所、纽约期货交易所等。"华尔街"一词现已超越这条街道本身，成为附近区域的代称，亦可指对整个美国经济具有影响力的金融市场和金融机构。

中文译文
Chinese Version

1 嗨，大家好！四年前的这个月，一场肇始于华尔街的危机几乎拖垮了我们的整个经济。我国最大的银行只差几天就要倒闭。股票市场以及数百万人的退休金账户都摇摇欲坠。信贷冻结，借贷停止。所有企业，无论大小甚至都不知道还能不能给员工发工资了。那种景象几乎没有多少美国人有过亲身经历。

2 今天，我们都知道这场危机最根本的原因就是房地产市场的草率行为。

3 成千上万的人们所做的事情正确而负责任——他们买房子，在自己的能力范围内妥善安排抵押贷款，按时还款——却被其他人毫不负责任的行为所伤害。这些人包括向没有还贷能力的家庭发放贷款的放贷人——而这些贷款买房人自己都不知道能不能还上贷款；还包括那些想赚快钱的投机者，以及将这些高风险的抵押品打包销售以骗取丰厚利润的银行。

4 当这样的游戏结束，房地产泡沫破裂了，我们的整个经济陷入到历史上严重的衰退之中，包袱却被甩给了中产家庭。

5 四年以后，房地产市场正在恢复。房屋销售和建设都有所回升。房价也开始上涨。有 100 多万个家庭今年年初拥有的房产的价值要低于他们承担的抵押贷款，现在也已开始解套了。

6 我们正沿着正确的方向前进。但是我们远未大功告成。现在仍然有成千上万的人们正在为他们的抵押而苦苦地奋斗，尽管是在这利率创历史低点的时刻。

7 现在，我知道有些人认为房主们的唯一选择就是坐视和期待市场触底反弹。我可不敢苟同。

8 正是因为如此，本届政府与各个州的大法官们联手调查让房主们受到坑害的卑劣行径，从我国最大的一些银行寻求安全的解决方案——因为这些银行曾得到纳税人的紧急援助——以便帮助这些家庭保住自己的房子。

9 正是因为如此，我们宣布了几项新的措施来帮助信用良好的房主做转按揭贷款。现在，已经有数十万身陷高利率贷款的人可以利用这一较低的利率，这样每年可节省数千美元。

10 这不仅仅对那些家庭有利，对我们的经济也有利。当人们在房屋抵押贷款上支出少一些，他们就能在当地企业上多支出一些。当这些企业有了更多的顾客，他们就能开始雇用更多的员工。

11 但是倘若国会愿意履行自己的职责，我们甚至还可以做得更多。

12 回首今年 2 月，我向国会提交了一个方案，给诚信的房主以较低的利率重做转按揭贷款的机会，让他们每年节省 3,000 美元。这个方案得到了无党派独立经济学家以及房地产行业领袖们的支持。但国会的共和党人拼命阻挠，甚至连投票表决的机会都不给。现在，七个月过去了，我们依然还在等待国会的表决。

13 这毫无道理。上周，抵押贷款利率降到了历史最低点。但国会非但没有帮助越来越多辛勤劳作的家庭利用这一利率良机，反而休假去了。看得出来，他们并不关心你们，他们已经回家考虑自己的选举大事去了。

14 事实是，我们房产市场的全面恢复尚待时日。但倘若国会继续阻挠，恢复的过程将需要更长的时间，并引发更多的伤痛。倘若你们同意我的观点，我希望你们表达自己的心声。给你们的议员们打电话，发电邮。去他们的市政厅，告诉他们，等他们重回华盛顿开始国会工作的时候，最好回来后就有所动作。你们都在竭尽全力履行自己的职责，他们也该如此。

15 谢谢，祝周末愉快！

第40周

Congress Should Keep America Moving Forward

October 6, 2012

国会应该不断推动美国向前发展

2012年10月6日

【摘要导读】

在本周的广播电视讲话中，巴拉克•奥巴马总统告诉美国民众，在遭遇大萧条以来最严重的经济危机四年之后，美国正在向前发展。尽管美国的企业在过去31个月里提供了520万个工作岗位，失业率也降低到他上任以来的最低水平，然而，仍然有诸多的工作有待完成。

演讲再现

Original Text

1 Hi, everybody. Four years after the worst economic crisis of our lifetimes, we're seeing signs that, as a nation, we're moving forward again.

2 After losing about 800,000 jobs a month when I took office, our businesses have now added 5.2 million new jobs over the past two and a half years. And on Friday, we learned that the unemployment rate is now at its lowest level since I took office. More Americans are entering the workforce. More Americans are getting jobs.

3 But too many of our friends and neighbors are still looking for work or struggling to pay the bills — many of them since long before this crisis hit.

4 We owe it to them to keep moving forward. We've come too far to turn back now. And we've made too much progress to return to the policies that got us into this mess in

the first place.

5 For example — two years ago, we put in place tougher, commonsense rules of the road for Wall Street to make sure that the kind of crisis we've been fighting back from never happens again.

6 These rules mean that big banks are no longer going to be able to make risky bets with your deposits. And if a big bank does make a bad decision, they pay for it — not taxpayers.

7 And we also put in place the strongest consumer protections in our history to crack down on the worst practices of credit card companies and mortgage lenders.

8 But for some reason, some Republicans in Congress are still waging an all-out battle to delay, defund and dismantle these commonsense new rules.

9 Why? Do they think undoing rules that protect families from the worst practices of credit card companies and mortgage lenders will make the middle-class stronger? Do they think getting rid of rules to prevent another crisis on Wall Street will make *Main Street*[1] any safer?

10 Republicans in Congress need to stop trying to refight the battles of the past few years, and finally start doing something to actually help the middle-class get ahead.

11 And here are three things they can do right now.

12 First, Congress needs to step up and guarantee that 98% of Americans and 97% of small business owners won't see their taxes go up next year. This is something that everyone says they agree on. It should have gotten done months ago. But Republicans in Congress are standing in the way. They're holding tax cuts for 98% of Americans hostage until we pass tax cuts for the wealthiest 2% of Americans. Ask them how that helps the middle-class.

13 Second, Congress needs to step up and provide every responsible homeowner a chance to save about $3,000 a year on their mortgage by refinancing at lower rates. I gave them a plan to do that — back in February. It's a plan that has the support of independent, nonpartisan economists and

Words & Expressions

put sth. in place 到位，落实到位，正在实施

deposit [di'pɔzit] *n.* 存款，保证金，沉淀物 *vt.* 使沉积，存放

crack down 对…采取严厉措施，镇压

defund [di'fʌnd] *vt.* 从…抽回资金，瓦解

dismantle [dis'mæntl] *vt.* 拆除，拆开，去除，废除

undo [ʌn'du:] *vt.* 取消，解开，破坏，扰乱

refight [ri'fait] *vt.* 再战

leaders across the housing industry. But Republicans won't even let that plan come to a vote. Ask them how that helps homeowners.

14 Third, Congress needs to step up and pass my plan to create a veterans jobs corps to help our returning heroes find work as cops, firefighters and park rangers in communities across the country. A few weeks ago, Republicans in the Senate voted that plan down. Ask them why someone who fights for this country abroad should have to fight for a job when they come home.

15 In other words, Ask them to get back to work and get these things done. If we're going to keep this economy moving forward, there's no time for political games. Even in a political season. Everyone needs to do their part. If you agree with me, let your Representative know where you stand. Tell them that if they want your vote, then they need to stand with you and not in the way of our recovery.

16 Thanks and have a great weekend.

park rangers 公园管理员，公园巡逻队员，护林员

do one's part 尽自己的职责，尽自己的本分

背景知识注释 Background Notes

1. Main Street　Main Street 一词在 20 世纪中进入美国的政治舞台，当时的共和党用 Wall Street 来描述自由派，以 Main Street 来代指保守派。2004 年总统竞选时，有一位民主党总统候选人约翰•爱德华兹 (John Edwards) 以平民主义的思想提出他的竞选纲领，主要提出了 Wall Street 和 Main Street 的两元经济论。这也是他在 2008 年再度竞选时的主要理念。所以自 2004 年开始，Wall Street 和 Main Street 的含义基本就定位在：Wall Street 指包括金融、投资在内的美国的巨型企业和富人的阶层，即表征富有阶层的利益或是少数富人的利益，Main Street 是指小企业、小作坊和平民阶层，即表征平民阶层的利益，或社会主要群体的利益。

中文译文 Chinese Version

1 嗨，大家好！在遭遇人生当中最严重的经济危机四年之后，我们看到的一些迹象表明我们的国家又继续向前发展了。

2 我上任时一个月约有80万人失业，自那以后的两年半时间里我们的企业增加了520万个工作岗位。周五，我们得知失业率已经降到我上任以来的最低水平。越来越多的美国人加入了劳动大军，越来越多的美国人走上了工作岗位。

3 但是，我们还有许许多多的朋友和邻居依旧在四处寻找工作或为支付账单而苦苦挣扎，他们中有很多人在这次经济危机爆发以前的很长一段时间里就已经如此了。

4 为了他们，我们应不断向前推进。我们已经取得了很大的进展，前进的步伐已经不可逆转。我们所取得的进展已经无法使我们重回最初让我们陷入这一泥淖的政策了。

5 例如，两年前，我们在华尔街实施了更加严格、更为符合常理的监管措施，以确保我们所抗击的金融危机不会再卷土重来。

6 这些措施意味着大型银行再也不能把大家的存款当做高风险的赌注。而且一旦大型银行做出了错误的决定，他们就得自食其果，而不是由纳税人埋单。

7 另外，我们还实施了史上最强有力的消费者保护措施，对信用卡公司和抵押贷款放贷人的恶劣行径进行严厉打击。

8 但由于某些原因，国会的一些共和党人依旧开展了一场全面的阻击战来延迟、瓦解乃至废除这些符合常理的新措施。

9 为什么？难道他们认为在保护人们免受信用卡公司和抵押贷款放贷人的恶行的欺诈上，少了这些监管措施能让中产阶级变得更为强大吗？难道他们认为在预防另一场华尔街危机上，取消这些措施能让中产阶级更加安全吗？

10 国会的共和党人应该停止在过去几年里一直在进行的斗争，开始做些实实在在的事情，帮助中产阶级成长壮大。

11 现在，他们尚有三件事情可以做。

12 其一，国会应该加紧工作，保证98%的美国人和97%的小微企业主明年的税赋不会上涨。在这件事情上所有人都表示同意的，本来应该在几个月前就完成的，但国会的共和党人却一直在阻拦。他们以为98%的美国人减税为要挟，想让我们先通过对2%最富有的人减税。请问为富人减税如何能帮助中产阶级呢？

13 其二，国会要加紧工作，为信誉良好的房屋贷款人提供一个机会，让他们可以利用当前的低利率进行转按揭贷款，这样每年可以节省3,000美元。我今年2月就向国会提交了这一计划。该计划得到了独立的、无党派经济学家以及房地产业领头人的支持。但对这一计划共和党人甚至没有让它进入投票程序。请问他们如何能帮助房屋贷款人呢？

14 其三，国会需要加紧工作，通过我提出的成立退伍军人就业促进会的提案，以此来帮助凯旋的英雄们找到一份工作，比方说全国各地都需要的警察、消防队员或公园护林人员等。几个星期前，参议院的共和党人否决了这一提案。请问他们为什么要让那些为国家在海外征战的人回到家乡还要为找到一份工作四处奔忙呢？

15 也就是说，请他们回到岗位上把这些事情办好。倘若我们想要推动我们的经济向前发展的话，那么我们就没有时间继续玩弄这类政治游戏了。即便在大选期间也是如此。每个人都需要尽职尽责。倘若大家同意我的看法，让你们的议员们知道你们的立场。告诉他们倘若他们需要你们的投票，那么他们就需要与你们站在一起，而不是成为经济复苏道路的障碍。

16 谢谢，周末愉快。

第41周

One Million American Jobs Saved and a Stronger American Auto Industry

October 13, 2012

百万民众重获工作岗位，汽车行业再现强盛辉煌

2012年10月13日

【摘要导读】

在本周的广播电视讲话中，巴拉克•奥巴马总统谈到了他曾经的决定。这一决定拯救了美国汽车产业，使其免于破产并挽救了100多万就业岗位。当时有人呼吁让底特律破产去吧，但现在美国的汽车产业又傲视全球，汽车销量也达到了四年来的最高值。奥巴马说在未来的日子里，具备更高燃油标准的新型美国汽车将进入市场，这会让中产家庭节省开支，对环境亦有好处；由于有了他联合两党提出的贸易协定，美国现在将汽车销售到了韩国等地。他还说汽车产业的经历向人们展示了，美国人民在哪里跌倒，就能在哪里爬起来，而且能变得更为强盛。

演讲再现 Original Text

Words & Expressions

roll out 铺开，滚出

entice [in'tais] v. 诱使，引诱

this time around 此时此刻，这一次

1 Hi, everybody.

2 Every year around this time, American car companies start rolling out their newest, shiniest models, hoping to entice you into buying one. It's Detroit's chance to show you what they've been working on — the latest and greatest. And this year is no exception. They've got some pretty good-looking cars coming out.

3 But something is different this time around — and it starts with the auto companies themselves.

4 Just a few years ago, the auto industry wasn't just

struggling — it was flatlining. GM[①] and Chrysler[②] were on the verge of collapse. Suppliers and distributors were at risk of going under. More than a million jobs across the country were on the line — and not just auto jobs, but the jobs of teachers, small business owners, and everyone in communities that depend on this great American industry.

5 But we refused to throw in the towel and do nothing. We refused to let Detroit go bankrupt. We bet on American workers and American ingenuity, and three years later, that bet is paying off in a big way.

6 Today, auto sales are the highest they've been in more than four years. GM is back. Ford[③] and Chrysler are growing again. Together, our auto industry has created nearly a quarter of a million new jobs right here in America.

7 And we're not just making more cars and trucks — we're making better ones.

8 After 30 years of inaction, we raised fuel standards so that by the middle of the next decade, cars and light trucks will average almost 55 miles per gallon — nearly double what they get today. That means you'll only have to fill up every two weeks instead of every week. It's good for your wallet, it's good for our economy, and it's good for the environment.

9 The technology that makes it happen will also help America stay on the cutting edge for decades to come. Just this week, GM announced they plan to hire 1,500 workers for a new research center in Michigan to help make sure the high-tech cars of tomorrow are designed and built right here in America.

10 I've also signed new bipartisan trade agreements into law, because I want to see more cars on the road in places like South Korea imported from Detroit and Toledo[④] and Chicago[⑤].

11 All of this is something the American people can and should be proud of. It's a reminder that when the American people put their mind to something, there's nothing we can't do.

12 So next time you see one of those brand new 2013

flatline ['flætlain] *vi.* 死亡，完全失效，失败

on the verge of 濒临于，接近于

distributor [di'stribjutə] *n.* 经销商，散布者，配电盘

go under 破产，沉没，屈服，失败

on the line 处于危险中，模棱两可，在电话线上

throw in the towel 认输，放弃

bankrupt ['bæŋkrʌpt] *adj.* 破产的 *n.* 破产者

fuel standards 燃油标准

put one's mind to 全神贯注于

brand new 全新的，崭新的

can-do spirit 敢做敢当的精神

at the pump 加油站

models on TV or on the lot, think about how far we've come together. Think about how — thanks to the hard work and can-do spirit of the American people — more of those cars and trucks are being manufactured by American workers at American companies in communities all across the country. And they're going to save you more money at the pump.

13 That's what America is all about. When we get knocked down, we get back up. We come back stronger. And as long as I'm President, that's what we'll keep doing.

14 Thanks, and have a great weekend.

背景知识注释 Background Notes

1. GM 即 General Motors Corporation 通用汽车公司，成立于 1908 年 9 月 16 日，自从威廉•杜兰特创建了美国通用汽车公司以来，先后联合或兼并了别克、凯迪拉克、雪佛兰、奥兹莫比尔、庞蒂克、克尔维特、悍马等公司，使原来的小公司成为它的分部。从 1927 年以来它一直是全世界最大的汽车公司。通用的总部在密歇根州的底特律市，另外厂房遍布美国 30 个州和世界 32 个国家。

2. Chrysler 克莱斯勒，仅次于通用汽车公司和福特，为美国第三大汽车公司。该公司创始人为沃尔特•克莱斯勒 (Walter Chrysler)，1875 年出生于美国衣阿华洲一个铁路技师家庭。

3. Ford 福特汽车公司，由亨利•福特先生创立于 1903 年，是世界上最大的汽车企业之一。1908 年福特汽车公司生产出世界上第一辆属于普通百姓的汽车——T 型车，世界汽车工业革命就此开始。1913 年，福特汽车公司又开发出了世界上第一条流水线，这一创举使 T 型车一共达到了 1,500 万辆，缔造了一个至今仍未被打破的世界纪录。福特先生为此被尊为“为世界装上轮子”的人。

4. Toledo 托莱多，位于美国俄亥俄州北部伊利湖畔，是卢卡斯县的县治所在。著名汽车品牌“吉普”于 1941 年在托莱多诞生。

5. Chicago 芝加哥，位于美国中西部，属伊利诺伊州，东临密歇根湖，是美国仅次于纽约市和洛杉矶的第三大城市。芝加哥地处北美大陆的中心地带，为美国最重要的铁路、航空枢纽。芝加哥同时也是美国最为重要的金融、文化、制造业、期货和商品交易中心之一，并逐渐成为在世界具有重大影响力的大都市之一。芝加哥常见的别名包括：“第二城”、“风城”、“芝城”等。芝加哥也是全球最重要的一个金融中心，是美国第二大商业中心区，也是美国最大的期货市场。

中文译文
Chinese Version

1 嗨，大家好！

2 每年的这个时候，美国的汽车厂商都会推出他们最新款、最炫目的车型，以期盼吸引你我购用。这是底特律向人们展示他们工作成果的机会：最新和最棒的汽车。本年度也不负众望。他们推出了一些相当惹人眼球的车型。

3 但这一次情况有所不同，它与汽车生产厂家有关。

4 仅仅几年之前，汽车产业不仅仅是在苦苦挣扎，而且几近崩溃了。通用和克莱斯勒濒临破产。供应商和分销商面临关门歇业的风险。全国各地100多万个工作岗位岌岌可危——不仅仅是汽车行业，而且还包括教师、小微企业主以及全社会依赖美国这一伟大行业的每一个人都面临窘境。

5 但我们不认输，不言弃。我们拒绝让底特律破产。我们相信美国工人和美国民众的聪明才智。三年后，那样的选择得到了丰厚的回报。

6 现在，汽车销售量达到了四年来的最高水平。通用挺过来了，福特和克莱斯勒东山再起再展宏图。总的说来，仅汽车行业就在美国本土创造了将近25万个工作岗位。

7 我们所生产的小汽车和卡车不仅数量更多——而且品质更好。

8 在经历了30年的沉寂之后，我们再次提高燃油标准。要求再过5年，小汽车和轻型卡车都达到每加仑燃料行驶55英里的标准，这将是现行标准的两倍。这就意味着你不需要每周都去加油，两周加一次就好了。这不仅能为大家省钱，而且对经济也有利，对环境亦如此。

9 促使这一切发生的技术将让美国在未来数十年里在该领域保持领先地位。就在本周，通用宣布了他们为密歇根的新研究中心聘用1,500名员工的计划。该中心将确保未来的高科技汽车将在美国本土完成设计并被生产出来。

10 我还签署了一项两党的贸易协定使之成为法律，因为我期盼看到更多的从底特律、特莱多和芝加哥进口的汽车在韩国等地的公路上奔跑。

11 所有的这一切都值得也应该让美国人民感到自豪。这表明了只要美国人民专心致力于某事，就没有什么事情我们做不到。

12 因此，倘若下次你们在电视上或展销会上看见这些新品牌的2013款汽车，不要忘了我们所取得的成就。想象一下，正是有了美国人民的辛勤付出和敢做敢当的精神，越来越多的这种汽车和卡车才能在全国各地的美国工厂由美国工人制造出来。它们将在油费上为大家节省一大笔开支。

13 这正是美国的真实写照。我们在哪里跌倒，就从哪里爬起来，而且变得比以前更为强盛。只要我还在总统的任上，这就是我们将继续努力的方向。

14 谢谢大家，周末愉快！

第42周

Congress Should Join the President to Help Responsible Homeowners

October 20, 2012

国会应当与总统齐心协力帮助那些信誉良好的房屋贷款人

2012年10月20日

【摘要导读】

在本周的广播电视讲话中，巴拉克•奥巴马总统敦促国会行动起来，通过帮助信誉良好的房屋贷款人重新转按揭贷款，从而每年节省3,000美元，以促进房地产市场的复兴。

演讲再现 Original Text

Words & Expressions

foreclosure [fɔːˈkləuʒə] *n.* 丧失抵押品赎回权

filing [ˈfailiŋ] *n.* 文件归档

hold the bag 独自承担责任，(无可奈何地)背别人摔掉的包袱，背黑锅

underwater [ˈʌndəˈwɔːtə] *adj.* 在水中的，水面下的 *adv.* 在水下

1 Hi, everybody. In recent weeks, you might have noticed something. Or maybe even heard the sound of it if you live close enough.

2 New homes are going up. In fact, construction workers are breaking ground on new homes in America at the fastest pace in more than four years.

3 At the same time, more homes are being sold. Home values are back on the rise. And foreclosure filings are at their lowest point in the five years since the housing bubble burst and left millions of responsible families holding the bag.

4 Now, we're not where we need to be yet. Too many homes are still underwater. Too many families are still having a hard time making the mortgage on their piece of the

American Dream.

5 But one of the heaviest drags on our recovery is getting lighter. Now we have to build on the progress we've made, and keep moving forward.

6 I never believed that the best way to deal with the housing market was to just sit back, do nothing, and simply wait for things to hit bottom. That would have been a disaster for all the responsible families who — through no fault of their own — were struggling to make ends meet.

7 Instead, I've made helping those homeowners a priority.

8 Since I took office, my Administration has taken action to help millions of families stay in their homes.

9 We teamed up with attorneys general in almost every state to investigate and crack down on the practices that caused this mess. And in the end, we secured a $25 billion settlement from the biggest banks — one of the biggest settlements in history — and used it to provide relief to families all across America.

10 We've taken action to help responsible homeowners refinance their mortgages. As a result, just this year hundreds of thousands of Americans who were stuck in high-interest loans have been able to take advantage of historically low rates and are saving thousands of dollars every year.

11 And now I want every homeowner in America to have that chance. I just wish it didn't require an act of Congress. But it does. So, back in February, I sent Congress a plan to give every responsible homeowner the chance to save about $3,000 a year on their mortgage by refinancing at historically low rates. That's the equivalent of a $3,000 tax cut.

12 It's a plan that we know will work. It has the support of independent, nonpartisan economists and leaders across the housing industry. It's a no-brainer that should have passed easily.

13 But Republicans in Congress banded together and kept this plan from even coming to a vote.

build on 依赖，依靠，建立于，把…建立于…，以…为基础

sit back 休息，不采取行动

hit bottom 向下探底，得到结论

team up with 与…合作

attorney [ə'tə:ni] *n.* 律师，代理人

attorneys general 司法部长，首席检察官

equivalent [i'kwivələnt] *adj.* 等价的，相等的，同意义的 *n.* 等价物，相等物

no-brainer 不伤脑筋的事，无需用脑的事

band [bænd] *vi.* 用带绑扎，聚集

14 They banded together and prevented millions of Americans — including many of you listening today — from saving $3,000 a year. That's money that could have gone back into the value of your home, or your kid's college savings account. That's money that could have gone into your local businesses, so they could hire and create more jobs in your town.

15 But Republicans in Congress still won't let that happen. And that's only held back the economy, when we should be doing everything we can to accelerate our economic engine.

16 Let's be honest — Republicans in Congress won't act on this plan before the election. But maybe they'll come to their senses afterward if you give them a push. So contact your Representative, especially if this plan will help you or somebody you know. Tell him or her that American homeowners have waited long enough. Tell them that it's time for Congress to stop standing in the way of our recovery and to start standing up for you. Thanks and have a great weekend.

中文译文 Chinese Version

1 嗨，大家好！最近几周，你们可能注意到了一些事情，或者倘若你就住在附近，也应该有所耳闻。

2 新建的房子正在拔地而起。实际上，在美国，建筑工人们正以四年多来的最快速度开建新房。

3 而与此同时，住宅成交量大增，价格回暖。五年前房地产泡沫破裂，致使成千上万信誉良好的房屋贷款人被迫背上包袱，而现在止赎案例已经降到了最低点。

4 然而，我们尚未实现我们必须达到的目标。还有许多房产仍然深陷困境；还有许多家庭，为实现自己那一份美国梦，依旧为偿还按揭月供苦苦地煎熬。

5 我从来就不相信处理房地产市场问题的最佳方案是坐视不管，等待市场触底。

6 这样对于那些负责任的家庭而言是一次灾难，他们并没有错，可却要为了实现收支平衡而苦苦地挣扎着。

7 反之，我一直都把帮助那些房主当成第一要务。

8 自从我出任总统以来，我的政府采取了行动，以帮助数以百万计的家庭保住自己的房子。

9 政府同差不多每个州的首席检察官组成团队联手调查和打击导致这次经济危机的恶劣行径，而且最终与一些最大的银行达成高达250亿美元的和解协议——有史以来最大的协议——这笔资金为全美各地家庭提供救助。

10 我们已经采取行动帮助信誉良好的房屋贷款人进行转按揭贷款。结果，仅今年一年，成百上千万过去身陷高利率贷款泥淖的房主们现在都能够享受史上最低的利率，从而每年节省了数千美元。

11 而现在我希望美国的每位房屋贷款人都有这样的机会。我希望这不需要国会的授权。但事实上却需要。所以，我在今年2月向国会提交了一份方案，让每一个信誉良好的房屋贷款人有机会在历史新低的利率下进行转按揭贷款，每年都可以节省3,000美元。这相当于3,000美元的减税。

12 我们知道，这个方案是可行的，而且得到独立的、无党派经济学家以及房地产行业领袖们的支持，而它本应轻而易举地获得通过。

13 可是，国会共和党人却拉帮结派，甚至连个投票的机会也不给。

14 他们拉帮结派，阻止数百万美国民众——包括今天正在收听演讲的各位——每年节省3,000美元。这些钱可以用于重新注入你房产的价值，或者存入你孩子上大学的储蓄账户，亦可以进入你们当地的企业，以便这些企业在当地雇用员工并创造更多的就业机会。

15 但是，国会的共和党人还是想法阻止该方案的实施。当我们竭尽所能加快经济发展的步伐的时候，他们的作为只能拖经济振兴的后腿。

16 老实说——在大选之前，国会的共和党人根本不想通过这一方案。但是，倘若大家敦促国会的共和党人，或许他们过后会良心发现。因此，倘若该提案有益于你或你所认识的人，联系你们的国会议员。告诉他或她，美国的房主们等得太久了。告诉他们，在振兴经济的道路上，国会是停止充当绊脚石，开始站出来帮助老百姓的时候了。谢谢大家，并祝各位周末愉快。

第43周

Protecting the American People with New Wall Street Reforms

October 27, 2012

用新的华尔街改革方案保护美国民众的利益

2012 年 10 月 27 日

【摘要导读】

在本周的广播电视讲话中，巴拉克•奥巴马总统强调他所推动设立的新的独立消费者保护机构的作用。该机构代表消费者的利益，保护他们免受掌控消费者信誉评分的公司所做的错误决定的侵害。他指出尽管这些消费者保护措施可以有效避免大型银行再次引发另一场金融危机，国会的共和党人却一直反对。奥巴马表示他是不会让这样的事情发生的，他将继续为美国工薪阶层努力抗争，并与大家一道推动国家向前发展。

演讲再现
Original Text

1 Hi, everybody. It's now been four years since a crisis that began on Wall Street spread to Main Street, hammering middle-class families and ultimately costing our economy 9 million jobs.

2 Since then, we've fought our way back. Our businesses have added more than 5 million new jobs. The unemployment rate has fallen to the lowest level since I took office. Home values are rising again. And our assembly lines are humming once more.

3 And to make sure America never goes through a crisis like that again, we passed tough new Wall Street reform to end taxpayer-funded bailouts for good.

Words & Expressions

hammer [ˈhæmə] *vi.* 锤击，反复敲打 *vt.* 锤打，严厉批评

hum [hʌm] *v.* 发低哼声，哼（曲子）*n.* 嗡嗡声

bailout [ˈbeilˌaut] *n.* 紧急（财政）援助，紧急融资

for good 永久地，一劳永逸地

4 Wall Street reform also created the first-ever independent consumer watchdog, whose sole job is to look out for you.

5 That means making sure you've got all the information you need to make important financial decisions like buying a home or paying for college. And it means going after anyone who tries to take advantage of you, or rip you off.

6 Starting this month, that includes the folks who come up with your credit score.

7 If you haven't checked out your credit score recently, you should. It can have a major impact on your life. It can determine whether or not you qualify for a loan or what kind of interest you have to pay. It can even affect your chances at renting an apartment or getting a job.

8 But here's the thing: the companies that put your credit score together can make mistakes. They may think you had a loan or a credit card that was never yours. They may think you were late making payments when you were on time. And when they mess up, you're the one who suffers.

9 Until this week, if you had a complaint, you took it to the company. Sometimes they listened. Sometimes they didn't. But that was pretty much it. They were your only real hope.

10 Well, not anymore. If you have a complaint about your credit score that hasn't been properly addressed, you can go to consumerfinance.gov/complaint and let the consumer watchdog know.

11 Not only will they bring your complaint directly to the company in question, they'll give you a tracking number, so you can check back and see exactly what's being done on your behalf.

12 And fixing your credit score isn't the only thing they can help with.

13 If you're opening a bank account, trying to get a student loan, or applying for a credit card and something doesn't seem right, you can let them know and they'll check it out.

watchdog ['wɔtʃdɔg] *n.* 看门狗，监察人

rip... off 偷窃，扯掉，欺诈，剥削

mess up 陷入困境，搞糟

in question 讨论中的，成问题的，考虑中的

a tracking number 跟踪号码

14 If you're looking to buy a home, and you want to know if you're getting a fair deal on your mortgage, you can give them a call and they'll get you an answer.

15 Their only mission is to fight for you. And when needed, they'll take action.

16 For example, alongside other regulators, they recently ordered three big credit card companies to return more than $400 million to folks who were deceived or misled into buying things they didn't want or didn't understand.

17 That's what Wall Street reform is all about — looking out for working families and making sure that everyone is playing by the same rules.

18 Sadly, that hasn't been enough to stop Republicans in Congress from fighting these reforms. Backed by an army of financial industry lobbyists, they've been waging an all-out battle to delay, defund and dismantle these new rules.

19 I refuse to let that happen.

20 I believe that the free market is one of the greatest forces for progress in human history, and that the true engine of job creation in this country is the private sector, not the government.

21 But I also believe that the free market has never been about taking whatever you want, however you can get it. Alongside our innovative spirit, America only prospers when we meet certain obligations to one another, and when we all play by the same set of rules.

22 We've come too far — and sacrificed too much — to go back to an era of top-down, on-your-own economics. And as long as I'm President, we're going to keep moving this country forward so that everyone — whether you start a business or punch a clock — can have confidence that if you work hard, you can get ahead.

23 Thanks and have a great weekend.

an army of 一大队，大量的

lobbyist [ˈlɔbiist] *n.* 活动议案通过者，说客

obligation [ˌɔbliˈgeiʃən] *n.* 义务，职责，债务

on-one's-own 靠自己的力量的，独自的

中文译文
Chinese Version

1 嗨，大家好！四年前，肇始于华尔街的危机蔓延至整个社会，重创了中产阶级家庭，最终让我们付出了 900 万人失业的惨重代价。

2 从那时起，我们就开始了绝地反击之路。现在，我们的企业又新增了 500 万个就业岗位。失业率也跌到我上任以来的最低点。房产价格又开始上扬。我们工厂里的生产线也再次轰鸣繁忙起来。

3 为了确保美国不会再次遭遇这样的危机，我们通过了新的更严厉的华尔街改革法案。这一法案永远地终结了用纳税人的钱来做紧急救助基金的做法。

4 华尔街改革还在历史上破天荒地设立了消费者保护机构。该机构唯一的职责就是保护广大消费者。

5 这意味着在大家做财务决定时，该机构可以确保你们可以获得所有的必要信息，比方说买房子或支付大学学费等，而且该机构还会调查任何想要占你们便宜或敲你们竹杠的人。

6 从本月起，调查范围还新增了给消费者信誉评分的人。

7 倘若你近期没有查过自己的信誉评分，你还是应该查一查。这些分数将对你的生活产生重大影响。信誉评分能决定你是否有资格获得贷款或你需要支付多高的贷款利率。信誉评分还能影响你租赁公寓或寻找工作的机会。

8 但问题在于：这些汇总你信誉分数的公司可能会犯错。它们可能认定你有一笔并不是属于你的贷款或一张并不是归于你的信用卡。他们可能认定你没有按时还款，而你却是按时还的。当他们把事情搞砸，受害的就是大家了。

9 直到今天，倘若你要投诉，你还是只能去找信用卡公司。有时候他们会倾听，有时候他们不理会。而情况大体上就是如此。但是他们是你唯一的希望。

10 这种情况已一去不复返了。倘若你有关于信誉评分的投诉没有得到合适的处理，可以访问 consumerfinance.gov/complaint 网站，让消费者保护机构为你主持公道。

11 他们不仅会把你的投诉直接交给有关公司，还会给你一个跟踪号码，这样你就可以跟踪核实他们是否为你把事情办了。

12 当然，订正你的信誉评分并不是他们唯一能够帮你做的事情。

13 倘若你想开设一个银行账户，申请获得助学贷款，或者是申请一张信用卡，不能顺利办好的话，你也可以告诉他们，他们会帮你查办的。

14 倘若你打算买房子，你想要知道你的抵押贷款是否公平合理，你也可以打电话向他们咨询，他们会给你解答。

15 他们唯一的任务就是为你们抗争。只要你们需要，他们就会采取行动。

16 比方说，最近，他们与其他监管方一起，敦促三家大型信用卡公司向消费者返还了四亿多美元，因为他们欺骗或误导消费者购买了他们全然不想要或根本不懂的东西。

17 华尔街改革大抵如此——保护我们的工薪家庭，并确保每个人都遵守同样的游戏规则。

18 不幸的是，这还不足以阻挡住共和党国会议员们反对这些改革的行动。他们在一伙金融行业游说者的支持下发动了一次全面战争来延迟、瓦解乃至废除这些新的规则。

19 但我绝不会坐视这类事情发生。

20 我坚信，自由市场是人类历史进步最伟大的推动力之一。在我们国家创造就业机会真正的引擎是私营企业而不是政府。

21 同时我也坚信，自由市场并不意味着你可以为所欲为，想干什么就干什么，想怎么干就怎么干。除了我们的创新精神之外，我们彼此还应尽职尽责，遵从同样的游戏规则，只有这样美国才能繁荣昌盛。

22 我们已经取得了长足的进展——并为此做出了巨大的牺牲——再也不可能回到那种自上而下，自给自足的经济时代了。只要我还在总统的任上，我们就将继续推动我们国家向前发展，这样每个人——无论你开办企业或按时上下班——都相信只要你努力工作，就能获得成功。

23 谢谢，周末愉快！

第44周

Recovering and Rebuilding After the Storm

November 3, 2012

加快飓风袭击之后的恢复和重建

2012年11月3日

【摘要导读】

奥巴马总统在本周的广播电视讲话中向在美国史上最严重的飓风中，夜以继日地工作、英勇无畏的紧急救援人员和国民警卫队员表示谢意。同时他也向受到“桑迪”影响的数百万美国民众承诺，在重建的过程中国家将始终与灾区人民在一起。另外，奥巴马总统指示相关机构简化行政流程，尽快运送物资，确保各州和地方紧急救援人员能及时得到所需的联邦救助资源。

演讲再现 Original Text

1 This weekend, millions of our fellow Americans are still picking up the pieces from one of the worst storms in our history.

2 I toured New Jersey on Wednesday with Governor *Christie* ①, and witnessed some of the terrible devastation firsthand. It's heartbreaking. Families have lost loved ones. Entire communities have been wiped away. Even some of the first responders who repeatedly put themselves in harm's way to bravely save the lives of others have suffered losses of their own.

3 Today, I ask everyone to keep them in your prayers. And as President, I promise them this: your country will be there for you for as long as it takes to recover and rebuild.

Words & Expressions

pick up the pieces 跌倒后重新爬起来，收拾残局

devastation [ˌdevəˈsteiʃən] *n.* 毁坏，荒废

4 Throughout the week, I've been in constant contact with governors and mayors in the affected areas, who are doing an excellent job in extraordinarily difficult circumstances. And we owe the first responders and *National Guardsmen* ② who have been working around the clock our deepest gratitude.

5 Our number one concern has been making sure that affected states and communities have everything they need to respond to and recover from this storm.

6 From the earliest hours, I ordered that resources be made available to states in the path of the storm as soon as they needed them. And I instructed my team not to let red tape and bureaucracy get in the way of solving problems — especially when it came to making sure local utilities could restore power as quickly as possible.

7 Before the storm hit, *FEMA* ③ pre-staged emergency response teams from North Carolina to Maine, and deployed resources like food, water, and generators up and down the coast. As the storm passed, thousands of FEMA personnel were on the ground responding to those in need. And by midweek, *the Department of Defense* ④ was ready to fly in cargo planes that could be loaded with trucks and equipment to help local power companies get up and running faster.

8 But recovery will be a long, hard road for many communities. There's a lot of work ahead.

9 If you've been directly impacted by this storm and need temporary assistance getting back on your feet, you can call 1-800-621-FEMA, or apply at DisasterAssistance.gov. If you know folks who are still without power, please spread the word and let them know.

10 And if you don't live in an affected area and want to help, supporting the Red Cross is the best and fastest way.

11 This week, we have been humbled by nature's destructive power. But we've been inspired as well. For when the storm was darkest, the heroism of our fellow citizens shone brightest.

12 The nurses and doctors at *NYU Medical Center* ⑤ who

work around the clock 夜以继日地工作

cargo planes 运输飞机，货机

humble ['hʌmbl] *vt.* 使谦恭，使谦卑，使温顺，压下…的锐气，使威风扫地

evacuated fragile newborns, carrying some down several flights of stairs.

13 The firefighters in *Queens*⑥ who battled an inferno from flooded streets, and rescued people from an apartment building by boat.

14 *The Coast Guard*⑦ crews from North Carolina who saved a sinking ship in stormy seas — and their rescue swimmer who, when he reached those in need, said, "I'm Dan, and I hear you guys need a ride."

15 That's who we are. We're Americans. When times are tough, we're tougher. We put others first. We go that extra mile. We open our hearts and our homes to one another, as one American family. We recover, we rebuild, we come back stronger — and together we will do that once more. Thanks, God bless you, and God bless America.

inferno [in'fə:nəu] *n.* 阴间，地狱

go that extra mile 特别付出努力以做某事

背景知识注释
Background Notes

1. Christie　即 Chris Christie 克里斯•克里斯帝 (1962.9.6 －)，是美国第 55 届新泽西州州长。克里斯•克里斯帝在 2009 年 11 月的州长选举，成为 12 年内第一个新泽西州赢得了全州选举的共和党员。克里斯•克里斯帝为一名律师，曾担任美国新泽西州区检察长和新泽西州莫里斯县自由保有权所有人。克里斯•克里斯帝在 2012 年共和党全国代表大会上发表了主题演讲。

2. National Guardsmen　美国国民警卫队，常简称为"国民兵"，是美国的一支预备役军事部队，由各州国民警卫队单位组成，不论有否转为现役，均受联邦政府认可。士兵皆为民兵，平常从事各行各业，旗下一分为二，有陆军国民警卫队及空军国民警卫队，分别是陆军和空军的预备队。国民警卫队由美国法典第十篇及美国法典第三十二篇创立，身为美国首层防线。它散驻各州和其他国土，听命于州长或民兵指挥官。遇有紧急状态及灾害如风灾、洪水或地震，州长或民兵指挥官可下令召集国民警卫队，不能跟其他专职军事作战训练的后备军队相混淆。美国国民警卫队负责管理军队事务，并与国防部紧密沟通，以使上令下达。

3. FEMA　即 Federal Emergency Management Agency 联邦紧急事务管理署，是美国防灾部，总部设在华盛顿哥伦比亚特区，负责减轻自然灾害的影响。2003 年 3 月 1 日 FEMA 并入美国国土安全部。

4. the Department of Defense　即 DOD 或 DoD，美国国防部，是美国联邦行政部门之一，主要负责统合国家安全与武装力量（美军），其总部大楼位于五角大楼，因此人们也常用“五角大楼”代称。国防部的行政首长是国防部长，依照美国法律由文官担任。美国国防部设有三个军事部门：陆军部、海军部与空军部，涵盖除海岸防卫队外的所有美国军队。除此之外，美国国防部亦设有若干国防幕僚与研究单位，同时管辖各军校。1947 年，美国政府将军队管理中央化，将军事指挥权统一交由新成立的“国家军事机构”(National Military Establishment)，除了将陆军部与海军部交由其管辖之外，同时将陆军航空队升格为独立的美国空军，建立一个直属于该机构的空军部。至 1949 年 8 月 10 日，国家军事机构才更名为国防部。美国国防部现在的组织是按照美国国会 1986 年通过的《戈德华特－尼科尔斯国防部改组法》来的。按照这个法案，军事命令是从美国总统通过美国国防部长直接到美国战区司令官。参谋长联席会议有责任管理美国武器和后备军人，参谋长联席会议主席也担任总统和国家安全委员会的首席军事顾问，但是参谋长联席会议没有指挥权。

5. NYU Medical Center　纽约大学医学中心。

6. Queens　皇后区，是美国纽约市的五个行政区之一，也是其中面积最大、人口第二多的行政区。其范围和纽约州皇后县相同。皇后区位于长岛的西半部，纽约市主要的三个机场中，两个就坐落于皇后区，分别是肯尼迪国际机场和拉瓜地亚机场。这些机场在世界上是数一数二忙碌的，这使得皇后区的上空成为全国最拥塞的空域。

7. the Coast Guard　即 USCG 美国海岸警卫队，是美国军队的一支，亦是美国七个纪律部队中的一员。海岸警卫队作为海事军队，专职处理各类海事执法事宜（职权涵盖 12 哩领海及国际水域）及执行联邦管制规定，地位特殊。和平时期部队受国土安全部管辖，如有需要美国总统可下令部队移交美国海军部指挥，国会亦有权在战时下达相同命令。首任美国财政部长亚历山大•汉弥尔顿早于 1790 年 8 月 4 日创立美国海关缉私船局，亦即后来的海岸警卫队，故而此部队视己为美国最悠久的海航部门。

中文译文 Chinese Version

1　本周末，在经历我国历史上最严重的飓风之后，数百万美国同胞依旧在收拾残局重整山河。

2　周三，我在克里斯蒂 (Christie) 州长的陪同下视察了新泽西州，亲眼目睹了一些惨烈的破坏现场。那场面令人肝肠寸断。有的家庭失去了他们心爱的亲人。有的社区整个被夷为平地。甚至还有一些紧急救援人员一次次舍生忘死地挽救他人的生命，而自己的亲人却在这次飓风中丧生。

3　今天，我提议大家都为他们祈祷。作为总统，我向他们保证：在恢复和重建的整个过程中，你们的祖国将永远与你们在一起。

4 整整一周，我都与灾区各州的州长、市长们一直保持着联系。他们在异常艰难的环境中完成了非凡的使命。紧急救援人员和国民警卫队员夜以继日不停地工作，让我们向他们致以最诚挚的谢意。

5 我们最为关心的事情就是确保受灾各州和各社区能得到抗灾救灾和恢复重建所需要的一切。

6 在风暴刚刚来袭时，我就命令风暴沿途各州准备好各种资源以备不时之需。我还责成我的班子简化妨碍解决问题的行政流程——特别是一定要确保地方电网尽快恢复供电。

7 从北卡罗来纳州到缅因州，联邦紧急事务管理署(FEMA)在飓风来袭之前就提前部署了应急救援队伍，同时在海岸沿线储备了食品、水和发电机等资源。飓风刚过，数千名紧急救援人员立即赶赴现场投入到救灾工作中。到周三，国防部也准备好用运输机向受灾地区运送卡车和设备，以帮助当地的发电厂尽快恢复发电。

8 但是对于多数社区而言，恢复重建的道路漫长而艰难。还有很多工作有待我们去完成。

9 倘若你受到这场风暴的直接影响，恢复重建需要临时帮助，请拨打1-800-621转联邦紧急事务管理署(FEMA)，或者在DisasterAssistance.gov网站上提出申请。倘若你知道还有人没用上电，请把消息转告给他们。

10 倘若你不在灾区生活，而想要出手相助，支持红十字会是最好和最快的方式。

11 本周，在大自然的重创之下我们显得十分渺小。但是我们也受到了启发和鼓舞。因为飓风越是凶狠，就越能彰显我们公民英雄主义的精神。

12 纽约大学医疗中心的医护人员们紧急疏散了许多名生命脆弱的新生婴儿，有些是被抱着从层层楼梯下楼的。

13 皇后区的消防员们在洪水肆虐的街道上与死神抗争，用小船营救出被困在一座公寓大楼里的人们。

14 北卡罗来纳州的海岸警卫队人员在风大浪高的大海里营救一艘正在下沉的船只——他们的救生人员靠近被困者后，大喊："我是丹(Dan)，我听见你们需要搭船的声音了。"

15 这就是我们的本色。我们是美国人。时局艰难时，我们显得更加坚忍不拔。我们先人后己，我们不惧辛劳。我们美国犹如一个大家庭，敞开心扉和家门欢迎他人。我们东山再起。我们再振雄风，并比以往更加强盛。让我们再次团结起来共同实现这些目标。谢谢大家，愿上帝保佑你们，愿上帝保佑美国。

第45周

Extending Middle-Class Tax Cuts to Grow the Economy

November 10, 2012

继续为中产阶级减税，促进经济增长

2012年11月10日

【摘要导读】

在本周的广播电视讲话中，巴拉克•奥巴马总统指出：为了98%的美国民众，国会应该尽快通过中产阶级减税法案，两党都认为这将给予98%的家庭和97%的小微企业安全感并促进经济增长，因此完全没有理由再等下去。他号召国会团结起来,帮助创造就业岗位并增强美国的经济实力。

演讲再现 Original Text

Words & Expressions

poll [pɔl] *n.* 大选

consensus [kən'sensəs] *n.* 一致，舆论，合意

bring in 引进，生产，增加

civic ['sivik] *adj.* 市的，公民的，市民的

input ['input] *n.*（资金、物资、精力等的）投入，（提供的）信息，意见，情况

1 Hi, everybody

2 On Tuesday, America went to the polls. And the message you sent was clear: you voted for action, not politics as usual. You elected us to focus on your jobs, not ours.

3 That's why I've invited leaders of both parties to the White House next week, so we can start to build consensus around challenges we can only solve together. I also intend to bring in business, labor and civic leaders from outside Washington to get their ideas and input as well.

4 At a time when our economy is still recovering from the Great Recession, our top priority has to be jobs and growth. That's the focus of the plan I talked about during the campaign. It's a plan to reward businesses that create jobs here in America, and give people access to the education and

training that those businesses are looking for. It's a plan to rebuild our infrastructure and keep us on the cutting edge of innovation and clean energy. And it's a plan to reduce our deficit in a balanced and responsible way.

5 This is even more important because at the end of this year, we face a series of deadlines that require us to make major decisions about how to pay down our deficit — decisions that will have a huge impact on the economy and the middle-class, now and in the future.

6 Last year, I worked with Democrats and Republicans to cut a trillion dollars' worth of spending, and I intend to work with both parties to do more. But as I said over and over again on the campaign trail, we can't just cut our way to prosperity. If we're serious about reducing the deficit, we have to combine spending cuts with revenue — and that means asking the wealthiest Americans to pay a little more in taxes. That's how we did it when Bill Clinton was President. And that's the only way we can afford to invest in education and job training and manufacturing — all the ingredients of a strong middle-class and a strong economy.

7 Already, I've put forward a detailed plan that allows us to make these investments while reducing our deficit by $4 trillion over the next decade. Now, I'm open to compromise and new ideas. But I refuse to accept any approach that isn't balanced. I will not ask students or seniors or middle-class families to pay down the entire deficit while people making over $250,000 aren't asked to pay a dime more in taxes. This was a central question in the election. And on Tuesday, we found out that the majority of Americans agree with my approach — that includes Democrats, Independents, and Republicans.

8 Now we need a majority in Congress to listen — and they should start by making sure taxes don't go up on the 98% of Americans making under $250,000 a year starting January 1. This is something we all agree on. The taxes on the middle-class should not go on. Congress should permanently extend the middle-class tax cuts right now. Even as we negotiate a broader deficit reduction package. It's a step that would give

the cutting edge 尖端，前沿

revenue ['revənu:] *n.* 税收，收入，税务局

ingredient [in'gri:diənt] *n.* 原料，要素，组成部分

millions of families and 97% of small businesses the peace of mind that will lead to new jobs and faster growth. There's no reason to wait.

9 We know there will be differences and disagreements in the months to come. That's part of what makes our political system work. But on Tuesday, you said loud and clear that you won't tolerate dysfunction, or politicians who see compromise as a dirty word. Not when so many of your families are still struggling.

dysfunction [dis'fʌŋkʃən] *n.* 功能失调

10 Instead, you want cooperation. You want action. That's what I plan to deliver in my second term, and I expect to find leaders from both parties willing to join me.

11 Thanks, and have a great weekend.

中文译文 Chinese Version

1 嗨，大家好！

2 本周二，美国迎来了总统大选。大选中所反映出来的信息是明确的：与以往一样你们投票选择的是实际行动而不是政治口号。你们之所以选择我们是希望能够致力于解决你们的就业问题，而不是我们自己的工作岗位。

3 正是因为如此，我邀请两党的领袖下周在白宫相聚，以便就当下只有两党共同合作才能解决的挑战达成共识。同时，我也打算邀请政府外的商界、劳工和民间团体领袖到白宫议政参政。

4 在我们的经济还处在大萧条后的复苏阶段里，促进就业和推动增长是我们的头等大事。这也是我在竞选期间提出的施政纲领的重心。这个纲领鼓励在美国本土创造就业岗位的企业，让民众有机会接受那些企业所需的教育和培训。这个纲领拟重建我们的基础设施，保持我国在科技创新、清洁能源等方面的领先地位。这个纲领还计划通过统筹兼顾而负责的方式减少我们的财政赤字。

5 尤为重要的是，到了年底我们将面临一系列政策的最后期限。这要求我们就如何减少赤字做出重大决定，这些决定将对我们的经济和中产阶级的现在和未来产生巨大影响。

6 去年，我与民主党和共和党人共同努力，削减了多达万亿的开支，现在我打算与两党携手再做一些工作。但是正如我在选战中反复强调的，通往繁荣之路不能仅仅依靠减少开支。倘若我们真想减少赤字，我们就必须在削减开支的同时增加税收——就是要求最富有的美国人略微增加一点税赋。比尔·克林顿担任总统时就采取这样的方式。这是我们得以投资于教育、职业培训和制造业的唯一途径——这些都是构成一个强盛有力的中产阶级和兴旺发达的经济的要素。

7 我已经提出来一个详尽的计划使我们能够在进行这些投资的同时还能在未来的十年里减少 4 万亿美元的赤字。我随时可以做出妥协并接受新的想法。但是我绝不会接受这种难以统筹兼顾的方案。我们不能要求学生、老人或中产阶级家庭为全部赤字埋单而不要求年收入超过 250,000 美元的人们多一点税款。这是竞选中的问题。在周二，我们发现大多数美国人赞同我的方案——包括民主党人、独立人士和共和党人。

8 现在，我们要让国会的大多数议员知道——并让他们采取行动确保 98% 的年收入低于 25 万美元的美国民众在明年元旦到来的时候税赋不会加重。在这点上我们意见一致。加在中产阶级身上的税不应再继续。即便我们还需对一个更为广泛的一揽子消减赤字方案进行磋商，国会也应该立即延长对中产阶级减税的政策。这一政策将让数百万美国家庭和 97% 的小微企业心中的石头落地，带来新的工作岗位和更快的增长速度。我们没有理由再犹豫不前了。

9 我们知道在未来的几个月里分歧和矛盾不可避免。这正是我们政治体系运作的方式之一。但是在周二，你们掷地有声地说出了自己的心声：绝不容许无所作为，绝不容忍那些视妥协为肮脏的政客。更不用说是在你们这么多家庭还在苦苦挣扎的时候了。

10 相反，你们需要的是精诚合作。你们需要的是付诸行动。这就是我在第二个任期内打算履行的计划。我期待两党领导人愿意与我合作。

11 谢谢，祝大家周末愉快！

第46周

Working Together to Extend the Middle-Class Tax Cuts

November 17, 2012

同心同德，共同延长中产阶级减税政策

2012年11月17日

【摘要导读】

在本周的广播电视讲话中，巴拉克·奥巴马总统敦促国会立刻就大家意见一致的一件事采取行动——即确保98%的美国民众和97%的小微企业年底时税收不会上涨。他说：周五，他和国会领袖举行建设性的会商，寻求削减赤字且又增强美国经济实力和保护中产阶级的途径。他期盼各方能够齐心协力一道完成这项工作。

演讲再现 Original Text

1 Hi, everybody.

2 Four years after the worst economic crisis of our lifetimes, our economy is growing again and creating jobs. But we have much more to do. Our task now is to build on that progress. Because this nation only succeeds when we've got a growing, thriving middle-class.

3 That's what drives me. That's what I campaigned on for the past year. That's what will guide me in our work over the next four years. And I'm willing to work with anyone of any party to move this country forward.

4 Because soon, we face a very clear deadline that requires us to make some big decisions on jobs and taxes; on investments and deficits. Both parties voted to set this

deadline. And I believe both parties can work together to make these decisions in a balanced and responsible way.

5 When it comes to taxes, for example, there are two pathways available.

6 One says, if Congress fails to act by the end of the year, then everybody's taxes automatically go up — including the 98% of Americans who make less than $250,000 a year. Our economy just can't afford that right now. You can't afford that right now. And nobody wants that to happen.

7 The other path is for Congress to pass a law right away to prevent a tax hike on the first $250,000 of anyone's income. That means all Americans — including the wealthiest Americans — get a tax cut. And 98 percent of Americans, and 97 percent of all small business owners, won't see their income taxes go up a single dime.

8 The Senate has already passed a bill like this. Democrats in the House are ready to pass one, too. All we need is for Republicans in the House to come on board.

9 We shouldn't hold the middle-class hostage while Congress debates tax cuts for the wealthy. Let's begin our work by actually doing what we all agree on. Let's keep taxes low for the middle-class. And let's get it done soon — so we can give families and businesses some good news going into the holiday season.

10 I know these challenges won't be easy to solve. But we can do it if we work together.

11 That's why on Friday I sat down with Congressional leaders to discuss how we can reduce our deficit in a way that strengthens our economy and protects our middle-class. It was a constructive meeting. And everyone agreed that while we may have our differences, we need to come together, find solutions and take action as soon as possible.

12 Because if anything, that's the message I heard loud and clear in the election.

13 Work as hard as you can to make our lives better. And do it together.

14 Don't worry about the politics. Just get the job done.

Words & Expressions

dime [daim] *n.*（美国、加拿大的）10分铸币，少数的钱

if anything 如果有什么区别的话，如果有什么的话

grit [grit] *n.* 砂砾，粗砂石，勇气，决心 *vt.* 覆以砂砾，咬紧牙关

resilience [ri'ziliəns] *n.* 适应力，弹性

decency ['di:sənsi] *n.* 正派，体面，庄重，合乎礼仪，礼貌

15 Everywhere I went in that campaign — from farms in Iowa to *the Vegas strip*①; from Colorado's *Rockies*② to the Florida coast — I was inspired by the grit and resilience of the American people, by your hard work and sense of decency. And it makes me want to work even harder for you. I saw it again this week in New York, where our fellow citizens are going through a really tough time, but are helping each other through it. And we're going to be there to help them rebuild.

16 Every single day, the good people of this country work as hard as you can to meet your responsibilities. Those of us you sent to Washington have to do the same.

17 Thanks and have a great weekend.

背景知识注释 Background Notes

1. the Vegas strip 即 the Las Vegas strip，拉斯维加斯大道，全长约 6.5 公里，是拉斯维加斯最繁荣的街道。这里汇集了最豪华的酒店、赌场、餐馆与购物场所，是拉斯维加斯的灵魂与象征。这里灯光璀璨，赌场中众生相尽收眼底。
2. Rockies 即 Rocky Mountain，落基山脉，它是纵贯北美（加拿大、美国）的山系。落基山脉又译做"洛矶山脉"，是美洲科迪勒拉山系在北美的主干，由许多小山脉组成，被称为北美洲的"脊骨"，从阿拉斯加到墨西哥，南北纵贯 4,500 多公里，广袤而缺乏植被。其名称源自印第安部落名。巍峨的落基山脉绵延起伏，自北向南，有数千公里之长。整个落基山脉由众多小山脉组成，其中有名称的就有 39 条。这条巨大的山脉南北狭长，北至加拿大西部，南达美国西南部的得克萨斯州一带，几乎纵贯美国全境。除圣劳伦斯河外，北美几乎所有大河都源于落基山脉，它是大陆的重要分水岭。

中文译文 Chinese Version

1 嗨，大家好！

2 在经历了有生以来最严重的经济危机爆发四周年之后，我国的经济又开始重新增长并创造就业机会。但是我们还有更多事情要做。当下我们的任务就是巩固现有的成就。因为只有拥有一个不断成长壮大而充满活力的中产阶级我们国家才能兴旺发达。

3 这正是一直鞭策着我的动力。这正是在过去一年里我竞选的目的。这也是在未来

的四年中引领我工作的指南。我愿意与任何党派里的任何人一道努力推动我们的国家向前发展。

4 由于我们不久就要面对一个非常明确的期限。这就要求我们就就业和税收、投资和赤字等问题做出一系列重大决定。这个最后期限是两党投票设定。我坚信，两党也可以共同努力以一种统筹兼顾而又负责任的方式做出这些抉择。

5 比方说，就税收而言，摆在我们面前的有两条道路可走。

6 一条是，倘若国会到年底还裹足不前，那么届时所有人的税赋将会自动上涨，这包括98%的年收入低于25万美元的人。我们的经济不堪承受如此重压。你们也不堪承受这般重负。谁都不希望这样的事情发生。

7 另一条是，国会应当马上通过一项法案，防止税收与任何一个人的首个250,000美元挂钩。这意味着所有美国人——包括最富有的美国人——税赋都减少了。98%的美国民众和97%小微企业主们会发现他们的税赋一个子也没有增加。

8 参议院已经通过了一项类似法案。众议院的民主党人也准备通过一项类似法案。现在我们需要众议院的共和党人也加入进来。

9 在国会讨论为富人减税问题的时候，我们不能把中产阶级作为“人质”。让我们就从大家都认同的事情开始吧。保持中产阶级的低税率，并尽快把这件事情办好——以便我们可以在即将来临的节日假期给很多家庭和企业带来一些好消息。

10 我深知解决这些难题并非易事。但是只要我们共同努力是肯定能做到的。

11 正是因为如此，周五，我与国会领导人们坐到一起，探讨如何在消减赤字的同时增强我国经济的实力并保护我们的中产阶级。这是一次建设性的会商。所有与会人员都认可这一点：即便我们之间存在分歧，我们仍需同舟共济，尽快找到解决方案并付诸实施。

12 因为这正是我在竞选过程中所能听见的最有力最清晰的呼声。

13 为了更为美好的生活，全力以赴地工作，并要共同努力。

14 不要沉溺于政治争斗。还是先把工作做好。

15 竞选期间，从爱荷华州的农庄到拉斯维加斯大道 (the Vegas strip)，从科罗拉多的落基山脉到佛罗里达的魅力海滨，在我所到过的每一个地方，美国人民英勇无畏与坚忍不拔的精神、不辞辛劳与诚实正直的风貌一直使我深受鼓舞，并促使我更加努力地为大家工作。本周，我在纽约再次看到这种精神风貌，尽管这里的民众仍在经受着苦难，但他们依然相互搀扶。我们一定会与他们一起重建家园！

16 日复一日，我国心地善良的百姓都在尽心尽力地履行自己的职责，而我们这些受你们委派来到华盛顿的人们更应该如此。

17 谢谢，周末愉快！

第47周

Wishing the American People a Happy Thanksgiving

November 24, 2012

祝愿全国人民感恩节快乐

2012年11月24日

【摘要导读】

感恩节之际，奥巴马总统利用每周讲话的机会向全美人民表示感谢并致以节日的祝福，同时对依然在世界各地执行任务保卫自由的英勇军人表达敬意。他说："在我们与亲人们一起度过节日的时候，我们不会忘记那些在今年时乖命蹇的人们，尤其是东北部在最近飓风中损失惨重的同胞们。今年的感恩节，朋友、家人以及全社会都将在团结共进的精神感召之下齐聚一堂，照料那些不幸的人们，帮助他们摆脱困境，一道向未来进发。"

演讲再现 Original Text

Words & Expressions

bounty [ˈbaunti] *n.* 慷慨，丰富，奖励金，赠款

passionate [ˈpæʃənit] *adj.* 热情的，热烈的，激昂的

set... apart 分开，区别，使与众不同

1 On behalf of the Obama family — Michelle, Malia, Sasha, Bo and me — I want to wish everyone a very happy Thanksgiving.

2 For us, like so many of you, this is a day full of family and friends; food and football. It's a day to fight the overwhelming urge to take a nap — at least until after dinner. But most of all, it's a time to give thanks for each other, and for the incredible bounty we enjoy this country.

3 That's especially important this year. As a nation, we've just emerged from a campaign season that was passionate, noisy, and vital to our democracy. But it also required us to make choices — and sometimes those choices led us to focus on what sets us apart instead of what ties

us together; on what candidate we support instead of what country we belong to.

4 Thanksgiving is a chance to put it all in perspective — to remember that, despite our differences, we are, and always will be, Americans first and foremost.

5 Today we give thanks for blessings that are all too rare in this world. The ability to spend time with the ones we love; to say what we want; to worship as we please; to know that there are brave men and women defending our freedom around the globe; and to look our children in the eye and to tell them that, here in America. No dream is too big if they're willing to work for it.

6 We're also grateful that this country has always been home to Americans who see these blessings not simply as gifts to enjoy, but as opportunities to give back. Americans who believe we have a responsibility to look out for those less fortunate — to pull each other up and move forward together.

7 Right now, as we prepare to gather around our dinner tables, there are families in the northeast who don't have that luxury. Many of them have lost everything to *Hurricane Sandy*① — homes, possessions, even loved ones. And it will be a long time before life goes back to normal.

8 But in the midst of so much tragedy, there are also glimmers of hope. Over the last few weeks, we've seen FEMA personnel, National Guard and first responders working around the clock in hard-hit communities. We've seen hospital workers using their lunch breaks to distribute supplies. Families offering up extra bedrooms. The fire department advertising free hot showers. Buses full of volunteers coming from hundreds of miles away. Neighbors sharing whatever they have — food, water, electricity — and saying again and again how lucky they are to have a roof over their heads.

9 It would have been easy for these folks to do nothing — to worry about themselves and leave the rest to someone else. But that's not who we are. That's not what we do.

10 As Americans, we are a bold, generous, big-hearted

put sth. in perspective 客观地看待某事

first and foremost 首先，首要的是

blessing [ˈblesiŋ] *n.* 神恩，神赐，恩惠，慈悲，恩典

all too 实在太

worship [ˈwə:ʃip] *vt.* 崇拜，尊敬 *vi.* 拜神，做礼拜 *n.* 崇拜，礼拜，尊敬

glimmer [ˈglimə] *vi.* 闪烁，发微光 *n.* 微光，闪光，少许

big-hearted *adj.* 慷慨的，宽大的，洒脱的

roll up one's sleeves 卷起袖子大干一场

recognition [ˌrekəgˈniʃən] *n.* 识别，承认，认出，重视，赞誉，公认

people. When our brothers and sisters are in need, we roll up our sleeves and get to work — not for the recognition or the reward, but because it's the right thing to do. Because *there but for the grace of God go I*[②]. And because here in America, we rise or fall together, as one nation and one people.

11 That's something to be grateful for — today and every day.

12 So to all the Americans doing your part to make our world a better place — it is my great privilege to serve as your President. To all our servicemembers — it is my honor to be your Commander in Chief. And from our family to yours, happy Thanksgiving, everybody.

背景知识注释 Background Notes

1. Hurricane Sandy 飓风“桑迪”，是形成于大西洋洋面上的一级飓风。2012年10月24日、25日、26日飓风“桑迪”袭击了古巴、多米尼加、牙买加、巴哈马、海地等地，造成大量财产损失和人员伤亡。北京时间2012年10月30日上午6点45分，飓风“桑迪”在新泽西州登陆，伤亡惨重，联合国总部亦受损。
2. there but for the grace of God go I 倘若不是神的眷顾我亦会遭此不幸。即人的命运都掌握在神的手里。此言据传出自约翰•布拉德福德 (John Bradford, 1510—1555)，他是英国改革家和殉道者。

中文译文 Chinese Version

1 我谨代表奥巴马家庭——米歇尔、玛莉亚、萨莎和小狗波——祝愿大家感恩节快乐！

2 对于我们而言，就像你们中的大多数人一样，这一天会在家人和朋友中度过，一道品尝感恩节食物，观看橄榄球比赛。这一天因忙忙碌碌总想找个时间小憩一会儿，至少晚饭后会有这种想法。但对大多数人来说，这一天都会彼此互致谢意，并感谢我们所享有的无穷无尽的馈赠。

3 这在今年尤为重要。作为一个国家，我们刚刚经历了一场情绪高涨、热闹纷呈并且对我们的民主体制而言至关重要的大选。但是这也要求我们还要做出一系列抉择——有时候

这些决策令我们关注那些造成我们四分五裂而不是使我们团结一心的事儿；关注我们支持什么样的候选人而不是我们同属什么样的国家。

4 感恩节让我们有机会客观地进行思考。要记住，尽管彼此之间存在着分歧，最重要的是我们是并且永远是美国人。

5 今天我们感激所获得的恩赐，在当今世界它们还是那么的稀缺和珍贵：我们可以与自己深爱的人一起度过美好的时光；我们可以自由表达我们的思想并追求我们的信仰；我们明白那些英勇无畏的军人正在世界各地为捍卫我们的自由而战；我们可以望着自己孩子的眼睛告诉他们，在美国这里，只要你愿意为之努力，一切梦想都可以成为现实。

6 我们心存感念，也是因为在这个国家，美国人不会简单地把恩赐当做礼物去享用，而是把它们当做机会去回馈。美国人相信我们负有责任去关心那些时乖命蹇的人，彼此拉对方一把，然后一道前行。

7 此时此刻，当我们准备围坐在餐桌旁时，我国的东北部还有很多家庭享受不到这次盛筵。他们中的很多人在飓风“桑迪”中失去了一切——房屋、财产甚至是亲人，而生活恢复正常还需要很长一段时间。

8 但是就是在如此严重的灾难之中，我们依旧看到了希望的光芒。在过去的几个星期里，我们看到了联邦紧急事务管理署的工作人员、国民警卫队和紧急救援人员在灾区不停工作忙碌的身影。我们看到了医院工作人员在午餐间隙分发救灾物资动人的景象。很多家庭腾出了自己家里空闲的卧室。消防部门通知大家可以免费洗热水澡。汽车上满载着从数百英里外赶来的志愿者。左邻右舍一道分享自己的食物、水、电等一切东西，并一遍又一遍地念叨着：能有个地方遮风挡雨是何等的幸运。

9 袖手旁观对这些人而言本是件再容易不过的事儿——只考虑自己，剩下的都留给别人去做。但我们绝非这样的人，我们也不会这么去做。

10 作为美国人，我们英勇无畏、宽厚慷慨、充满大爱。当我们的兄弟姐妹遭遇困难的时候，我们就会卷起袖子出手相助——并不是为了赞誉或奖赏，而是因为这是我们应该做的事情。因为这是上帝对我们的恩典。因为在美国，作为一个国家和民族，我们唇齿相依休戚与共。

11 这是今天乃至今后每一天我们都要心存感念的。

12 因此，对于所有各尽其职把我们的家园建设得更加美好的美国民众，我想说，能担任你们的总统，我感到无上荣光。对于我们所有的部队指战员，我想说，能担任你们的总司令，我感到无比荣耀。最后，我再次代表我的家人祝愿大家感恩节快乐！

Urging Congress to Extend the Middle-Class Tax Cuts

December 01, 2012

敦促国会延长中产阶级减税政策

2012年12月1日

【摘要导读】

在本周的广播电视讲话中，巴拉克•奥巴马总统在宾夕法尼亚州一家繁忙的工厂与美国民众谈论有关通过削减中产阶级税赋法案的紧迫性。他说：削减中产阶级税赋将给准备过节众多家庭和企业迎接新年所需的安全感；民主党人和共和党人必须携起手来通过大家都认同的一个法案——为98%的美国家庭和97%的小微企业减税；他们完全没有理由踌躇不前。奥巴马敦促国会采取行动帮助发展美国的经济并加强中产阶级的实力。

演讲再现 Original Text

Words & Expressions

tick [tik] *vi.* 发出滴答声，标以记号 *n.* 滴答声，记号，赊欠

have to do with 与…有关

1 Hi, everybody. I'm here on the factory floor of a business in *Hatfield*[①], Pennsylvania, where folks are working around the clock making toys to keep up with *the Christmas rush*[②].

2 And I came here because, back in Washington, the clock is ticking on some important decisions that will have a real impact on our businesses — and on families like yours.

3 The most pressing decision has to do with your taxes. See, at the end of the year, middle-class tax cuts are set to expire. And there are two things that can happen.

4 First, if Congress does nothing, every family will see their income taxes automatically go up at the beginning of next year. A typical middle-class family of four will see their

income taxes rise by $2,200. We can't let that happen. Our families can't afford it, and neither can our economy.

5 The second option is better. Right now, Congress can pass a law that would prevent a tax hike on the first $250,000 of everybody's income. Everybody. That means that 98 percent of Americans and 97 percent of small businesses wouldn't see their income taxes go up at all. And even the wealthiest Americans would get a tax cut on the first $250,000 of their incomes.

6 Congress can do that right now. They can give families like yours a sense of security going into the New Year. They can give companies like this one some certainty about what to expect down the road. And with the issue behind us, we'll have more time to work out a plan to bring down our deficits in a balanced way — including by asking the wealthiest Americans to pay a little more, so we can still invest in the things that make our nation strong, like education and research.

7 So let's begin by doing what we all agree on. Both parties say we should keep middle-class taxes low. The Senate has already passed a bill to keep income taxes from going up on middle-class families. Democrats in the House are ready to do the same thing. And if we can just get a few House Republicans on board, I'll sign this bill as soon as Congress sends it my way.

8 But it's unacceptable for some Republicans in Congress to hold middle-class tax cuts hostage simply because they refuse to let tax rates go up on the wealthiest Americans. And if you agree with me, then I could use your help. Let your congressman know what $2,000 means to you. Give them a call. Write them an email. Or tweet them using the hashtag "*My2K*③." That's My2K.

9 You and your family have a lot riding on the outcome of this debate. We all do. And as citizens, we all have a say in the country we want to build — not just on election day, but every day. So make your voice heard. I promise, it makes a difference. Thanks, and have a great weekend.

down the road 将来，今后

on board 支持某人的，赞同某人的政策/路线的

unacceptable [ˌʌnək'septəbl] *adj.* 不能接受的，不受欢迎的

hashtag ['hæʃtæg] *n.* 标签

riding ['raidiŋ] *n.* 骑马，乘车，自找麻烦，自讨苦吃

have a say 有发言权

make a difference 有影响，有关系

背景知识注释
Background Notes

1. Hatfield 哈特菲尔德，宾夕法尼亚州蒙哥马利县的一个区，面积 1.66 平方公里。

2. the Christmas rush 圣诞节购物热潮。

3. My2K 我的 2,000 美元，为了通过中产阶级延长减税法案，酷爱新媒体的美国总统奥巴马 11 月 28 日继续借助推特的力量，在网上发起“My2K”的活动，试图通过民间和网友向国会施压。

中文译文
Chinese Version

1 嗨，大家好。我现在正在宾夕法尼亚州哈特菲尔德 (Hatfield) 一家工厂的生产车间，这里的工人正在加班加点生产圣诞节购物热潮所需的大量玩具。

2 我之所以来此，是因为时间正在滴答滴答作响，可是在华盛顿尚有一系列重要决策仍未落实，而这些决策将对我们的企业乃至各位的家庭产生实质性的影响。

3 而这其中最为紧迫的便是大家的税赋问题。就是说，到今年年底，中产阶级的减税政策就要到期了。接下来只有两种结果。

4 首先，倘若国会无所作为，新年伊始所有家庭都将面临所得税自动上涨的问题。一个普通的四口中产之家的所得税将上涨 2,200 美元。我们不能让这样的事情发生。我们的家庭乃至我们国家的经济都无法承受如此的重负。

5 第二种选择要好一些。当下，国会可以通过一项法案来防止税收与每个人收入的首个 250,000 美元挂钩。这对每个人都一视同仁。这将意味着有 98% 的国民和 97% 的小微企业的所得税税率不会上涨。即便对于最富有的美国人而言，他们首个 250,000 美元收入也可以享受减税政策。

6 国会现在就可以行动了。他们可以给予各位的家庭在迎接新年时一份安全感。他们可以给予像这家公司一样的企业一颗定心丸来筹划未来一段时间的发展。解决了这些问题，我们就有更多的时间来制订计划寻求一种平衡的方式降低我们的财政赤字，这其中就包括要求最富有的美国人多缴纳一点税收，这样我们才能继续对教育和研究等有利于国家发展壮大的领域进行投资。

7 因此，让我们一起着手办好已达成共识的事情。两党都认为我们应该保持较低的中产阶级税率。参议院已经通过了一项法案防止中产阶级所得税增加。众议院的民主党也准备通过这一法案。倘若我们可以争取到部分众议院共和党人的支持，我将在国会呈报之后尽快签署使之生效。

8 但对于国会有些共和党人以为中产阶级减税为要挟，以此拒绝提高最富有的美国人的税赋，这是不可接受的。倘若你们同意我的意见，请帮助我。让你们的国会议员知道

2,000 美元对你们意味着什么。打电话给他们，发电子邮件给他们，或在推特上用“我的两千块”给他们留言。这是我的两千块。

9 对于这场辩论的结果，你们和你们的家庭都有很多的期待。人人如此。作为公民，对于国家的发展，我们都有发言权，不仅在选举日，而是在每一天。大声疾呼吧！我敢肯定，这必将带来改变。谢谢大家，周末愉快！

第49周

Congress Must Extend the Middle-Class Tax Cuts

December 8, 2012

国会必须延长中产阶级减税政策

2012年12月8日

【摘要导读】

在本周的广播电视讲话中，巴拉克·奥巴马总统敦促国会立即对98%的美国民众和97%的小微企业延长中产阶级减税政策，并明确表示若要达成一项平衡的赤字削减方案，国会的共和党人必须同意让最富有的美国人缴纳更多的税赋。

演讲再现 Original Text

Words & Expressions

lose sight of 忽略，不再看见

expire [ekˈspaiə] *vi.* 期满，终止，死亡，呼气

drag down 使（某人）身体衰弱（或情绪低落），使健康状况变坏，拖垮

1 Hello, everybody. Over the last few weeks, there's been a lot of talk about deadlines we're facing on jobs and taxes and investments. But with so much noise and so many opinions flying around, it can be easy to lose sight of what this debate is really about. It's not about which political party comes out on top, or who wins or loses in Washington. It's about making smart decisions that will have a real impact on your lives and the lives of Americans all across the country.

2 Right now, middle-class tax cuts are set to expire at the end of the year. Time is running out. And there are two things that can happen.

3 First, if Congress does nothing, every family in America will see their income taxes automatically go up on January 1st. A typical middle-class family of four would get a $2,200 tax hike. That would be bad for families, it would be bad for businesses, and it would drag down our entire

economy.

4 Now, Congress can avoid all this by passing a law that prevents a tax hike on the first $250,000 of everybody's income. That means 98 percent of Americans and 97 percent of small businesses wouldn't see their income taxes go up by a single dime. Even the wealthiest Americans would get a tax cut on the first $250,000 of their income. And families everywhere would enjoy some peace of mind.

5 The Senate has already done their part. Now we're just waiting for Republicans in the House to do the same thing. But so far, they've put forward an unbalanced plan that actually lowers rates for the wealthiest Americans. If we want to protect the middle-class, then the math just doesn't work.

6 We can and should do more than just extend middle-class tax cuts. I stand ready to work with Republicans on a plan that spurs economic growth, creates jobs and reduces our deficit — a plan that gives both sides some of what they want. I'm willing to find ways to bring down the cost of health care without hurting seniors and other Americans who depend on it. And I'm willing to make more entitlement spending cuts on top of the $1 trillion dollars in spending cuts I signed into law last year.

7 But if we're serious about reducing our deficit while still investing in things like education and research that are important to growing our economy — and if we're serious about protecting middle-class families — then we're also going to have to ask the wealthiest Americans to pay higher tax rates. That's one principle I won't compromise on.

8 After all, this was a central question in the election. A clear majority of Americans — Democrats, Republicans and Independents — agreed with a balanced approach that asks something from everyone, but a little more from those who can most afford it. It's the only way to put our economy on a sustainable path without asking even more from the middle-class. And it's the only kind of plan I'm willing to sign.

9 Everyone agrees we need to bring down our deficit and strengthen our economy for the long-term. The question

math [mæθ] *n.* 数学，数学运算，公式

bring down 降低，打倒，打死，击落

entitlement spending 福利开支，权益支出

on top of 另外，在…之上，紧接着

sustainable [sə'steinəbl] *adj.* 可持续的，合理利用的，养得起的，可承受的

is whether we can do it in a responsible way that allows us to keep investing in the things that have always made America strong. I'm convinced we can. And if both sides are willing to compromise, I believe we can give businesses and families a sense of security going into the New Year.

10 Thanks, and have a great weekend.

中文译文
Chinese Version

1 嗨，大家好。在过去的几周里，全国上下都在谈论我们面对的就业、税收和投资的最后期限。但是由于噪声嘈杂、议论满天，人们难免迷失方向，不知道这场辩论的实质。这不是哪个政党能取得压倒性优势，或哪个人入主白宫的问题。这是关于能否做出明智的决策从而对大家乃至全国各地的人的生活产生积极影响的问题。

2 现在，中产阶级的减税政策即将在年底到期。时间正在流逝。接下来只有两种可能。

3 首先，倘若国会无所作为，明年元旦所有家庭都将面临所得税自动上涨的问题。一个普通的四口中产之家的所得税将上涨 2,200 美元。这对各家各户都不是什么好事，对所有企业亦不是什么好事，而且会拖累我们的整个经济。

4 当下，国会可以通过一项法案来防止税收与每个人收入的首个 250,000 美元挂钩。这将意味着有 98% 的国民和 97% 的小微企业的所得税税率一个子也不会上涨。即便对于最富有的美国人而言，他们首个 250,000 美元收入也可以享受减税政策。全国各地的家庭将因此得到些许安宁。

5 参议院已经履行了自己的职责。现在我们期待着众议院的共和党人也为此做出努力。但是迄今为止，他们推出的不是一个统筹兼顾的法案。这个法案实际上仅仅降低了最富有的美国人的税赋。倘若我们打算保护中产阶级，那么他们这个如意算盘则行不通。

6 除了延长中产阶级减税政策之外，我们能够也应该做出更多的努力。我随时准备和共和党人携手推出一项刺激经济增长，创造就业机会并且减少赤字的计划。这个计划让双方都有所收获。我希望找到不损害依赖医保的老年人和其他美国人的利益且降低医疗成本的各种方法。在我去年签署的削减 1 万亿美元支出的基础上，我也希望削减更多的应享权益支出。

7 但是倘若我们审慎考虑减少我们的赤字同时坚持在诸如教育和科研之类对我们的经济发展举足轻重的领域投资——审慎地考虑保护中产阶级家庭——那么我们就不得不要求最富有的美国人略微增加一点税赋。在这个原则上我绝不会让步。

8 毕竟这是本次选举中的中心议题。绝大多数美国人——民主党人、共和党人和独立人士——都赞同一个统筹兼顾的途径，要求每个人都有所付出，但是要求有能力的人承担略微多一点。这是让我们的经济在走上可持续发展之路的同时避免让中产阶级受到更多影响的唯一途径。这也是我唯一愿意签署的方案。

9 所有人都认为从长远来看我们应该降低赤字并增强我们的经济实力。但问题是我们是否能够以一种负责任的方式实现这个目标，使我们能够继续对那些一直使美国保持强盛的领域进行投资。对此，我充满信心。倘若两党双方都愿意做出让步，我坚信我们可以让企业和家庭在迎接新年到来时都能有一份安宁的心情。

10 谢谢，祝周末愉快！

第50周

Nation Grieves for Those Killed in Tragic Shooting in *Newtown*[①], CT

December 15, 2012

举国哀悼康涅狄格州纽敦枪击案悲剧的罹难者

2012年12月15日

【摘要导读】

在本周的广播电视讲话中，巴拉克•奥巴马总统说美国人民惦挂着星期五康涅狄格州纽敦枪击案悲剧失去至亲的人们并为他们祈祷祝福。

演讲再现 Original Text

Words & Expressions

grieve [gri:v] *vi.* 悲痛，哀悼 *vt.* 使悲伤，使苦恼

devote one's life to 献身于

tear away 拉掉，撕掉，拉走，夺走，把(某人)勉强拉开，忍痛离去

1 On Friday, we learned that more than two dozen people were killed when a gunman opened fire in an elementary school in Newtown, Connecticut.

2 Most of those who died were just young children with their whole lives ahead of them. And every parent in America has a heart heavy with hurt.

3 Among the fallen were also teachers — men and women who devoted their lives to helping our children fulfill their dreams.

4 So our hearts are broken today. We grieve for the families of those we lost. And we keep in our prayers the parents of those who survived. Because as blessed as they are to have their children home, they know that their child's innocence has been torn away far too early.

5 As a nation, we have endured far too many of these tragedies in the last few years. An elementary school in

Newtown. A shopping mall in Oregon. A house of worship in Wisconsin. A movie theater in Colorado. Countless street corners in places like Chicago and Philadelphia.

6 Any of these neighborhoods could be our own. So we have to come together and take meaningful action to prevent more tragedies like this. Regardless of the politics.

7 This weekend, Michelle and I are doing what I know every parent is doing — holding our children as close as we can and reminding them how much we love them.

8 There are families in Connecticut who can't do that today. And they need all of us right now. Because while nothing can take the place of a lost child or loved one, all of us can extend a hand to those in need — to remind them that we are there for them; that we are praying for them; and that the love they felt for those they lost endures not just in their own memories, but also in their community, and their country.

9 Thank you. God bless you!

take the place of 代替，取代，接替…的位置

背景知识注释 Background Notes

1. Newtown 纽敦，是美国康涅狄格州西南部费尔菲尔德县一座市镇。费尔菲尔德县成立于1666年，是康涅狄格州最早的四个县之一，县名来自当地海岸的盐沼。纽敦建于1705年，2012年12月14日，此地发生美国史上死亡人数第二多的枪击案。

中文译文 Chinese Version

1 本周五，我们惊悉在康涅狄格州纽敦城的一所小学，一名枪手开枪射击，造成二十几人丧生。

2 大多数罹难者还只是些生命之花尚未绽开的孩子们。全美上下每一位为人父母的无不为此肝肠寸断。

3 罹难者中还有几位老师——那些致力于帮助我们的孩子们实现他们的梦想的男男女女们。

4 因此，今天我们痛彻心扉。我们为那些失去亲人的家庭悲伤欲绝。我们为那些幸存

下来的孩子的父母切切祈祷。因为尽管孩子平安回家甚为幸运，他们却不得不面对孩子的天真无邪被过早撕裂的现实。

5 作为一个国家，我们近几年已经经历了太多类似的悲剧：无论纽敦城的一所小学，还是俄勒冈的一座购物中心，抑或威斯康星州的一个教堂，或是科罗拉多州的一座电影院，还是无数像芝加哥和费城街头那样的地方。

6 或许我们的社区在某一天亦像这些社区那样遭受袭击。因此，我们必须齐心协力，抛开政治成见，采取有意义的行动以防止更多的这类悲剧再度发生。

7 这个周末，米歇尔和我将做我所知道的、所有父母们都将做的事情——紧紧地把我们的孩子搂在怀里，让她们知道我们是多么爱她们。

8 然而，康涅狄格州的有些家庭今晚却已无法做到这一点了。他们现在就需要我们大家。因为没有什么能够取代一个失去的孩子或失去的亲人，我们都应向那些需要帮助的人伸出援手——告诉他们，我们就在他们的身边，为他们祈祷；他们对逝者的爱不仅永远留在他们的记忆中，也留在他们的社区和他们的国家里。

9 谢谢，上帝保佑！

第51周

The President and First Lady Extend a Holiday Greeting and Thank the Troops for Their Service

December 22, 2012

总统和第一夫人节日的问候与诚挚的谢意

2012 年 12 月 22 日

【摘要导读】

在本周的广播电视讲话中，巴拉克•奥巴马总统和第一夫人米歇尔•奥巴马祝愿美国人民圣诞快乐，假期愉快。他们还对美国部队和家属所做的奉献表示谢意。奥巴马总统和夫人还请美国民众访问JoiningForces.gov网页，寻找向退伍军人和军属表示敬意和支持的方式。他指出美国人民必须像往常一样齐心协力在此节日期间相互关照。

演讲再现 Original Text

1 **THE PRESIDENT:** Hi everybody. This weekend, as you gather with family and friends, Michelle and I want to wish you a Merry Christmas and a Happy Holidays.

2 **THE FIRST LADY:** We both love this time of year. And there's nothing quite like celebrating the holidays at the White House. It's an incredible experience and one that we try to share with as many folks as possible.

3 This month, more than 90,000 people have come through the White House to see the holiday decorations. And our theme for this year's holiday season was "Joy to All" — a reminder to appreciate the many joys of the holidays: the joy of giving… the joy of service… and, of course, the joy of homecomings.

4 **THE PRESIDENT:** That's right. This weekend,

Words & Expressions

decoration [ˌdekəˈreiʃən] *n.* 装饰，装潢，装饰品，奖章

parents are picking up their kids from college — and making room for all that laundry they bring with them. Children are counting down the hours until the grandparents arrive. And uncles, aunts and cousins are all making their way to join the family and share in the holiday spirit.

5 **THE FIRST LADY:** That's what makes this season so special — getting to spend time with the people we love most.

6 **THE PRESIDENT:** And this year, that's especially true for some of our military families. You see, the war in Iraq is over. The transition in Afghanistan is underway. After a decade of war, our heroes are coming home. And all across America, military families are reuniting.

7 So this week let's give thanks for our veterans and their families. And let's say a prayer for all our troops — especially those in Afghanistan — who are spending this holiday season overseas, risking their lives to defend the freedoms we hold dear.

8 **THE FIRST LADY:** And remember, when our men and women in uniform answer the call to serve, their families serve right along with them. Across this country, military spouses have been raising their families all alone during those long deployments. And let's not forget about our military kids, moving from base to base — and school to school — every few years, and stepping up to help out at home when mom or dad is away.

9 Our military families sacrifice so much on our behalf, and Barack and I believe that we should serve them as well as they serve this country. That's why *Dr. Jill Biden* ① and I started *Joining Forces* ② — an effort to rally all Americans to honor and support our veterans and military families. Just go to joiningforces.gov to find out how you can show your gratitude for their service.

10 **THE PRESIDENT:** Because that's what this season is all about. For my family and millions of Americans, it's a time to celebrate the birth of Christ. To reflect on His life and learn from His example. Every year, we commit to love

laundry [ˈlɔːndri] *n.* 洗衣店，洗衣房，要洗的衣服，洗熨，洗好的衣服

count down 倒读数，倒计时

true for 对…来说是正确的，对…成立

transition [ˌtrænˈziʃən] *n.* 过渡，转变，转换，变调

underway [ˈʌndəˈwei] *adj.* 进行中的，起步的，航行中的

deployment [diˈplɔimənt] *n.* 调度，部署

step up 提高，增加，走近，加紧，加快

help out 帮助…摆脱困难

rally [ˈræli] *vt.* 团结，集合 *vi.* 团结，重整，恢复 *n.* 集会

one another. To give of ourselves. To be our brother's keeper. To be our sister's keeper. But those ideas are not just part of our faith. They're part of all faiths. And they unite us as Americans.

11 **THE FIRST LADY:** In this country, we take care of each other. And in this season of giving, it's inspiring to see so many people all across America taking the time to help those most in need.

12 **THE PRESIDENT:** That's part of what makes us such a compassionate nation. And this year, I know many of you are extending that kindness to the families who are still picking up the pieces from Hurricane Sandy and extending your prayers to the people of Newtown, Connecticut.

13 **THE FIRST LADY:** So thank you for all that you've done this year on behalf of your fellow Americans.

14 **THE PRESIDENT:** And on behalf of my favorite Americans — Michelle, Malia, Sasha and Bo — Merry Christmas, everybody.

15 **THE FIRST LADY:** Happy holidays.

compassionate [kəm'pæʃənət] *adj.* 慈悲的，富于同情心的

背景知识注释 Background Notes

1. Dr. Jill Biden　吉尔•拜登博士 (1951.6.3—)，教育工作者，美国第47任即现任副总统约瑟夫•拜登的太太，第二夫人。

2. Joining Forces　支持军队，为美国第一夫人米歇尔与副总统拜登的夫人吉尔博士联手发起的一项全国性运动，旨在动员全社会的力量支持和关心军人家庭。

中文译文 Chinese Version

1 **总统：**嗨，大家好！这个周末你们将与家人和朋友团聚，我和我的夫人祝各位圣诞快乐，节日愉快！

2 **总统夫人：**我们都热爱每年的这一段时光。再也没有什么能比得上在白宫里庆祝圣诞了。这是一段不可思议的经历，我们想和尽可能多的民众共同分享。

3 这个月里，累计超过9万人来到白宫参观节日装饰，感受节日气息。我们今年圣诞节的主题是"全民同乐"，以此提醒我们来感激在节日里得到的诸多快乐：感激奉献带来的

愉悦，感激为他人服务的乐趣，当然了，还有回家团聚的喜悦。

4 **总统：**的确，本周末父母们都把孩子从大学接回家中，并为他们携带回来所有换洗的衣服腾出空间。而小孩子们则在默默倒计时，等待爷爷奶奶的到来。同时，叔舅、姑姨和堂表兄妹都一路赶来参与到家庭聚会中来，共享节日的欢快。

5 **总统夫人：**与我们的至爱共享浓浓亲情，这个节期之所以如此特殊莫概于此。

6 **总统：**而今年，对于我国部分军人家庭来讲，尤其如此。瞧，伊拉克战争结束了。阿富汗过渡时期也在进行中。经过了十年战事，我们的英雄正在班师回朝，全国各地的军人家庭终于可以再次团聚了。

7 所以在本周，让我们向退伍军人及其家属致谢，让我们为我们所有的部队祈福——特别是对那些在阿富汗的军人们——他们此次假期驻扎在海外，冒着生命危险守护可贵的自由。

8 **总统夫人：**让我们记住，当那些身着军装的男女士兵响应号召做出牺牲的时候，他们的家庭也随即与他们踏上了为美国奉献的道路。全国军人配偶都是在另一方长年部署他地时独自抚养孩子的。让我们记住，我们军人家庭的子女们。他们每隔几年都要从一个基地迁移到另一个基地，从这所学校转往另一所学校，并要在母亲或父亲不在身边时帮助料理家务。

9 我们的军人家庭为我们做出如此巨大的牺牲，巴拉克和我都希望我们也应该如同他们为我们国家奉献一般为其服务。这就是我和吉尔博士启动 Joining Forces 的初衷。我们希望通过努力号召美国人民向我们的退伍军人和军人家庭表示敬意，并支持他们。您只需访问 www.JoiningForces.gov 网站就知道该做些什么来表达您对他们投身军旅的感激之情了。

10 **总统：**因为这正是这个节期的宗旨所在。对于数以百万计的美国民众和我的家庭来说，这就是一个纪念耶稣诞生的日子。回忆耶稣的一生，能在他身上学到很多。每年，我们都承诺关爱彼此，承诺奉献自我，承诺守护我们的兄弟，承诺守护我们的姐妹。但是，这些信念不仅仅是我们信仰的一部分，更是所有信仰的一部分。正是这些信念让所有的美国人团结一心。

11 **总统夫人：**在美国，我们关爱彼此，相互照顾。特别是在这个感恩的季节里，看到全国上下那么多的民众向那些最需要帮助的人伸出援手，让我们备受鼓舞。

12 **总统：**正是因为如此，我们的国度充满同情与怜惜。特别是在今年，我知道你们当中很多人都在帮助深受飓风“桑迪”之苦的灾民重整山河，为在康涅狄格州纽敦镇 (Newtown) 校园枪击案罹难者家庭切切祈祷祝福。

13 **总统夫人：**我代表全体美国人民为你们今年所做的一切表示感谢。

14 **总统：**我谨代表我最热爱的美国人民，代表米歇尔、玛利亚、萨沙，以及狗狗小波，祝各位圣诞快乐。

15 **总统夫人：**节日快乐。

第52周

Congress Must Protect the Middle-Class from Income Tax Hike

December 29, 2012

国会必须保护中产阶级免受增税冲击

2012年12月29日

【摘要导读】

在本周的广播电视讲话中，巴拉克•奥巴马总统敦促国会遵循期限履行职责，保护中产阶级免受增税冲击，为未来经济更大的发展和消减赤字奠定基础。

演讲再现
Original Text

1 Hi, Everybody. For the past couple months, I've been working with people in both parties — with the help of business leaders and ordinary Americans — to come together around a plan to grow the economy and shrink our deficits.

2 It's a balanced plan — one that would protect the middle-class, cut spending in a responsible way, and ask the wealthiest Americans to pay a little more. And I'll keep working with anybody who's serious about getting a comprehensive plan like this done — because it's the right thing to do for our economic growth.

3 But we're now at the point where, in just a couple days, the law says that every American's tax rates are going up. Every American's paycheck will get a lot smaller. And that would be the wrong thing to do for our economy. It would hurt middle-class families, and it would hurt the businesses

Words & Expressions

shrink [ʃriŋk] *vt.* 使缩小，使收缩 *vi.* 收缩，畏缩 *n.* 收缩

comprehensive [ˌkɔmpriˈhensiv] *adj.* 综合的，广泛的，有理解力的

that depend on your spending.

4 And Congress can prevent it from happening, if they act now. Leaders in Congress are working on a way to prevent this tax hike on the middle-class, and I believe we may be able to reach an agreement that can pass both houses in time.

5 But if an agreement isn't reached on time, then I'll urge the Senate to hold *an up-or-down vote* ① on a basic package that protects the middle-class from an income tax hike, extends vital unemployment insurance for Americans looking for a job, and lays the groundwork for future progress on more economic growth and deficit reduction.

6 I believe such a proposal could pass both houses with bipartisan majorities — as long as these leaders allow it to come to a vote. If they still want to vote no, and let this tax hike hit the middle-class, that's their prerogative — but they should let everyone vote as well. That's the way this is supposed to work.

7 We just can't afford a politically self-inflicted wound to our economy. The economy is growing, but keeping it that way means that the folks you sent to Washington have to do their jobs. The housing market is healing, but that could stall if folks are seeing smaller paychecks. The unemployment rate is the lowest it's been since 2008, but already, families and businesses are starting to hold back because of the dysfunction they see in Washington.

8 You meet your deadlines and you meet your responsibilities every day. The folks you sent here to serve should do the same. We cannot let Washington politics get in the way of America's progress. We've got to do what it takes to protect the middle-class, grow this economy, and move our country forward.

9 Thanks, everybody.

both houses 参众两院

package ['pækidʒ] *n.* 包，包裹，有关联的一组事物，一揽子交易（计划、建议等），（通过劳资集体谈判取得的合同上的）一揽子福利条件（如退休金、养老金等）

prerogative [pri'rɔgətiv] *n.* 特权 *adj.* 有特权的

self-inflicted ['selfin'fliktid] *adj.* 自己造成的，加于自身的

stall [stɔːl] *vi.* 停转，拖延 *vt.* 拖延，使停转，使陷于泥中 *n.* 货摊，畜栏

hold back隐瞒，退缩，抑制，阻止

dysfunction [dis'fʌŋkʃən] *n.* 功能紊乱，机能障碍，官能不良

背景知识注释 Background Notes

1. an up-or-down vote　直接投票表决，指美国参议院或众议院对某一修正案或法案的直接投票表决。这种表决并非就某一相关程序投票，而是直奔主题，直接就某事投赞成票或反对票。

中文译文
Chinese Version

1 嗨，大家好！在过去的几个月里，在众多商界领袖和普通美国民众的支持下，我与共和民主两党进行了广泛合作，并形成了一份保持经济增长并降低财政赤字的方案。

2 这是一份统筹兼顾的方案——不仅可以保护中产阶级，并以负责任的方式削减开支，还要求最富有的美国人略多缴纳一点税收。我将继续与任何希望真正落实这类综合计划的人合作——因为只有这样做才有利于我们经济的增长。

3 但是我们现在处于一个微妙的时间点。再过几天，按法律规定每个人的税率都将上升。每个国人的收入都要蒙受不小的损失。这对我们的经济不是什么好事。

4 倘若国会闻风而动，他们有能力阻止这类情况的发生。国会领袖们正在为防止税收上涨冲击中产阶级商讨方案，我相信我们应该能按时达成一项协定并获得参众两院的通过。

5 但是倘若我们未能及时达成一项协议，我将敦促参议院就一揽子基本方案进行直接投票，这包括保护中产阶级免受增税冲击，延长对于正在求职的国人而言事关重大的失业保险，并为未来的经济更大的发展和消减赤字奠定基础。

6 我相信这个提案将会在参众两院以两党绝对多数的优势获得通过，只要国会领袖批准其进入投票议程。倘若他们依然否决这一方案，让中产阶级的税收上涨，这也是他们的权力——但他们至少应该让所有人参加投票。这本来就是应当遵循的模式。

7 我们绝不能容忍我国的经济受到这种政治上自我伤害的波及。经济仍在增长，但是保持这种增长意味着那些华盛顿的民选官员们应履行自己的职责。房市正在回暖，但是倘若人们的收入减少，这种势头可能会再次受阻。失业率处于2008年以来的最低水平，但是很多家庭和企业在目睹了华盛顿的无动于衷之后已经开始紧缩开支了。

8 你们每天都按时守信履行义务。你们选举出来的那些为国家服务的人也应该这么做。我们不能让华盛顿的政治问题挡住美国前进的道路。我们必须竭尽全力保护中产阶级、促进经济增长、推动国家向前发展。

9 谢谢诸位。